JOURNAL FOR THE STUDY OF THE NEW TESTAMENT
SUPPLEMENT SERIES

31

Executive Editor
David Hill

Publishing Editor
David E. Orton

BIBLE AND LITERATURE SERIES

15

General Editor
David M. Gunn

Assistant General Editor
Danna Nolan Fewell

Consultant Editors
Elizabeth Struthers Malbon
James G. Williams

Almond Press
Sheffield

This book is dedicated to
my mother, Lois, and my aunt, Ethel,
with profound affection
and appreciation

The STRUCTURE of MATTHEW'S GOSPEL

A Study in Literary Design

David R. Bauer

The Almond Press · 1989

Bible and Literature Series, 15

General Editor: David M. Gunn
(Columbia Theological Seminary, Decatur, Georgia)
Assistant General Editor: Danna Nolan Fewell
(Perkins School of Theology, Dallas, Texas)
Consultant Editors: Elizabeth Struthers Malbon
(Virginia Polytechnic Institute & State University, Blacksburg, Virginia)
James G. Williams
(Syracuse University, Syracuse, New York)

First published by Almond Press 1988
Reprinted 1989

Published by Almond Press
Editorial direction: David M. Gunn
Columbia Theological Seminary
P.O. Box 520, Decatur
GA 30031, USA
Almond Press is an imprint of
Sheffield Academic Press Ltd
Mansion House
19 Kingfield Road
Sheffield, S11 9AS
England

Printed on acid-free paper in Great Britain
by Cromwell Press
Melksham, Wiltshire

British Library Cataloguing in Publication Data

Bauer, David R.
    The structure of Matthew's Gospel.
    1. Bible. N.T. Matthew - Commentaries
    I. Title   II. Series   III. Series
    226´.207

    ISSN 0143-5108
    ISSN 0260-4493

    ISBN 1-85075-104-8

CONTENTS

PREFACE

Within the past fifteen years, the discipline of literary criticism has assumed a central role in biblical studies, especially in the United States and Great Britain. Throughout this formative period, this new discipline has explored a number of issues that relate to the literary character of the final form of the biblical text. And yet there is a clear sense among literary critics that only the slightest beginnings have been made in the exploration of these issues. The present volume deals with one of the questions to which literary criticism has addressed itself, that of literary structure.

Concurrent with the emergence of literary criticism has been a renewed interest in the Gospel of Matthew. This book, which for centuries was known as 'the church's Gospel', because of its preeminent standing within the community of believers, was forced to take second station to the Gospel of Mark (at least in New Testament scholarship) when Marcan priority became the accepted solution to the synoptic problem. But now the First Gospel has become an object of intense interest and thorough investigation among New Testament scholars. And one of the major issues that has arisen within recent Matthean studies is that of the literary structure of the Gospel. The structure of Matthew has been a center of controversy and debate. There is currently no consensus whatsoever on the structure of this Gospel.

We contend that the wide range of views regarding Matthean structure stems from the application of diverse methodologies to the question of Matthew's structure, and that the discipline of literary criticism offers a solution to this vexing problem. Literary criticism, with its focus upon the final form of the text, is uniquely qualified to deal with the issue of the structure of Matthew's Gospel, since in fact literary structure has to do with the arrangement of materials in the final document. Moreover, one of the concerns of literary criticism is the identifiction of rhetorical elements that point to the literary structure of books and passages.

The aim of the present study is to identify and describe various rhetorical features that relate to literary structure, and to discern the structure of Matthew's Gospel by examining certain of these rhetorical features employed in the Gospel of Matthew. We also wish to draw theological implications (particularly in terms of christology and salvation history) from our study of Matthean structure.

Of the many who have contributed to the publication of this book, I want to express my gratitude especially to the following: Professor Jack Dean Kingsbury, who directed my doctoral dissertation on the structure of Matthew's Gospel, and whose knowledge and encouragement helped me to see that project as well as the present volume through to completion; Professor Robert A. Traina, who, in the tradition of the Biblical Seminary in New York, introduced me to many of the compositional relationships set forth in Chapter 1; Professor David M. Gunn, of the Almond Press, who graciously accepted this work for publication, and provided much in the way of fine editorial guidance; finally, my mother, Lois E. Bauer, and my aunt, Ethel M. Odson, who assisted in typing and proof-reading, and to whom this volume is affectionately dedicated.

David R. Bauer

ABBREVIATIONS

AB	Anchor Bible
ATR	*Anglican Theological Review*
BHTh	Beiträge zur historischen Theologie
BR	*Biblical Research*
BS	*Bibliotheca Sacra*
BTB	*Biblical Theology Bulletin*
BW	*Biblical World*
BZ	*Biblische Zeitschrift*
CBQ	*Catholic Biblical Quarterly*
CBQMS	Catholic Biblical Quarterly Monograph Series
CL	*Communicantes et Liturgies*
CTM	*Concordia Theological Monthly*
Exp	*The Expositor*
FRLANT	Forschungen zur Religion und Literatur des Alten und Neuen Testaments
HTR	*Harvard Theological Review*
ICC	International Critical Commentary
Int	*Interpretation*
JAAR	*Journal of the American Academy of Religion*
JBL	*Journal of Biblical Literature*
JR	*Journal of Religion*
JSNT	*Journal for the Study of the New Testament*
JSOTS	Journal for the Study of the Old Testarnent, Supplement Series
JTS	*Journal of Theological Studies*
LB	*Linguistica Biblica*
NICNT	New International Commentary on the New Testament
NTS	*New Testament Studies*
PRS	*Perspectives in Religious Studies*
RB	*Revue Biblique*
RSR	*Religious Studies Review*

SBLDS	Society of Biblical Literature Dissertation Series
SBLMS	Society of Biblical Literature Monograph Series
SBS	Stuttgarter Bibelstudien
SE	*Studia Evangelica*
SNTSMS	Society for New Testament Studies Monograph Series
TDNT	*Theological Dictionary of the New Testament*
TD	*Theology Digest*
TU	Texte und Untersuchungen zur Geschichte der altchristlichen Literatur
ZThK	*Zeitschrift für Theologie und Kirche*

Chapter 1

INTRODUCTORY CONSIDERATIONS

The subject of this book is the literary structure of Matthew's Gospel and its relevance for understanding the theology of the Gospel. The method of the book may be broadly termed 'literary critical'.

A. Matthean Structure and Literary Criticism

There is as yet no consensus regarding the literary structure of the Gospel of Matthew. Four general views of Matthew's structure have been suggested and today vie for supremacy in Matthean studies.[1]

First, a number of scholars have offered topical outlines which are primarily concerned with the contents of individual sections and have little to say regarding the flow of thought or movement of the book as a whole. Consequently, no implications regarding the theology of the Gospel can be drawn.[2]

Second, many scholars follow the structure advanced by B.W. Bacon (1930: 82, 265-335). This view stresses the role of the discourses in Matthew. Bacon himself divided the Gospel into five 'books', based upon the division of the Pentateuch. Each book culminates with a discourse closed by the formula 'and it happened when Jesus finished' or the like,[3] and these books are preceded by a prologue (chs. 1-2) and followed by an epilogue (chs. 26-28). Bacon drew the conclusion that Matthew was a converted rabbi, a Christian legalist, who presented Jesus as the new Moses delivering a new law to combat the antinomianism rampant in his church. Thus, Bacon perceived the Matthean Jesus as a teacher and argued that Matthew sub-ordinated everything else to this didactic role.

Third, other scholars[4] argue that Matthew breaks down into a threefold division based upon the formulaic sayings in 4.17 and 16.21, 'From that time Jesus began'. Thus, 1.1-4.16 is 'The Preparation for Jesus'; 4.17-16.20 is 'The Proclamation of Jesus'; and

16.21-28.20 is 'The Passion and Resurrection of Jesus'. In this case, 4.17 and 16.21 are general headings which are expanded in their respective divisions, and the book moves toward culmination in the death and resurrection of Jesus, and especially in his missionary commissioning (28.16-20). Those who advocate this structure tend to emphasize christology over ecclesiology and see Jesus as Messiah, Son of God, rather than as Teacher.

Fourth, within the past twenty-five years a number of scholars have abandoned the notion of a topical outline for the Gospel of Matthew and have seen Matthew's concept of salvation history as the key to the composition of the Gospel. Thus, Georg Strecker (1971: 45-49, 184-88), taking his cue from the work of Hans Conzelmann on Luke, argues that Matthew divided salvation history into three epochs: the ages of prophecy, of Jesus, and of the church. In a significant footnote (1967: 220), Strecker brushes aside both the fivefold division of Bacon and his successors and the threefold division with breaks at 4.17 and 16.21. The topical outline has been replaced by a conception of salvation history around which Matthew has arranged his material. Wolfgang Trilling (1964), Rolf Walker (1967), William G. Thompson (1974), and John P. Meier (1975) follow similar proposals.

Virtually all the scholars mentioned above have made use of the discipline of redaction criticism. Indeed, some of the differences which have arisen regarding the literary structure of Matthew's Gospel can be traced to difference emphases in the application of this method. That is to say, these differences in the understanding of the Gospel's structure are to some degree methodologically determined. Bacon focuses upon changes or additions Matthew has made to received traditions (the *process* of redaction), whereas Jack Dean Kingsbury, who is a chief advocate of the threefold structure of Matthew, stresses the final composition of the work (the *product* of redaction). The salvation-history proponents generally emphasize specific uniquely Matthean passages, especially 10.5; 15.24; 21.43; 28.16-20.

The growing interest in literary criticism in biblical studies, with its focus upon the final form of the text, suggests a way past this impasse. In literary criticism, attention is centered upon the literary character of the text as it stands and the way in which the reader construes, and responds to, this text. As such, it focuses upon the form of the final work as a literary object, rather than upon questions about the unity or integrity of the work (which are assumed), the historical situation out of which the text arose, or the redactional processes that stand behind the final text (though all these may be legitimate points of inquiry in the broad task of exegesis).[5] This disciplines deals with a broad range of issues relating to the literary character and meaning of the extant text, including the issue of rhetorical elements that point toward the structure of the work.[6]

Our concern is centered upon that dimension of literary criticism which has to do with literary structure. Here the term 'literary structure' is used to refer to the relationship between constituent parts of a literary unit. The ultimate literary unit in this case is the biblical book, the Gospel of Matthew. The task of the investigation of literary structure is thus twofold: (a) to determine the major units and sub-units within the Gospel, and (b) to identify the structural relationships within and between these units. The latter relates to the unique structural contour that defines the composition of the Gospel of Matthew. That is the burden of this study.

In particular, we will direct our attention to certain rhetorical features of the text by which we will be able to discern the structure of the Gospel in its final form. These rhetorical features, or 'compositional relationships', are specifically and directly applicable to the question of literary structure. These categories are drawn from various sources, and many of them are simply assumed in the investigation of literary structure.[7] Yet they need to be explicitly identified and explained, with examples given. Their usefulness in meeting the demands of the examination of Matthean structure will be demonstrated in the remainder of the book, especially in Chapters 3 through 7.

B. *Categories of Compositional Relationships*

These categories are designed to aid in dealing with the two components of literary structure. They are employed to determine the distinct units (that is, to indicate limits of units), and to reveal the relationships both between and within these units.

a. *Repetition* (*recurrence*) involves the repetition or re-occurrence of the same or similar terms, phrases, or other elements.[8] Repetition usually indicates emphasis.

William Freedman (1971: 123) declares that one of the major concerns of recent literary investigation has been 'to discern clusters or families of related words or phrases that, by virtue of their frequency and particular use, tell us something about the author's intentions, conscious or otherwise'.

Of course, frequency alone is not determinative of repetition as a major structural device; the notion of 'particular use' must always be considered, that is, the function of the repeated element in the movement of the text. Some constantly repeated elements (such as prepositions or conjunctions) may have little structural significance, and yet elements that recur only a few times can carry great weight. Freedman (1971: 126-27) gives four criteria for structurally significant and literarily effective repetition: avoidability or unlikelihood in the content being communicated (not simply part of the 'color'); significance of contexts; coherence between various references to the motif; and, with regard to symbolic motifs, appropriate representation to the thing being symbolized.

Repetition is a most common device in the literary structure of biblical materials. The book of Joshua is tied together through repetition of the theme of inheritance,[9] even as 'witness-testify' is a repeated element in the Gospel of John.[10]

b. *Contrast* is the association of opposites or of things which are dissimilar.[11]

Psalm 1 is structured according to the principle of contrast (note the two ways). The book of Judges is composed around a repeated contrast between the covenant faithfulness of God and the unfaithfulness of Israel, between the God of Israel and the gods of the surrounding nations, and between Israel and its neighbors.[12] Contrast is also quite often noted or assumed in works of literary criticism (as in Culpepper, 1983: 125; Gros Louis, 1982: 18).

c. *Comparison* is the association or juxtaposition of things which are alike or at least essentially similar.

Since the days of F.C. Baur, many scholars have argued that the book of Acts includes a comparison between Peter and Paul.[13] There is also a repeated comparison between Joshua and Moses in the book of Joshua,[14] and between Paul and the Thessalonian Christians in 1 Thessalonians (1.2-10; 2.1-35; 3.6-8).

d. *Causation* and *substantiation*. *Causation* represents the movement from cause to effect.

Again, examples of this relationship abound in biblical materials. Ephesians is structured around causation: the declarations of chs. 1-3 produce or lead to (form the basis of) the exhortations in chs. 4–

6. Here the 'therefore' (οὖν) of 4.1 makes this relationship explicit. Repetition of causation is found in 1 Kings: there obedience and righteousness (covenant faithfulness) produce well-being, whereas disobedience and wickedness (covenant unfaithfulness) produce destruction. Here, of course, the element of contrast is also involved.[15]

Substantiation involves the movement from effect to cause. It thus involves the same components as causation, only here they operate in reverse order.

One may view the book of Revelation in terms of substantiation. It is possible that the injunctions made to the seven churches of Asia Minor in chs. 2–3 are substantiated (that is, reasons are given why these injunctions should be obeyed) through the panoramic view of the flow of history toward its culmination in judgment for the wicked and blessing for the righteous in chs. 4–22. The notion of 'for' or 'since' is involved in substantiation, though these, of course, are often not explicitly included.

e. *Climax* is the movement from the lesser to the greater to the greatest (or most intense). It comes from the word meaning 'ladder' or 'staircase' and hence suggests the element of climbing. It is the movement toward a culmination and usually comes at or near the end of a unit.[16] Climax is almost ubiquitous in narrative material. The arrival of Paul in Rome and his house arrest there (with some degree of freedom to proclaim the gospel) climaxes the book of Acts (28.30-31; compare 1.7-8); the crucifixion forms the climax to the Gospel of Mark;[17] and the book of Exodus comes to a climax in the dedication of the tabernacle (40.34-38; compare 7.16; 8.20).

Climax always involves two other relationships implicitly: causation and the repetition of causation.

f. The *pivot* involves a radical reversal or turning around—a change of direction—of the movement of the material.[18] In its purest form, the latter movement virtually cancels out the previous movement. It thus involves more than a change of emphasis. There are two types of pivots.

The negative pivot begins with positive development, with the reversal involving a downturn.

This type of pivot may be found in 2 Samuel. David's period of general prosperity and good fortune in chs. 1–10 are reversed in the debacles of chs. 12–24, following upon the sin David perpetrated against Bathsheba and Uriah in ch. 11.

In the positive pivot, the negative development precedes the upturn.

This phenomenon may be present in the description of Paul in Acts. Paul is a persecutor of the church and an enemy of Christ prior to his conversion in 9.3-19a (7.58; 8.1; 9.1-2), but after this event he becomes a mighty herald of the gospel (9.19b-31; 13.1-28.31). The pivot always implicitly contains two other relationships—causation and contrast; but precision demands that this phenomenon be described as pivot rather than as contrast and causation.

g. *Particularization* and *generalization*, as in the case of causation and substantiation, involve the same components used in different sequence. *Particularization* involves a movement from the general to the particular.

It is possible to argue as, for instance R. Alan Culpepper (1983: 89-97) does, that the prologue to the Gospel of John is a general statement that is expanded, or 'particularized' in the remainder of the Gospel. Also, Mk 1.1 may be a general statement which is expanded, or made specific, in the rest of the Gospel of Mark.[19] In the segment Mt. 1.1-17, whatever one may wish to say regarding the broader function of 1.1, there is little doubt that v. 1 serves as a general statement that is particularized in the specific notations of generations which follow in vv. 2-16.

Generalization designates the movement from the particular to the general.

Acts is structured around generalization. It moves in progressive stages from narrow geographical confines (especially Jerusalem) to 'the uttermost parts of the earth' (1.8; 13.1-28.31). The book of Ruth also evidences generalization; events leading to the birth of Obed are set forth in 1.1-4.17, which is followed by a genealogy of the descendents of Perez from Hezron through Obed to David in 4.18-22.

h. *Statement of purpose.* The statement of purpose involves the movement from means to end; this statement has to do with both the end or purpose and the means whereby that end is achieved (Culpepper, 1983: 201; Talbert, 1982: 9-10). The Gospel of John contains a statement of purpose in 20.31: 'these things are written in order that you may believe that Jesus is the Christ, the Son of God, and that believing you might have life in his name'. John thus declares that his Gospel has been structured or composed according to the intention to lead (or confirm) his readers into faith in the

Messianic Son-ship of Jesus, with the further purpose that they may thereby experience life. In this case, the Gospel of John as a whole serves as the means, with the purpose just stated functioning as the end. Another example is the statement of purpose found in Luke 1.1-4. Here Luke identifies an orderly account of the things related (Gospel of Luke as a whole) as the means, with the end that Theophilus may know the truth concerning these things. Any understanding of the arrangement or structure of the Gospel of Luke must keep this statement of purpose in mind.

i. *Preparation (introduction)* is the inclusion of background or setting for events or ideas.[20] When that for which preparation is made comes about, it may be said to be realized. By setting forth the background according to which the rest of the book is to be read and understood, Job 1-2 forms the introduction to the book as a whole. Likewise, the events which took place in Transjordan in the book of Joshua (chs. 1-2) prepare the reader for the main concern of the book, the conquest of Canaan (chs. 3-24). One of the most common forms of preparation is the prediction which comes to fulfillment later in the narrative; a prime example is the repeated preparation (and subsequent realization) of the Marcan passion predictions in 8.31; 9.31; 10.33-34.

j. *Summarization* is an abridgement or compendium (summing up) of a unit of material.[21] Summarization is similar to the general component in generalization or particularization. A général statement is usually less precise, more vague and indefinite, with fewer details. Summarization is a more deliberate attempt to bring into the statement in abridged form the various components of that which is being summarized.

Joshua 23.1-24.13 is a summary of Israel's experience recorded in 1.1-22.34. The unit Judges 2.6-16.13 is summarized in 2.6-3.6; and 2 Kings is summed up in 17.7-23.

k. *Interrogation* is the employment of a question or problem followed by its answer or solution. It is found in two forms: (a) The question raised, followed by an answer, either explicit or implicit. This is the simplest form. (b) The statement of a problem, followed by the solution to the problem. This is more subtle and implicit than the question-answer type.

One way of looking at the book of Genesis involves the element of interrogation, whereby the problem of sin and the curse in chs. 1-11 is solved by the covenant and blessing in chs. 12-50.

Mark 13 may also be understood as a case of interrogation. While recognizing that the material of vv. 5-37 goes beyond an answer to the question of v. 4, these verses do contain an answer to the question, and it is no doubt appropriate to see the structure of this chapter composed around the question-answer format.

l. *Inclusio* involves the repetition of features, words, phrases, and so on at the beginning and the ending of a unit, thus having a 'bracket' function.[22]

Psalm 8 is clearly structured according to *inclusio*; at the very beginning and the very end the phrase 'O Lord, our Lord, how majestic is thy name in all the earth' is repeated (8.1, 9). Matthew 19.30 and 20.16 may form an *inclusio* around the intervening parable.

m. *Interchange* involves the exchanging or alternation of certain elements (a, b, a, b, a). Interchange is often used to strengthen contrasts or comparisons. This alternation is repeated, and thus interchange implies repetition.

The opening chapters of 1 Samuel are an example of interchange to strengthen contrast. There, the description of Hannah and Samuel is alternated with the picture of Eli and his sons (1.1–12.25). The opening chapters of Luke offer another example of interchange, perhaps to strengthen comparison. In Hebrews there is interchange between argument and exhortation.[23]

n. *Chiasm* has to do with the repetition of elements in inverted order (a, b, b', a').

According to N.W. Lund (1942: 97-99), Psalm 67 may be structured according to chiasm. One clear New Testament example in a very small unit (a verse unit) is Mt. 5.45b: 'he makes his sun rise on the evil and on the good, and sends rain on the righteous and on the unrighteous'. Here chiasm is used to strengthen the contrast between the good and the evil; God's universal love is demonstrated precisely through this contrast.

o. *Intercalation* is the insertion of one literary unit in the midst of another literary unit (a, b, a).[24] This usually means the 'splitting apart' of a narrative in order to interpose another narrative within it.

The Gospel of Mark offers the best examples of this phenomenon. In Mk 5.21-43 the story of the healing of the woman with a flow of blood stands in the middle of the pericope on the raising of the centurion's daughter; and the cleansing of the temple stands in the middle of the account of the cursing of the fig tree in Mk 11.12-25.

Structural relations found in a text may be either implicit or explicit. Implicit relations are present with no expressly stated connections or earmarks. Implicit relations involve the often discussed issues of asyndeton and peritactic construction, and this type of relationship demands an inference from the nature of the components and the context.

Another distinction which should be made is that between simple and complex relationships. A simple relationship is one relationship, for instance, causation. There is normally more than one component structuring a unit, but sometimes two or more relationships are so closely bound up with one another in the material that it is advantageous to use them in combination. Some of the examples cited above have involved complex relations; for instance, we noted that Judges is structured according to repeated contrast (repetition and contrast). It might be noted that the movement from particular to general in Acts parallels the movement toward the climax to the book; hence, Acts contains generalization with climax.

A distinction should be made between general and more specific relationships. Some relationships are by their very nature less precise or specific than others. Preparation, for instance, is a rather general relationship, since it is present in several other relationships, such as causation and interrogation. For the sake of precision, one should be careful to identify the most specific relationship used in a given unit of material.

The value of observing these relationships in order to come to grips with literary structure is manifold. A few of the reasons for employing these relationships follow.

First, these relationships are rooted in art (and hence in the process of human thinking) in general. Laws such as repetition, comparison, contrast, and so on may be found not only in literature, but also in music, painting, sculpture, and architecture (Kuist 1947: 37-39, 58, 161-81). This observation suggests a possible bridge between so-called deep structure and surface structure.

Second, these relationships are clearly present in biblical literature as a whole. The examples included above are drawn from every part of the canon, indicating that these relationships apply to literature produced over a long period of time, by many 'authors', and included in both the Old and New Testaments.

Third, all these relationships apply to units of various sizes and lengths: the book, the section, the sub-section, the segment, the paragraph, and even (for the most part) the verse or sentence. They are broad enough to include all these literary levels. Because this study deals with the structure of the Gospel of Matthew in general, most of the examples above came from macrostructures, but they could have been illustrated (and in a few cases were) from segments and even verses.

Fourth, these relationships are not limited to a certain type of literature, such as narrative, but apply to all literature. The examples included material from the Psalms, apocalyptic, and epistolary material as well as from narrative. This breadth is extremely important when dealing with the Gospels, which are not entirely narrative in form. The Gospels of Matthew and John especially include large sections or blocks of discourse.

C. *Steps of Procedure*

Having set forth some basic methodological considerations, we wish now to outline the steps of procedure which we will follow in the remainder of the book.

Chapter 2 contains a survey of the history of research dealing with the literary structure of Matthew. The various structural approaches will be analyzed and grouped insofar as grouping is possible, and points of concern and problems will be identified.

Chapters 3 through 7 examine the structure of the Gospel of Matthew from the standpoint of literary criticism. This examination pays special attention to the relationship between the narrative and discourse material. Thus, the structure of the First Gospel will be discerned.

Chapter 8 draws out the implications of this structure for the study of Matthean theology. Some conclusions regarding the christology and the view of salvation history of Matthew's Gospel will thus be set forth. Although these theological conclusions have sometimes been reached by scholars working with the Gospel on the basis of redaction criticism or composition criticism, they are here put forward as the result of our literary-critical examination of the structure of Matthew's Gospel. This convergence of theological conclusions based upon the application of different methods to the text of the Gospel underscores the validity of these conclusions. This last chapter also contains a summary of our study.

Chapter 2

SURVEY OF INVESTIGATIONS
INTO MATTHEW'S STRUCTURE

Almost all scholars agree that Matthew has carefully, even meticulously, structured his Gospel. W.D. Davies (1966: 14) speaks for many Matthean students when he declares,

> there are documents which are so closely knit that their parts can only be adequately understood in the light of the whole. Such is the Fourth Gospel, and such also is Matthew. It reveals not only a meticulous concern, numerically and otherwise, in the arrangements of its details, but also an architectonic grandeur in its totality.

But if careful composition and fine architecture is widely recognized in the Gospel, there is anything but unanimity when it comes to determining the nature of this structure. This chapter attempts to survey the history of research into this question and to place the major structural approaches into appropriate categories. The purpose of this categorization is twofold: (a) to create a framework by which this diverse and extensive material may become manageable; and (b) to determine the main lines of investigation and the major concerns with which scholars have approached the problem of Matthean structure.

These various structural studies fall into three general categories. First, most of the earlier scholars as well as a few recent exegetes have divided the Gospel according to *geographical* or *chronological* references within the book. Second, most twentieth-century investigators have adopted some form of *topical* outline. Several have followed Bacon's programmatic work, which divides the Gospel according to the alternation of narrative and discourse material. We shall see that there are many variations on Bacon's theme. Others have argued that chiasm is the basis of Matthew's structure. Some have identified three major divisions, marked off by a repeated formula at 4.17 and 16.21. Other topical arrangements have also emerged. Third, in the last thirty years several scholars have rejected the notion of a topical outline, or for that matter, any sort of linear divisions within the Gospel, in favour of an arrangement that is built around some crucial theme or *concept*. Both salvation history and Matthew's didactic purpose have been identified as the central concern around which Matthew has composed his Gospel.

Before examining these structural programs, it will be helpful to state three general observations regarding this survey.

To begin with, the procedure involves not only a classification of the various structural approaches into major groups, but also an examination of methodological and literary presuppositions, arguments advanced by proponents of the respective structures, theological implications, and brief evaluations in which both positive and negative elements are identified. At the close of the chapter we suggest some of the main points of concern which have arisen in the course of scholarly investigation.

Another general observation regarding this survey is that scholars are not always consistent in their presentation of structure. For example, Robert Gromacki (1974: 173-75) declares that the outline of Jesus' ministry in Matthew has a 'double thrust', represented by the formulaic statements at 4.17 and 16.21, yet in his outline of the Gospel he follows the alternating five-speech pattern, completely passing over these two references. Again, Alfred Wikenhauser (1958: 184) states, 'Thus it was the evangelist's intention that the Sermon on the Mount and the "miracle cycle" should form a unity'. Yet in his outline of Matthew (1958: 174) he makes a clear separation between these two sections. When such incongruity is encountered we shall categorize the scholar according to his to her formal outline rather than according to other statements made in the course of the discussion.

Finally, one of the by-products of the attempt to pigeonhole various structural approaches is the necessity to generalize. Only the major thrusts and tendencies of the several programs will be presented in the text of the chapter; individual divergencies and exceptions will be noted in the footnotes.

A. *Geographical-Chronological Structures*

As stated above, almost all the earlier (prior to 1930) structural investigations of Matthew's Gospel have focused upon geographical or chronological elements. An unbroken, though thin line of scholars down to the present has also adopted this approach. The following outline by Willoughby C. Allen and L.W. Grensted (1929: 23) is representative of the divisions advocated by these scholars:

  i-ii.   Birth and Infancy of the Messiah
  (a)   iii.1-iv.11. Preparation for His Ministry (=Mk i.1-13)
  (b)   iv.12-xv.20. Work and Teaching in Galilee(=Mk i.14-
          vii.23)
  (c)   xv.21-xviii.35. Work outside Galilee (=Mk vii.24-ix.50)
  (d)   xix.1-xx.34. A Journey to Jerusalem (=Mk x)
  (e)   xxi-xxviii. Last days of the Messiah's Life (=Mk xi-xvi.8).

Although these scholars agree regarding the general divisions of the Gospel, there is disagreement as to the specific points in Matthew's narrative where these divisions occur. Most mark the beginning of the Galilean ministry of Jesus at 4.12; yet some point to 4.17, or to 5.1.[1] The inauguration of the journey to Jerusalem is usually identified at 19.1, but also at 16.13, at 16.21, and at 17.1.[2] Furthermore, there are some who do not mark off the journey to Jerusalem as a separate unit.[3]

The early conservatives who adopted this structural approach identified the Gospel with the Apostle Matthew and accepted the final form of the text as the basis for the study. of its literary structure. No less than their liberal colleagues, however, were they caught up in the spirit of the times, at least in the sense that they viewed the Gospels primarily as a means to discover the historical Jesus. In other words, they had adopted a 'life-of-Jesus' orientation through which they read the synoptic Gospels, and especially Matthew, a Gospel they believed had come from the pen of an eye-witness.[4]

Ironically, some of the most ardent advocates of Marcan priority also divided the Gospel according to a geographical-chronological outline. But, of couse, they divided the Gospel in this way for entirely different reasons. These early source critics were enamored of the relatively new discovery that Matthew had drawn upon Mark not only for details of his Gospel but for its general narrative framework, as well. On the basis of this emphasis, these scholars investigated the structure of Matthew's Gospel according to its continuity with Mark's outline. In the Introduction to his Commentary on the First Gospel, Allen (1912: xiii) declares, 'In making the Second Gospel the framework of his own, the editor has adopted the gereral outline and plan of that Gospel'. Allen then presented his outline of Matthew along with parallel references to Mark.[5]

Other scholars, both early and more recent, have adopted this framework because of a putative theological significance given to geography, sometimes in analogy to studies on Mark's use of geography.[6]

Certain theological implications are drawn from the geographical-chronological structure, and these implications are clearly connected to the major emphasis of this approach, namely, that of the story of Jesus' movement from Galilee to Jerusalem, coming to a climax in his death, resurrection, and the commissioning of his disciples.

With regard to christology, all these scholars understand Jesus primarily in terms of the title 'Christ'.[7] Categories and titles related to 'Christ' are also much employed, such as 'king',[8] 'Son of David' (e.g. Kerr, 1892: 23; Wikenhauser, 1958: 186), and even 'Son of God'.[9] This accent upon the christological function of Jesus is closely connected to an emphasis upon his fulfillment of Old Testament messianic prophecies and his rejection by the Jews.[10] Thus, Matthew's explicit use of the title 'Christ', his repeated references to the fulfillment of Old Testament prophecy, his presentation of Jesus' desire to fulfil his messianic vocation by going from Galilee to Jerusalem, and the emphasis upon the Jews' rejection of their Messiah in Jerusalem and the consequent turning over of the kingdom of God to the Gentiles all point, in the minds of these scholars, in the direction of this christological category.

The emphasis upon the messianic role of Jesus in the fulfillment of prophecy leads also to strong implications regarding salvation history. These scholars discern that Matthew views the Old Testament period as the age of preparation, followed by the age of fulfillment or of salvation (as Moffatt, 1918: 244). Although they offer no explicit comments regarding a twofold or threefold view of the history of salvation, one may infer that their conclusions on this matter would differ, depending upon how much emphasis a given scholar has placed upon the establishment of the church as the community of the Messiah in consequence of the rejection of Jesus by the Jews. An emphasis upon the role of the church would lead to a threefold view of salvation history (the time of prophecy, of Jesus, and of the church), as opposed to the twofold view (the time of prophecy, and the time of fulfillment).

The advocates of this structure generally say little regarding either ecclesiology or (future) eschatology. Most of these scholars (e.g. Meinertz, 1950: 168-69; Plummer, 1909: xxv-xxi) believe Matthew wrote with an apologetic aim in mind: to demonstrate to Jewish Christians experiencing a time of painful transition that Jesus is the Christ of Old Testament prophecy and that the rejection of Jesus by the Jews does not destroy the messianic credentials of Jesus, but rather explains the universal appeal of the gospel.

As mentioned above, this view of Matthean structure, although most popular in the first three decades of this century, has not won many advocates of late. This general abandonment by the New Testament scholarly community points to weaknesses in the geographical-chronological framework.

First, the methodological presuppositions are problematic. Source criticism has demonstrated to the satisfaction of most that Matthew is dependent upon Mark and is therefore not a primary (eye-witness) source or an independent authority for the earthly life of Jesus. Furthermore, form criticism has shown that none of our Gospels reflects a historical life-of-Jesus orientation, and redaction criticism has confirmed this conclusion. The Gospels represent kerygmatic concerns, both in the history of the tradition and in the work of the final redactors, and were not written as biographies of the life of Jesus in the modern sense of the term.

Moreover, although scholarship has continued to maintain that Matthew largely adopted Mark's broad narrative patterns, it has become increasingly apparent that Matthew did much more than simply copy Mark. Redaction criticism has tended to emphasize the changes Matthew has made to his Marcan exemplar, and thus the focus has turned to discontinuity rather than continuity between Matthew and Mark. It will be shown below that this emphasis has led to an entirely different understanding of Matthew's structure. At any rate, in the judgment of the literary critics, it is methodologically unsound to begin an examination of the structure of one Gospel by comparing it to another.[11] According to literary criticism, one begins with an investigation of the Gospel itself before moving on to comparison with other Gospels.

Second, X. Léon-Dufour (1965: 167) and Kingsbury (1975: 1-2), among others, have discovered that these geographical outlines fail to grasp the dynamic theological force of the Gospel. According to Léon-Dufour, 'a purely geographical framework, taken over from the one which is supposed to be found in Mark, seems to be empty and does not bring out the wealth of the Gospel'.

Third, one should note that geographical divisions within the Gospel of Matthew are apparently not very well defined. There is, after all, a great deal of disagreement among advocates of this view regarding precisely where the various geographical and chronological shifts take place.

Positively, these geographical outlines point out three crucial elements in Matthew which must be addressed in an investigation of the structure of the First Gospel. In the first place, this view of Matthew's structure stresses the narrative character of Matthew and raises the issue of the ultimate nature of the Gospel: Is Matthew essentially narrative in plan and purpose, or does the writer merely use narrative material as background for other (for instance, didactic) features? Furthermore, it relates the issues of the fulfillment of prophecy, and the rejection of Jesus by his people and the consequent replacing of the Jews with the church to the question of Matthew's structure. These are issues which we shall meet again. Finally, these geograpical outlines invite us to look more carefully at the structural and theological significance of geography in the First Gospel.

B. *Topical Structures*

'Topical structures' represents the view which identifies discrete divisions within the text according to the various topics treated. As we indicated in our introduction to this chapter, the major share of research into Matthean structure over the past half-century falls within this category. By far the majority of scholars who have dealt with Matthew according to topical outlines have more or less followed Bacon, arguing that the alternation between narrative and discourse material forms the basis of Matthew's structure. Other voices, however, have been raised. Some of these favor a chiastic arrangement; others invite us to read the Gospel according to a threefold division in which Mt. 1.1 and the two repeated statements at 4.17 and 16.21 serve as 'headings' for the following material. Several other topical outlines, not easily classified into groups, have also been suggested. In this section, we will examine each of these topical structures in turn.

1. *Topical Outlines Based on Alternation of Narrative-Discourse Material*

Perhaps the most significant event in the history of investigation into Matthew's structure occurred in 1930 with the appearance of Bacon's *Studies in Matthew*. This volume, along with two or three other works from the pen of this Yale New Testament professor,[12] radically changed the direction of studies into Matthew's structure. With this change in the conception of structure came also developments in the way scholars thought about the nature of Matthew's Gospel and its theology.

The Work of B.W. Bacon. Bacon was engrossed in the problem of written sources lying behind our Gospels and argued strongly for the dependence of Matthew upon Mark and Q. In this conviction Bacon agreed with scholars like Alfred Plummer and A.H. McNeile. But whereas Plummer and McNeile used Matthew's dependence upon Mark to argue for structural continuity between the two Gospels, Bacon emphasized the differences between the two; he focused upon the changes, rearrangements, and additions Matthew had made to his Marcan source and thereby saw in Matthew a structure entirely different from the geographical-chronological frame which Plummer, McNeile, and others had discerned.

In the area of structural determination, Bacon operated with two basic methodological presuppositions: he believed that structure is essentially a matter of the writer's use of his sources; and he asumed that the changes and additions a writer has made to sources are much more significant for determining structure than the material which the writer has simply adopted intact from the received tradition. Accordingly, in *Studies in Matthew*, Bacon has placed his discussion on structure within the chapter entitled 'Mt's Use of Mark'.

Thus, Bacon examines the structure of the Gospel from the viewpoint of Matthew's redactional activity. In this connection, he makes several observations.

He notes (1930: 80) that Matthew has added a great deal of material to his Marcan exemplar, including an 'introduction' and 'large amounts of teaching material'. Matthew has grouped the bulk of this teaching 'stuff' into five large discourses (1930: 82). The evangelist precedes each of these discourses with an introductory narrative and closes each discourse with a 'stereotyped formula':

'And it happened when Jesus finished these words', or the like (1930: 81). This formula is concluding or terminating, rather than transitional, thus indicating major breaks in the text. Bacon discerns five narrative-discourse complexes in Matthew. Bacon notes, moreover, that toward the close of each discourse Matthew has inserted a note on the future judgment (1928: 205).

As regards narrative redaction, Bacon observes that Matthew has greatly rearranged Marcan pericopae up to Mt. 13.52, after which point he follows Mark more closely (1930: 80). He infers that Matthew has taken these great efforts in order to give primary position to the sermon on the mount (1928: 208), thereby creating a theological orientation which sets the stage for the rest of the book. Moreover, Matthew has consistently abridged the narrative material he has taken over from Mark in favor of discourse (1930: 80).

Bacon includes many other redactional observations. For example, he notes that at three crucial points Matthew has added the word 'lawlessness'.[13] He observes (1928: 205), furthermore, that Matthew has added a farewell commissioning of Jesus to his disciples in which Jesus orders them to 'teach all that I have *commanded* you' (28.19).

Bacon directs his keen sense of redactional activity to several individual pericopae which Matthew has taken over from Mark. Here he scrutinizes every detail Matthew has omitted, changed, or added to his Marcan source. In 15.22 Bacon notes that 'by a minute touch . . . Mt elminates the whole (unhistorical) journey of Jesus into Gentile territory' (1930: 88). And with regard to 19.16-22, Bacon promises (1930: 89),

> The following example will illustrate how by unobtrusive alterations Mt succeeds not merely in removing an utterance of apparent self-depreciation placed by Mk in the mouth of Jesus, but (far more significant!) in reversing the sense of Mk's teaching that Pharisean obedience to the commandment, however lovable in itself, gives no real claim to 'eternal life'.

Bacon immediately draws the theological conclusion that 'Mt's change produces a neo-legalistic doctrine which only differs from that of the scribes and Pharisees by the substitution of a "righteousness" which exceeds theirs by greater inwardness and greater emphasis on "good works"' (1930: 80).

The upshot of all these observations (1918: 65) is that the body of Matthew's Gospel is comprised of five 'books', each book containing a narrative section followed by a discourse section, which is closed by the repeated formula 'And it happened when Jesus finished these words', or the like. Matthew has added an introduction or 'preamble' to the whole which announces the advent of Jesus into the world (chs. 1-2), and has appended an 'epilogue', which describes the departure of Jesus (chs. 26-28).

Bacon concluded that Matthew's church was plagued by anti-nomianism, and in his attempt to stem this tide of lawlessness the evangelist, himself a converted rabbi and Christian legalist, has presented Jesus as a new Moses declaring a new Torah to his church. Matthew has 'tipped his hand' by imitating the structure of the Pentateuch, for according to Bacon each of the five books of Moses contains narrative describing the mighty acts of God followed by a discourse of legal instructions (1930: 81). Matthew has placed these instructions within the literary atmosphere of apocalyptic judgment, therby urging his readers to measure up to the legal requirements of this new Moses by warning that failure to do so will bring swift judgment (1928: 205).

The following outline (Enslin, 1931: 84 n. 11) reflects Bacon's presentation of the major divisions within the Gospel:

Preamble: Chapters 1-2
Book I. Concerning Discipleship (3.1-7.29)
    Div. A. Introductory Narrative (3.1-4.25)
    Div. B. First Discourse (5.1-7.29)
Book II. Concerning Apostleship (8.1-11.1)
    Div. A. Introductory Narrative (8.1-9.35)
    Div. B. The Discourse (9.36-11.1)
Book III. Concerning the Hiding of the Revelation (11.2-13.53)
    Div. A. Israel is Stumbled (11.2-12.50)
    Div. B. Teaching in Parables (13.1-53)
Book IV. Concerning Church Administration (13.54-19.1a)
    Div. A. Jesus and the Brotherhood (13.54-17.21)
    Div. B. The Discourse, Church Administration (17.22-19.1a)
Book V. Concerning the Judgment (19.1b-26. 2)
    Div. A. Jesus in Judea (19.1b-22.46)
    Div. B. Discourse on Judgment to Come (23.1-26.2)
Epilogue: 26.3-28.20.

Bacon thus sees Jesus as a Teacher and, more specifically, as a new Moses, the supreme legislator. Bacon's concept of salvation history is not spelled out, but we may conclude that according to this scheme salvation history is subordinated to the law; that is, salvation history must be understood in light of Matthew's presentation of the law.[14] The period of the old Moses and the old Torah was the time of preparation for the fulfillment of the new Moses and the new Torah. Although the concept of new law would suggest a certain salvation-historical break, Bacon himself tends to emphasize the continuity between the old Mosaic legislation and the new law promulgated by Jesus (1928: 226-27). The teaching of the Matthean Jesus differs from that of the scribes and Pharisees only insofar as Jesus requires *more* righteousness of his followers; the teachings of the Jewish leaders should be obeyed (23.2-3), but the followers of Jesus are to add to those demands the command of Jesus for a righteousness that is inward and that allows no incongruity between motive and action.

This period of the new law is moving toward its culmination on the day of judgment when all (including those in the church) will be judged according to their obedience to this new Torah (1928: 216, 223-24). In the meantime, the twelve have scribal authority in the church, corresponding to the authority of the scribes and Pharisees in Judaism (1928: 230).

Successors to Bacon's Structural Approach. Bacon has had many followers in his understanding of Matthew's structure. Some have remained truer to the overall program of Bacon than others. In this section, we wish to survey this work in order to identify points of continuity and discontinuity between these scholars and Bacon and to discuss some of the issues which have caused division in the camp.

As one persues the many presentations which fall into this category, one finds that several of the same positions appear again and again. For instance, virtually everyone who adopts the alternating pattern follows Bacon in supporting this structure by means of recourse to the formula repeated at the end of the great discourses.[15] In terms of method, practically all these scholars base their investigations into Matthew's structure on changes Matthew has made to his (Marcan) *Vorlage*, as Bacon had done.[16] In this regard, Meier (1980: xi) speaks for many other scholars when he says that Matthew:

> recast and combined the two major liturgical and catechetical
> documents of his church: the gospel of Mark and a collection of
> Jesus' sayings which scholars call 'Q'... It was by skillfully
> combining and editing these three sources that the author created

the theological masterpiece we call the gospel of Matthew. In the commentary which follows we will seek to understand the author's own thought by carefully tracing the process by which he welded disparate sources into an original and meaningful unity. Comparing what the author says by what his sources said will be the main way by which we will enter into the author's mind.

Furthermore, practically all these scholars follow the lead of Bacon in emphasizing ecclesiology and future eschatology.[17] Some have gone beyond Bacon by finding additional evidence for the alternating pattern, such as Matthew's penchant for 'numerical' grouping,[18] and by tying together the new Pentateuch theme more closely than did Bacon to the note of fulfillment in the Gospel as a whole.[19]

Despite this unity, many differences of opinion have arisen around some of Bacon's main contentions. For one thing, these scholars disagree on the number of discourses in the Gospel. While most, like Bacon, find five, several scholars have argued that ch. 23 forms a sixth discourse, and some have even opted for seven.[20]

This observation relates to another problem faced by advocates of this structure: the role of ch. 23. Some hold, along with Bacon, that ch. 23 is part of the eschatological discourse (with chs. 24–25).[21] yet many argue that it belongs to the narrative material preceding the discourse.[22]

Although there is no doubt about the endings of the various discourses, there is disagreement surrounding the exact spot where the several discourses begin. Terence Keegan (1982) has recently dealt with this problem, and he has demonstrated that there is no consensus at all on this significant question.

If scholars argue about the beginnings of the various discourses, they are also at odds over the question of the relationship between the discourses and the surrounding narrative material. Bacon clearly maintained that the narratives prepared for the following discourses and were therefore to be paired with them. Many of the scholars who hold to the alternating structure agree with Bacon on this point;[23] yet others argue that the narratives are to be linked with the preceding discourses;[24] and still others declare that the various narrative sections belong to both the preceding and following discourses, that is, that the structure is 'striped', or at least that the discourses serve to connect the continuing narrative.[25]

Leaving for the moment differences of opinion having to do

primarily with the form of the Gospel, we see that there is no greater
agreement on the issues of the purpose of the Gospel or of the new
Pentateuch ideology in Matthew. As far as the purpose of the Gospel
is concerned, G.D. Kilpatrick (1946; also F. Green, 1936: 2) argues
that Matthew contrasted Jesus with Moses and that the Gospel arose
out of liturgical use in the church. Krister Stendahl (1968: 11-35)
maintains that the Gospel was actually the product of a school of
Christian scribes who set about to produce a manual for church
administration and discipline.[26] Perrin and Duling (1982: 266; also
Harvey, 1977: 56-57) suggest an apologetic purpose relating to the
current attacks from Jamnia. For Marxsen (1968: 146-53), Matthew
is a 'book' which, through a historicizing tendency, mediated the
sermons of the exalted Christ to Matthew's church. For Meier (1980:
xi), the Gospel arose out of a need to address the influx of Gentiles
into the chuch and the separation of Jewish Christians from the
synagogue. Finally, A.W. Argyle (1963: 3-5) has found a multiplicity
of aims and functions standing behind the composition of Matthew.

Many of those who adopt some form of Bacon's alternating
structure have abandoned the notion of a 'new Moses' or 'new
Pentateuch' theology in the Gospel as David Barr (1976: 351, 357)
and Donald Guthrie (1970: 31) have done. Austin Farrer (1954: 179)
argues that the alternating pattern suggests a new Hexateuch rather
than Pentateuch, and he consequently discerns a 'new Joshua'
christology in the Gospel. Yet most of these scholars continue to
accept Bacon's new Moses and new Pentateuch orientation,
substantiating this conclusion by reference to the 'mountain' from
which the sermon on the mount, or new law, was given (5.1),
allusions to Old Testament and intertestamental Moses stories in ch.
2, Matthew's redaction of the transfiguration scene (17.1-8), and the
enunciation of the antitheses in 5.17-48.[27]

Evaluation of the Alternating Pattern. This structural approach has
not gone unchallenged by scholars. Indeed, many of its adherents
themselves point out weaknesses. At this point, we wish to present
some of the major problems with the 'Baconian' structure.

First, several critics have pointed out that it is illegitimate to speak
of the infancy, and passion and resurrection narratives as 'prologue'
and 'epilogue'.[28] The terms themselves suggest secondary status, and
indeed those who strongly advocate Bacon's view are unable to deal
with them as integral parts of the Gospel. Kingsbury (1984) has show

by a careful analysis of the flow of Matthew's narrative that the Gospel comes to a climax in the death, resurrection, and missionary commissioning of chs. 26–28. The genealogy and infancy narratives provide the setting for all subsequent events (see below). Often advocates of Bacon's structure sense this problem and hence speak of the passion and resurrection as 'climax' to the Gospel,[29] yet they consistently fail to relate this observation to their other structural arguments and sometimes even fall into at least apparent inconsistency.[30] Furthermore, this deprecation of the final chapters undercuts the sense of history and historical development in Matthew.

Second, a perusal of the books of the Pentateuch reveals that they are not structured according to a clearcut narrative-discourse sequence, as Bacon insisted. Genesis, Leviticus, and Numbers do not correspond at all to this kind of sequence. Furthermore, Davies (1966: 19) has pointed out that the discourses in Matthew cannot properly be said to contain merely legislative material. Indeed, a large proportion of their contents have no legal orientation whatsoever. Davies also notes that 'legal' material is found outside the discourses, for instance, in ch. 15.

Related to this difficulty is the question of the 'new Moses' typology. We have seen that the new Moses typology has not been accepted by all who advocate Bacon's structure. Critics of Bacon's approach often point out that the new Moses conception is not dominant enough to determine the structure of the First Gospel.[31] Although there may be allusions to Moses in ch. 2, the genealogy and infancy narratives clearly and explicitly relate Jesus to other Old Testament figures, such as Abraham and David (1.1-17, 20).

Third, if the relationship between Matthew and the books of Moses is thus weakened, it is questionable whether it is appropriate to see the formula repeated at the ends of the discourses as concluding rather than simply transitional. B.H. Streeter (1925: 262), one of the first to identify Matthew's use of this formula, judged its function to be that of providing a transition or bridge to the narrative material which follows. We have seen above that those who advocate the alternating pattern do not agree among themselves about the relationship between the narratives and discourses. Some of these scholars judge that this formula actually links the discourses to the following narratives.[32] At any rate, it cannot simply be assumed that this formula is terminative rather than transitional.

This observation leads into a further difficulty: the relationship between the narratives and discourses in Matthew. If Matthew is to be seen as structured according to five books, it would seem necessary to discern clearly the elements that bind each of these sections together in terms both of form and content. Those who argue that the narratives precede the discourses in these divisions are able to suggest only that the narratives 'prepare' for the following discourses.[33] Sometimes specific elements of preparation are identified. For instance, the following elements are identified by various scholars as preparatory for the sermon on the mount: the calling of the disciples in 4.18-22; the attraction of the crowds to the preaching of John in 3.1-8; the introduction of the concept of a 'higher righteousness' in ch. 3; the 'beginning of Jesus' ministry'.[34] One notes, first of all, that the existence of some of these elements is dubious, such as the conception of a 'higher righteousness' in ch. 3. Furthermore, all these elements prepare for the remainder of the book, not specifically for the sermon on the mount. Moreover, there are elements within this 'introductory' material that have no direct bearing upon the sermon on the mount, such as the ministry of John the Baptist. These difficulties are experienced in the narratives preceding other discourses also. The relationship between 19.1-23.39 and 24.1-25.46 is especially hard to grasp.

For those who argue that the discourses go with the following material, the road is no easier. Although this framework works better with the relationship between the sermon on the mount and the ten healings in chs. 8-9, it runs aground when the relationship between the eschatological discourse and the passion and resurrection narrative is pursued. In order to relate these units, Jean Radermakers (1972: II, 22) finds it necessary to interpret the parousia described in chs. 24-25 as an existential presence of the crucified and resurrected Lord with his church throughout history. Barr (1976: 349-59) and James L. Price (1961: 194-95) have seen this problem and have attempted a solution by arguing that the narratives belong equally to the preceding and following discourses.

It is important to recognize that it is not enough for these scholars to indicate points of contact between the discourses and the narrative material which surrounds them. If Matthew is a unity, as virtually everyone maintains, it is inevitable that the discourses would correspond at least in a general way to the material around them. To argue, however, for the pairing off of narrative-discourse complexes into discrete units within Matthew requires a much more persuasive presentation of unity of theme and other elements of structural binding than has thus far been forthcoming.

Fifth, we noted above that there is a good deal of disagreement among these scholars as to the number of discourses in Matthew. Many identify five speeches, others six, and some as many as seven. Whatever number one finally decides upon, there is a gnawing suspicion that if the 'meticulous' Matthew deliberately wished to structure his Gospel according to the alternation of narrative and discourse, he would have maintained a clearer division between these two types of material. The confusion over the roles of chs. 11 and 23 is especially problematic.

Sixth, there is a problem with the suggestion that the Matthean Jesus is understood primarily in terms of Teacher, as Bacon and many of his followers have argued. A glance at the concordance reveals that Jesus is addressed as 'teacher' or 'rabbi' in Matthew only by Judas (26.25, 49), strangers, or opponents (for instance, 8.19; 12.38). The disciples typically address Jesus as 'Lord'. Indeed, the Matthean Jesus does 'teach' (for instance, 4.23-25; 9.35), but to identify 'Teacher' as the primary christological category, or to espouse a structure of the Gospel according to which such a conclusion is practically inevitable, seems to fly in the face of Matthew's use of this term.

Finally, we must put forth the same question regarding methodology as that raised in the discussion of the geographical-chronological approach. It is methodologically inappropriate to begin an examination of literary structure with an investigation into Matthew's use of Mark. Such a comparision has a place and is essential in the broad task of exegesis. But if one is interested in the structure of the extant form of the literary text as a literary entity, rather than the structure of the redactional process, the appropriate place to initiate the examination is with a study of the literary dynamics within the Gospel itself.

On a positive note, the alternating structural approach has indicated the phenomenon of large blocks of teaching material in Matthew and the existence of the repeated formula at 7.28; 11.1; 13.53; 19.1; 26.1. Even if these elements might not form the primary structural base of the Gospel, any investigastion of Matthew's structure must deal with them.

2. *Topical Outlines Based Upon Chiastic Structure (a-b-c-b'-a')*
A few scholars have identified the main structural thrust of the
Gospel as Matthew's use of chiasm. The most concise description of
chiasm comes from the pen of Charles H. Lohr (1961: 424):

> In this scheme the elements are arranged so that one section—the
> most prominent—forms the centre about which the rest are
> grouped in carefully balanced blocks, the first corresponding to the
> last, the second to the second from the end, the third to the third
> from the end, and so on.

Since virtually all the works which belong in this section are more
or less dependent upon the alternation of narrative and discourse
material, it would be possible to include this discussion within the
preceding section. But those who advocate a chiastic structure go far
beyond simply advocating this alternation; the alternating structure
is assumed in their work, but it is not the main concern. Furthermore,
the emphasis upon chiastic arrangement leads to literary and
theological conclusions quite distinct from those of Bacon and the
scholars who have followed him in Matthew's structure. For these
reasons, the chiastic framework receives separate treatment.

Chiastic patterns in Matthew can generally be divided into two
groups, according to the identification of the central or 'pivotal'
passage (the 'c' passage). This turning point has been located in the
middle of ch. 13 and at ch. 11.

Chiastic Patterns with Turning Point at 13.35-36
Most of the advocates of the chiastic structure fall under this
category. Among these scholars, Peter F. Ellis (1974) has produced
the most thorough and representative work.[35]

The assumptions of Ellis are quite apparent. Although he indicates
(1974: 8-9, 14) that his methodological procedure is that of
'composition criticism', which begins by looking at the book as a
whole in its present form ('vertical') and moves then to the secondary
consideration of examining the relation of the book to other books
and sources ('horizontal'), we discover that in practice his approach
depends a great deal upon Matthew's use of Mark and especially
upon the changes Matthew has made to his Marcan exemplar. Thus,
in his method, Ellis employs the same approach as others who
emphasize the alternating pattern.

Ellis proceeds according to a number of literary observations. He
notes, following Lohr, that Matthew is characterized by symmetry

(1974: 11). He also argues that there is a balance of length among the discourses, which corresponds to a balance of themes. On the basis of this observation, Ellis pairs the discourses (and their introductory narratives) as follows (1974: 12-13):

(a) Chs. 5-7 (Blessings of True Discipleship)
    Chs. 23-25 (Curses for False Disciples)
(b) Ch. 10 (Mission of Apostles)
    Ch. 18 (Apostles' Exercise of Authority in the Church)
(c) 3.8-12 (linked by reference to 28.18-20 'baptism')

Chapter 13 forms the middle element, and the division of ch. 13 between vv. 35 and 36 marks also the main division of the Gospel. The break between 13.35 and 13.36 relates to Jesus' change of activity (1974: 13):

> Up to 13.35 Jesus speaks to all the Jews. After 13.35, as in Mk. 8.27-46, Jesus bestows the major part of his attention upon the disciples, who, in contrast to the Jews, listen and understand him. Thus, in ch. 13, Jesus turns from the pseudo-Israel which will not accept him (cf. chs. 11-12) to the Church, the true Israel, which believes in him.

Ellis finds five major discourses and two minor speeches (3.8-12; 28.18-20). Since Matthew is fond of the number seven, it is not surprising that this chiastic framework contains seven speeches. The number has theological significance; it represents perfection, and hence in Matthew points to the fulfillment of Christ (1974: 13).

The narratives are subservient to the discourses; they lead up to and prepare the reader for the discourses. Therefore, it stands to reason that there is a correspondence between the narratives, just as there is a correspondence between the discourses. But since the narrative material is selected and arranged by Matthew in light of the discourses and is consequently relegated to a secondary role, the parallel between the narratives is secondary and supportive (1974: 16-17).

Although ch. 13 serves as the turning point for the Gospel, the book moves toward the climax of the commissioning scene of 28.18-20. Matthew has a proclivity toward emphasizing the final element, and what is true for individual pericopae is true also for the Gospel as a whole. Ellis substantiates this climactic movement further by insisting that christology is the primary moving force behind Matthew's Gospel (1974: 19-25). The main concern of this final scene is Jesus' fulfillment of the Danielic Son of man vision (Dan. 7.13-14). Therefore, the central christological category in Matthew is Son of man (1974: 24, 111-13).

The crucial passage for salvation history, however, is the turning point of Jesus' ministry at 13.35-36. There the old Israel was rejected as the people of God, owing to its rejection of the Messiah, while the disciple circle, representing the church of Christ, entered into kingdom participation.

Three questions arise regarding this proposal by Ellis. To begin with, it is doubtful that 13.35-36 can bear the weight which Ellis places upon it. Jesus teaches his disciples exclusively in ch. 10, and at least according to 5.1 the audience for the sermon on the mount was the disciples. This is not to say that there is not a movement in Matthew toward greater concentration on the circle of disciples, but a clear break at 13.35-36 is not immediately apparent.

In addition, Ellis's subordination of narrative to discourse is problematic. Ellis himself identifies the climax of the Gospel at 28.18-20 as christological; but since according to his own account the discourses do not focus on christology, one must assume that this climactic movement is due for the most part to the narratives. And if the narratives are the primary conveyors of the climactic movement, is it appropriate to relegate them to secondary status? This ambiguity surrounding the respective functions of narrative and discourse is reflected also in the unclear relationship between 13.35-36 and 28.18-20. Is 13.35-36 the crucial passage in the light of which we are ultimately to interpret the entire Gospel, or does that distinction belong to 28.18-20? The answer to this question has implications for the center of Matthew's theology: ecclesiology and discipleship, or christology.

Finally, some of the correspondences Ellis discerns are forced. For example, chs. 5-7 do contain 'blessings of true discipleship', but these blessings are for the most part contained in the first twelve or at most sixteen verses. The remainder of the sermon has mostly to do with instructions. According to Ellis, chs. 23-25 correspond to the sermon on the mount as 'curses for false disciples'. But the curses are found in ch. 23, and there they are not directed to disciples at all, but to Jewish leaders. The disciples are warned against apostasy in chs. 24-25, but one could hardly say that the primary focus of these chapters is upon the *cursing* of the derelict disciples. The attempt to connect 3.8-12 to 28.18-20 by reference to baptism in both seems unable to move beyond a merely formal parallel.

Chiastic Patterns with Turning Point at Ch. 11
The major advocate for a chiastic framework which revolves around
ch. 11 is H.B. Green (1968). Green bases this hypothesis on two
observations. First, although it is generally argued that Matthew
begins to follow Mark's narrative in a thoroughgoing way after Mt.
13.52, a more careful analysis reveals that this change actually occurs
in ch. 12. Second, ch. 11 contains a summary of the entire Gospel. It points
back to John the Baptist (v. 10), to the miracles of chs. 8–9 (v. 5), and
it comes to a climax in the witness Jesus makes to himself (vv. 25-30).
On the other hand, the chapter points ahead to the rejection of Jesus
and to the establishment of the elect.

Moving out from the center of ch. 11, Green notes the chiastic
parallels as follows:

Ch. 11

(a)	Ch. 10	Chs. 12–13
	(Rejection of Proclamation)	
(b)	Chs. 8–9	Chs. 14–18
	(Miracles Performed and Miracles Rejected)	
(c)	Chs. 5–7	Chs. 19–23
	(Teaching of the Sermon and its Rejection)	
(d)	Chs. 3–4	Chs. 24–25
	(Manifestation of Christ to Israel, and Manifestation at the last time)	
(e)	Chs. 1–2	Chs. 26–28
	(Infancy narrative and Passion narrative)	

Again, problems appear with this chiastic framework. In the first
place, it is inappropriate to determine the structure of the Gospel
largely from Matthew's redactional adherence to the order of Mark's
narrative. That Matthew begins to follow Mark more closely at ch.
12 may be accurate, but the necessary connection between that
observation and the determination of literary structure is not clear.

Moreover, the correspondences between the paired sections are
quite weak, weaker even than in Ellis's proposal. With regard to (a),
the proclamation of ch. 10 is that of the disciples; Jesus is the
proclaimer in chs. 12–13. If one tries to unite the proclamation of
Jesus with that of the disciples, one is forced to conclude that ch. 10
deals in some sense with the rejection of Jesus' message and,
according to Green, belongs on the other side of the pivotal ch. 11.
The connection Green makes between chs. 8–9 and chs. 14–18 fails

to account at all for ch. 18. Even Green (1968: 55-58) realizes that the relationship suggested in (c) is difficult; it is hardly clear that the rejection of Jesus in chs. 19-23 is motivated specifically by antipathy toward the statements of Jesus in the sermon. With regard to (d), one can see how it would be just as easy to argue for the linking of chs. 3-4 with chs. 19-23 as it is to argue for the correspondence which Green presents. The former would allow one to say that the manifestation of Jesus to Israel corresponds to the rejection of Jesus by Israel.

General Evaluation of the Chiastic Patterns
There are basically two problems with the chiastic approaches of both Ellis and Green. To begin with, it is reasonable to suppose that for chiasm to have its effect as a literary device, it must be at least relatively clear and discernible. This conclusion follows from the purpose of chiasm as identified by Lohr: memory. Chiasm is not meant to be esoteric; it has a utilitarian function for the reader. The chiastic parallels cited by both Ellis and Green are insufficiently conspicuous and clear to serve such a function. This is evident from the fact that these two scholars themselves disagree about how this chiasm achieves its purpose and where the central turning point lies. Other scholars have identified different chiastic arrangements in the Gospel as a whole.[36]

Further, if in fact Matthew is a literary unity, as most scholars argue, one may assume there are recurrences and frequent interconnections within the material. Accordingly, it is only to be expected that there will be echoes and points of contact between almost any two sections of the Gospel. The observation that Green finds chiastic parallelism between ch. 10 and chs. 12-13, whereas Ellis finds chiastic parallelism between ch. 10 and ch. 18 suggests that the correspondences which each finds are due less to the chiastic plan of Matthew than to repetition of congruent elements which characterize unified narratives.

These chiastic studies do point out, however, that in individual pericopae and sections Matthew often uses chiasm. Furthermore, the parallels drawn by Ellis and especially Green between the infancy narrative and the passion narrative deserve to be explored more thoroughly.

Topical Outline based upon 'Superscriptions' at 1.1; 4.17; 16.21
Although several scholars over the past century have adopted a

threefold division of the Gospel according to the repeated formulaic statements at 4.17 and 16.21, 'From that time Jesus began', by far the most consistent and thorough presentation has come from Kingsbury's *Matthew: Structure, Christology, Kingdom.*[37] Hence, the following survey focuses upon this work.

Kingsbury produced his research on Matthew's structure in order to deal with the relationship of this structure to Matthew's christology and his view of salvation history (p. 1). In examining Matthew's structure, Kingsbury employs a type of redaction criticism which places greater emphasis upon the final form of the Gospel than upon editorial changes Matthew has made to his sources.

After arguing against Bacon's fivefold division (pp. 2-5), Kingsbury presents his own structure for Matthew's Gospel. He acknowledges that the fivefold formula is significant in the Gospel, yet both the content and the transitional character of these formulae deny them an ultimately determinative role in Matthew's structure (pp. 5-6).

In contrast to the fivefold formula, the phrase 'from that time Jesus began' at 4.17 and 16.21 does qualify as a structural indicator. This phrase, found only four times in the New Testament (also in Matthew 26.16 and Luke 16.16), always marks off a new period of time (p. 8). Kingsbury declares that the 'begin' (ἄρχομαι) here is not pleonastic; it actually means to begin or start (p. 8).

Whereas the formula, 'and it happened when Jesus finished' is simply transitional and cannot be pressed thematically, the formula at 4.17 and 16.21 actually sums up the material that follows in each case (p. 9). A corollary of this position is that 1.1 is also a 'superscription' for 1.1-4.16. Accordingly, Kingsbury argues for this conclusion over against those who would limit 1.1 to the genealogy or first chapter alone or those who would see it as a title for the entire Gospel (pp. 9-11). Rather, Matthew has taken over the phrase 'book of the generation' from Gen. 2.4a and 5.1b (LXX). where it serves as a heading for both genealogical and narrative material (p. 11).

A detailed analysis of 1.1-4.16 reveals both that 1.1 admirably serves as a superscription to this division and that this section forms a closely knit unity. In ch. 1, Jesus is presented as the Messiah, Son of Abraham and Son of David. Yet there are also allusions to his status as Son of God: he is conceived by the Holy Spirit (1.18, 20), and through the prophet God calls him 'Emmanuel' (1.23) (p. 12). In ch. 2, he is described as the ruler of God's eschatological people, and here again there is allusion to Son of God; although Matthew consistently refers to Jesus as 'the child' after v. 7 (vv. 8-9, 11-14, 20-21), he breaks this pattern in v. 15 when Jesus is called 'my Son' through another prophetic passage (p. 12). The climax to this first division is therefore the direct acknowledgment from God of Jesus' divine Sonship at the baptism (3.17).

The temporal and topical switch at 3.1 does not destroy the unity of 1.1-4.16. John the Baptist is clearly the forerunner, and his ministry as well as everything else which is recounted in this section occurs before the public proclamation of Jesus to Israel (4.17) (pp. 13-14). Furthermore, this division ends not at 4.11, but at 4.16, as careful attention to grammatical phenomena indicates. Kingsbury also points out that 4.13-16 is connected to 2.23 in terms both of content and form (pp. 15-16).[38]

Kingsbury argues that 4.17-16.20 and 16.21-28.20 demonstrate the same continuity with their respective 'superscriptions' and the same unity as obtained for 1.1-4.16. 'The Proclamation of Jesus' (4.17-16.20) is tied together by three summary passages (4.23-25; 9.35; 11.1) and by a logical progression leading up to the climax of Peter's confession at 16.13-20 (pp. 17-20). 'The Suffering, Death, and Resurrection of Jesus Messiah' (16.21-28.20) is also bound together by three summaries: predictions of Jesus' death and resurrection (16.21; 17.22-23; 20.17-29). 'Jerusalem' is explicitly mentioned at 16.21, and this geographical-theological reference to the passion and resurrection of Jesus establishes the overall theme which pervades these chapters. The climax to this section comes with the death and resurrection of Jesus and especially his final commissioning in 28.16-20 (pp. 22-23).

This structure points to Jesus as Son of God. The first major division, which presents the 'Person of Jesus Messiah' is pervaded throughout by the divine Sonship of Jesus and climaxes in the declaration from God at the baptism that Jesus is, in fact, his Son (3.17). The second major division closes with Peter's confession that Jesus is the Son of God (16.16). The third major division climaxes with the death of Jesus, which emphasizes his divine Sonship (27.40, 54); and the book comes to an ultimate climax at 28.18-20, where Jesus commands his disciples to baptize in the name of the Son (v. 19). Moreover, this divine Sonship is given content by three passages which stand at crucial points in the Gospel: 1.23; 18.20; 28.20. These passages, pointing to the presence of Jesus (or God) in the midst of his people, indicate that for Matthew God has drawn near to dwell with his people in the person of his Son, Jesus Christ (pp. 42-83).

Kingsbury concludes from his structural and exegetical investigations that Matthew conceived of salvation history in two epochs. He notes that Matthew is interested in salvation history, for he gives more weight to temporal terms and notions than did Mark (pp. 27-28). A close examination of these expressions in their contexts reveals that Matthew uses 'in those days' (3.1; 24.19-22, 29), to refer to the eschatological period before the final day of consummation (p. 31). Since this expression is used both of the appearance of John in Judah heralding the arrival of Jesus (3.1) and of the period just before the parousia of Christ, Matthew views the entire period (John–Jesus–church) as one major division of salavation history. This conclusion is supported by the Gospel's climactic emphasis upon the abiding presence of Jesus in his church (28.16-20), the correspondence between the earthly Jesus and the exalted Lord of the church's confession, the observations that Matthew (in contrast to Luke) has no ascension narrative nor does he emphasize the work of the Holy Spirit in the age of the church, and the fact that the structure of the Gospel points toward an emphasis upon the story of Jesus as one who ushers in the age of the kingdom (pp. 32-33).

Several major objections have been raised against Kingsbury's structural position.

Some scholars, such as Barr (1976: 350) and Rolland Philippe (1972: 166), have rejected the break at 16.21 because it separates 'the three Petrine episodes proper to Matthew, in which Jesus is proclaimed Son of God (14.25; 16.13-16; 17.24-27)'. The crucial item here is obviously the last passage, since 14.25-33 and 16.13-16 stand within Kingsbury's second major division. A glance at 17.24-27 reveals, however, that Jesus is not there proclaimed Son of God at all. Furthermore, this criticism assumes a fact not placed in evidence by these scholars, namely, that these three passages are of primary structural significance.

Again, Barr (1976: 350) objects that because 16.21 corresponds to Mk 8.31, a passage which indicates crucial recognition and reversal and divides that Gospel into two halves, it is unlikely that 16.21 has the same function in Matthew: 'Thus, if Kingsbury is right, Matthew and Mark have essentially the same structure. Possible, but dubious'.

But this criticism is also problematic. To say that Matthew and

Mark share one divisional break is not to say that they have the same overall structure. Furthermore, as was indicated above, it is methodologically unsound, and it is certainly contrary to Barr's stated method of literary criticism, to base the interpretation of the structure of one Gospel on the structure of another Gospel.

Other criticisms, too, have been put forward. Reginald Fuller and Pheme Perkins (1983: 82) and also Donald Senior (1983: 25) raise the objection that Kingsbury places too much weight on the phrase 'from that time', and that he does not deal adequately with the problem that this same construction appears in 26.16. Senior asks,

> But do two uses in the entire Gospel enable one to label a phrase a 'fixed formula?' And if Matthew wanted to give such importance to these two verses in his Gospel, is it likely that he would pen a very similar expression in 26.16?

This is not a convincing criticism, for Kingsbury does deal with the problem (p. 8), and the existence of a similar expression in ch. 26 does not exclude the possibility that the phrase as used in 4.17 and 16.21 marks off major divisions in the Gospel. For one thing, the formula at 4.17 and 16.21 is asyndetic, wheras the 'and' (καί) in 26.16 links the phrase 'from that time' with the preceding. Moreover, 4.17 and 16.21 are linked by the repetition not only of the phrase 'from that time', but of the further expression 'Jesus began', plus the infinitive. These latter phenomena are not present in 26.16.

Again Barr (1976: 351) has objected that although 4.17 and 16.21 indicate major breaks in Matthew's presentation of the life of Jesus, the development of Jesus' life or activities is not necessarily to be equated with the literary structure of Matthew's Gospel. This criticism, of course, points to another more fundamental question, namely, whether the Gospel of Matthew is essentially narrative, and if so, what are the implications of this narrative character for structure? Among other things, this question has to do with the relationship between narrative and discourse in Matthew.

The relationship between narrative and discourse stands behind another criticism of Kingsbury's position, namely, that he too easily dismisses the fivefold formula and the function of the large blocks of discourse material in Matthew, as Fuller and Perkins argue (1983: 82). Even if one looks only at the Gospel of Matthew (without turning an eye toward Mark), the long speeches of Jesus represent a significant literary feature. We agree that the function of these speeches in Kingsbury's threefold structure needs to be addressed more directly and more fully.

Finally, Jean Claude Ingelaere (1979: 24) has suggested that more needs to be done in terms of working out the structure of the large divisions according to Kingsbury's plan. Ingelaere declares that Kingsbury has not yet adequately shown the unity of these sections or the relationship of the structure of these sections to that of the Gospel as a whole.

Positively, one may conclude that Kingsbury deals carefully with the final form of the text and has argued cogently for his threefold division. It seems to present fewer serious problems than the other approaches examined above. The programmatic nature of Kingsbury's work and the fact that this structural view has not been adopted by the majority of scholars make further investigation into the structural patterns Kingsbury has identified crucial.[39]

C. *Conceptual Structures*

By 'conceptual structures' we mean those attempts to define Matthew's structure according to a theme or central idea around which Matthew has arranged his materials. Those who advocate these conceptual structures deny topical arrangement in the Gospel; the Gospel is not designed according to discrete sections, but according to an idea or a purpose in the mind of the evangelist, which is reflected in the Gospel as a whole.

Most scholars who belong in this camp identify this central concept with Matthew's view of salvation history.[40] Although virtually all of them argue that Matthew understands (at least generally) salvation history in three epochs (Israel–Jesus–church), they differ according to the precise shape of this salvation-historical understanding and consequently in the way Matthew has structured his Gospel to reflect his salvation-historical views.

1. *Georg Strecker*
According to Strecker, Matthew wrote during a time of changing Christian self-understanding. This period of second-generation Christians was characterized by the beginnings of 'early Catholicism' and by the concern over an indefinitely delayed parousia, that is, the continuing nature of human history (1967: 219; 1971: 41-49). Therefore, Matthew redacts his traditional material according to

three principles: historicization, ethicization, and institutionalization. Matthew deals with the problem of history through his process of historicization. It was his purpose to establish a time line extending from Abraham, or the fathers, through the time of the prophets, to the time of Jesus, who stands as the fulfillment of the preceding periods (1971: 89-93). The time of Jesus is set apart from the time of the church, just as it is separate from the time of the fathers and the prophets which preceded. Matthew presents the time of Jesus as entirely past, an ideal period standing in the middle of time (1967: 223).

Matthew engages in 'temporal' historicization. He has expanded his Marcan *Vorlage* by adding the genealogy and infancy narratives, thereby revealing that he is reflecting on the past as such. In this regard, Matthew parallels Luke (1967: 220). Matthew has also edited Mark in terms of chronology. To his Marcan source, Matthew has added the phrase 'from that time' (4.17; 16.21; 26.16). According to Strecker, this formula does not reflect development in the life of Jesus, but is intended rather to emphasize the linear time line in contrast to the kerygmatic nature of the traditional material (1967: 220).

At this point Strecker addresses directly the question of topical outlines. He rejects both the threefold structure suggested by Edgar Krentz (and later Kingsbury) and Bacon's fivefold approach. Strecker's objections to the outline put forward by Krentz concern the designations or titles which Krentz has given to the main sections of the Gospel. To Krentz's notion that 4.17-16.20 concerns the proclamation of the kingdom, Strecker responds that 'kingdom' is no more the theme of the first main division than it is of the second (18.23; 21.33). In like manner Strecker rejects Krentz's designation of 16.21-28.20 as 'The Son of Man on his way to resurrection', because Jesus is just as much Son of man in 4.17-16.20 as he is in the final main section of Matthew. We agree that the designations Krentz employs for these two units could be more felicitous,[41] but this criticism from Strecker does not deal with the central issues surrounding the division of the Gospel. Since Strecker is no more impressed with Bacon's outline than he is with that of Krentz, he concludes that 'Matthew, instead of working out and arranging a detailed composed structure, was rather concerned to constitute the Gospel as a whole in terms of a continuous line, which can be fixed temporally and geographically' (1967: 220 n. 2).

2. *Survey of Investigations*   47

In addition to 'temporal' historicization, Matthew also engages in 'geographical' historicization. Strecker argues that 'house', which in Mark is linked to the messianic secret and represents the place of revelation, is employed by Matthew in a geographical rather than a topological-theological sense (1967: 221; 1971: 93-98).

The formula quotations also serve this historicizing function. They are continually linked to events in Jesus' *life*, and they consequently serve to reinforce the biographical nature of the narrative. Matthew therefore uses the formula quotations to present the history of Jesus as a unique, unrepeatable event, separate from his own time (1967: 221-22; 1971: 107). Matthew further reinforces this understanding of the unique, separate time of Jesus by inserting two references to the restriction of the ministry of Jesus to 'the lost sheep of the house of Israel', and by employing 'Son of David' in order to indicate the confinement of Jesus to Israel.

The idealization of the disciples also serves to separate the (past) time of Jesus from the present time of the church. Furthermore, like Jesus, the mission of the disciples in Matthew's story is limited to the people of Israel (1967: 221-23; 1971: 107). John the Baptist, coming in 'the way of righteousness', also belongs to this ideal period (1967: 223).

The meaning of this 'historicization' is found in Matthew's 'ethicization'. The time of Jesus was also the time of the proclamation of the eschatological demand for a greater righteousness. This demand was central to the constitution of the people of Israel in the time leading up to Jesus, yet they failed to realize its goal. But that demand is required of the church in the time following Jesus. As it obeys the commands of Jesus and follows his example, the chuch 'represents the ethical demand in time' (1967: 230). Matthew's institutionalization is reflected in concern for church officials and church administration and in the presentation of the sacraments (1967: 228-29).

Strecker's study contains three problematic areas. To begin with, Strecker appears to be interpreting Matthew in light of Luke, specifically as Hans Conzelmann has understood Luke–Acts and its concept of salvation history (1967: 220). It is possible, of course, that Matthew, writing at approximately the same time as Luke, wrote with the same concerns and for the same purpose, but the differences between the two Gospels must be given due weight.

Furthermore, there are good reasons to think that Matthew

wished to establish more continuity between the time of Jesus and
the time of the church than Strecker allows. Strecker himself admits
that the figure of Peter represents the Christian in the age of
Matthew (1971: 205). There are also indications in the Gospel that
Matthew in some ways coalesced the earthly Jesus and the exalted
heavenly Christ.[42] The exalted Jesus is 'with' his church (28.20) and
is thus associated with the earthly Jesus (compare 18.20). Moreover,
Kingsbury (1966: 502-504) has drawn attention to the problems
associated with the use Strecker makes of the genealogy and formula
quotations.

Finally, Matthew's concept of 'Son of David' seems to emphasize
the messianic function of Jesus toward the people of Israel and
Israel's blatant rejection of the mercies of the time of fulfillment (as
Kingsbury, 1977: 53-55) rather than a biographical demarcation
separating Jesus from the time of the church.

2. *Wolfgang Trilling*

If Strecker identified the central concept in the Gospel of Matthew as
the earthly Jesus—the middle of time, Trilling finds it in Matthew's
understanding of the 'true Israel'. For Trilling, the main contention
of the Gospel is that the church has replaced the Jews as the 'true
people of God' (1968: 95-96). Trilling's investigation revolves around
two elements: (a) the community which passed on the traditions, and
(b) Matthew's redactional activity. With these concerns in mind,
Trilling devotes a section in each major unit of his monograph to an
exegesis of a relevant passage or passages, followed by a thematic
section drawing out the theological implications.

The key to Matthew's Gospel is the great commission (28.18-20).
There the main themes of Matthew are summarized: Christ's
lordship over his church relating to the Old Testament concepts of
the kingdom of God and the people of God, universalism, discipleship,
and a 'fulfilled eschatology' (1968: 49-51).

The negative background for the status of the church as the true
Israel is found in the judgment of historic Israel. The refusal of Israel
to accept the Messiah led to its condemnation. This guilt and
condemnation are especially reflected in 21.43 and 27.15-26. All
Israel is collectively guilty. Her judgment is twofold: loss of the
kingdom (21.43), and the destruction of Jerusalem (22.1-14). There is
no hope for the future conversion or restoration of the Jewish people
(1968: 95-96).

The positive background of the role of the church as the true Israel is found in the revelation of the Old Testament. Mt. 10.5-6 serves as proof of the messiahship of Jesus and does not nullify the Gentile mission (1968: 92-102, 130-31). Matthew's understanding is found in 15.24, where Jesus is sent to the lost sheep of the house of Israel in order to fulfill his messianic role and to seal the guilt of Israel. The universalism of Matthew's Gospel is rooted in the Old Testament concepts of (a) the election of the people in order to serve as a light to the nations (1968: 99-105), and (b) the kingdom of God (1968: 162-63).

Finally, the task of the true Israel is to obey the will of God. His will is a 'righteousness which exceeds that of the scribes and Pharisees' (5.20). This involves perfection (19.21; 5.48), perfection of love toward neighbors. This ethic is bound up with the notion of promise and fulfillment; the will of God, not the law, is to be fulfilled (1968: 185-86).

By way of critical evaluation, we note that the methodology Trilling has employed is somewhat troublesome. It is doubtful that even a passage so significant in Matthew as 28.18-20 can bear all the weight which Trilling places upon it. His almost exclusive attention to five or six 'key' passages makes one suspect that he fails to give due weight to the Gospel text as a whole. Furthermore, if the notion of 'true Israel' is so central in Matthew's theology and structure, it seems strange that the expression is not once found on the pages of the Gospel. Finally, Trilling's proposal has difficulty fitting all the evidence. He must conclude, for example, that the command of 5.19 comes from an erstwhile discussion within Matthew's church regarding the Torah in Jewish Christianity and does not express the opinion of the evangelist. The explanation of 10.5-6 is too brief to be persuasive. And Trilling admits that ch. 18 does not quite fit his schema; for it is a teaching piece on church administration (1968: 106-23, 154-58). In short, although the rejection of the nation of Israel in favor of the church as bearer of the kingdom of God is found in Matthew, the notion of 'true Israel' is not the best way to understand this conception, and this notion is not sufficiently dominant to account for all (or even the majority) of the material in Matthew and to determine the structure of the whole.

3. *Rolf Walker*

Walker, like Strecker, sees in Matthew a historicizing tendency.

Matthew is a Gentile Christian writing to a Gentile-Christian church. The issue facing this writer is not the problem of contemporary Jewish persecution; he does not write a polemic against the synagogue or an apology for Christianity in light of the Jewish rejection of Jesus. The Gospel of Matthew is rather a kerygmatic history book, providing an etiology for the Gentile mission with which his church was so well acquainted (1967: 10-11, 114-20, 145-49).

Walker notes that Matthew groups together disparate parties of Israel's representative leadership, especially 'Pharisees and Sadducees' (1967: 11-38). This uniting of the Pharisees and Sadducees cannot reflect the contemporary situation of the evangelist, and it does not refer to the Old Testament people of God. It must refer to the representatives of Israel at the time of Jesus. This disparate grouping is no ignorant mistake, but it is rather a skillful theological touch. All Israel is guilty; the generation marking the end of Israel's salvation history is a unity of evil (1968: 38-74). Therefore, the Gentiles take over as the people of God; this substitution took place with the destruction of Jerusalem in 70 CE. Walker notes that Israel is not included in Mt. 25.31-46 (1967: 114-27).

Thus, Matthew's scheme of salvation history is clearly defined. For Matthew, as for Luke, Jesus is the middle of time; yet Matthew inserts his 'Acts of the Apostles' into the very structure of the Gospel itself (1967: 114). Salvation history in Matthew runs from the time of Abraham to the parousia. Within this time line are three distinct epochs, and this division is reflected in the structure of the Gospel: (1) the pre-history of the Messiah (chs. 1-2); (2) the summoning of Israel (chs. 3-23, 'middle of time'); (3) the transition to the Last Time (chs. 24-28, Matthew's time) (1967: 114-27).

Several problems can be found with Walker's approach. For one thing, it is by no means clear that the Gospel of Matthew is a Gentile-Christian work, written for a Gentile-Christian community. Furthermore, Walker is unable to account for much material in the Gospel; ch. 18 is particularly problematic for him. David Hare (1970: 371-72) has suggested, moreover, that the redactional references to the persecution of Christians are more easily accounted for on the basis of historical experience than abstract theological inquiry.

Again, this threefold breakdown of the structure of the Gospel is not reflected by literary clues or indicators. Finally, the emphasis upon the fall of Jerusalem of 70 CE is problematic, since that event is

not narrated in the Gospel. Although Matthew (apparently) points to
the fall of Jerusalem in chs. 22 and 24, it is not emphasized in the
Gospel as a whole. The emphasis Walker places on this event
therefore leads to a playing down of the story of Jesus which the
Gospel of Matthew presents.

4. *Hubert Frankemölle*

Frankemölle agrees with Strecker and Walker that Matthew was
written by a Gentile Christian to a community of the same make-up.
His purpose in writing, however, was related to *apologia*. The dual
situation of the rejection of Jesus by the Jews and the destruction of
the Jerusalem temple produced consternation among the members of
Matthew's church. These events raised the problem of the faithfulness
of God to his promises and to his people (1974: 1-6).

Matthew met this theological problem by asserting that the church
had replaced Israel as the covenant people of God (1974: 7-82, 309).
Matthew has composed a work of 'covenant theology' explaining the
ways of God and the judgment of God upon his people similar to that
of the Old Testament works of the Deuteronomist and the Chronicler.
Frankemölle argues that the speech-narrative complex in the Gospel
as a whole prepares for the paschal meal and the death of Jesus; as
such, the discourses serve as 'departure speeches' (1974: 335-36).
There are both Jewish and Hellenistic examples of this form, but the
clearest parallels come from Chronicles and especially Deuteronomy
(1974: 339-42). Furthermore, Frankemölle finds correspondence
between the speech complexes in Deuteronomy and those in
Matthew, especially in terms of the repeated formulae associated
with the Deuteronomic speeches (1974: 340).[43] God has renewed his
covenant by coming to dwell with his people, the church.[44] It is
therefore the responsibility of this new covenant people to obey the
will of God (1974: 273-307).

But Frankemölle disagrees with Strecker and Walker when he
argues that Matthew was not interested in the past as such; he was
interested only in kerygma. The past facts have no significance in
themselves at all. Matthew is not interested in dividing salvation
history up into discrete epochs; Matthew's salvation history is rather
to be understood in terms of the categories of prophecy and
fulfillment (1974: 360-91).

Problematic here is Frankemölle's total disregard for the distinction
between the time of Jesus and the time of the church. As we saw

above, there is a certain degree of coalescing or assimilation of the earthly Jesus and the disciples to the exalted Lord of the church and members of Matthew's community; yet there is not sufficient evidence to conclude that Matthew wishes to de-historicize totally the events of the past. Furthermore, when one examines the 'parallels' Frankemölle discerns between Matthew and the Old Testament works of the Deuteronomist and the Chronicler, one finds that the correspondence is stretched; there are many points of discontinuity. Finally, Kingsbury (1975: 38) has pointed out that Matthew assumes what Frankemölle believes the first evangelist set out to prove: 'On the basis of Matthew's use of the OT, the faithfulness of God and the continued validity of his promises are exactly what Matthew accounts as certain'.

5. *William G. Thompson*

From an analysis of the form of Mt. 24.4b-14 Thompson discerns three stages in the history of salvation (1974: 245-50): (1) previous events from the standpoint of Matthew (vv. 4b-8); (2) current experience of Matthew's church (vv. 9-13); and (3) the future (v. 14). When Thompson examines Matthew's redactional activity in chs. 24 and 10 in relation to his Marcan *Vorlage*, he discovers that Matthew has moved sayings regarding Jewish opposition in Jewish territory from ch. 24 (= Mark 13) to ch. 10. Thompson suggests that the reference to the 'nations' in ch. 10 refers to Gentiles who live in Jewish territory. Matthew 10 thus relates to the restrictive earthly ministry of Jesus and his disciples, whereas ch. 24 refers to the contemporary experience of Matthew's church, when the Gentile mission was in full swing (1974: 250-56).

For Matthew, this change from Jewish missionary enterprise to that directed toward the Gentiles occurred at the resurrection. In the missionary commissioning at 28.16-20, Jesus commands his disciples to 'make disciples of all nations' (1974: 259-60). But Matthew is concerned not only with the missionary activity of his church, but he also gives advice concerning divisions within his church, especially in the section 17.22–18.35 (1970; 1974: 260-62). Thompson suggests that this historical perspective of Matthew may provide the ultimate clues to the composition of Matthew's structure (1974: 262).

The major problem with Thompson's work is that it fails to account for all the evidence, especially material found in ch. 10. The notion that references to the 'nations' in that passage indicate

Gentiles who live in Jewish territory is forced. Furthermore, there are injunctions of a general nature which Jesus gives in ch. 10; it is not clear how these can be limited to the ministry of Jesus and his disciples (vv. 8-42).

6. *John P. Meier*

Meier takes his cue from the relationship between 10.5, 6 and 15.24, which restrict the ministry of Jesus and the disciples to Israel, and 28.16-20, where Jesus commands these disciples to 'make disciples of all nations'. This apparent incongruity suggests a radical turning point in salvation history at the resurrection of Jesus. References earlier in the Gospel which tend to contradict the exclusiveness otherwise found there are said to be 'proleptic' (1975: 204-207).

This salvation-historical turning point at the resurrection is substantiated by two other observations. At 28.16-20 the reference Jesus makes to baptism, rather than circumcision, suggests that with the resurrection obedience to the Mosaic law is no longer required. Again, breaks in the earlier requirement of the law are said to be proleptic. By literary analysis, Meier argues that Matthew ties together the death and resurrection by associating both with apocalyptic devices used to portray the beginning of the new age (1975: 205-206). Meier concludes that the kingdom of God did not fully arrive until the death-resurrection. There are thus three stages in the coming of the kingdom (1975: 207-10): (a) the inbreaking with the earthly ministry of Jesus; (b) the full inbreaking with the death-resurrection of Jesus; (c) and 'full manifestation' of the kingdom at the end of time.[45]

The repeated appeal Meier makes to 'proleptic' elements in Matthew weakens his case. This appears to be a catch-all category for the evidence which does not fit his thesis. Beyond Meier's hypothesis, there are no reasons in the text to think these references are proleptic. Jesus' reference to baptism at 28.19 is thin evidence for a radical turning point regarding obedience to the law. Moreover, there is a line of narrative separating the death and resurrection in Matthew, including the women (27.55-56), the burial (27.57-61), and the securing of the tomb (27.62-66). Finally, the evidence from the Gospel as a whole points overwhelmingly to the conclusion that the kingdom of God has fully come with the ministry of Jesus; it awaits only its consummation (for instance, 12.28). It is difficult to conceive a more complete inbreaking of the kingdom than the circumstance that in Jesus God was and continues to be with his people (1.23). Meier points to no passage where such a three-tier notion of salvation history can be found comparable to the references to the 'gospel of the kingdom' linking the ministry of Jesus (4.23) to that of the post-Easter disciples (24.14).

All these salvation-history studies emphasize ecclesiology over christology. In this regard, they stand in continuity with the ecclesiological emphasis found among advocates of the alternating structural pattern. We shall argue in Chapters 3 through 7 that the Gospel is a story about Jesus; if, indeed, this understanding is correct, the emphases of these studies are wrong. Further, virtually all these critics argue that salvation history is divided into three epochs, making a division between the time of Jesus and the time of the church. But it will be shown in the following chapters of our study that Matthew coalesces the earthly Jesus and the exalted Lord while at the same time maintaining the historical integrity of the former, and that the Matthean concept of Christ abiding 'with' his church is central to Matthew's theology. If this is correct, it follows that the radical salvation-historical break between the time of Jesus and the time of the church is problematic. Moreover, the rejection of discrete topical divisions within the Gospel is appropriate only so long as such divisions cannot be clearly and persuasively identified. Finally, one should note that outside of the general three-epoch framework, there is lack of agreement among these scholars regarding the way in which salvation history has shaped the structure of the First Gospel.

Yet this approach helps us to see that salvation history is a significant element in Matthew's theology. Beyond that, it rightly insists that there is no doubt an organic relationship between Matthew's structure and his view of salvation history.

D. *Conclusion*[46]

This survey of Matthean structure shows that there is still no consensus regarding the structure of Matthew's Gospel. We have discovered, however, that there is a clear relationship between the determination of structure and the understanding of Matthew's theology. We have also seen that a definite connection exists between the type of method employed and the type of structure discerned. We have noted, further, that none of these structural approaches is without its problems.

Yet these structural presentations point to several relevant issues which must be addressed in any investigation of the structure of Matthew's Gospel: (1) the significance of geographical and chronological references for the structure of Matthew's Gospel; (2) the relationship between narrative and discourse material, including the structural significance of the fivefold formula at 7.28; 11.1; 13.53; 19.1; 26.1; (3) the meaning of the formula repeated at 4.17 and 16.21, and the relationship between this formula and the fivefold formula; (4) the relevance and function of characteristic Matthean literary devices, such as chiasm, inclusio, numerical arrangement, for the problem of Matthew's macrostructure; (5) the existence of discrete topical units within the Gospel and, if in fact these units exist, their unity and interrelationships; (6) the implications of Matthew's structure for his theology, especially in terms of christology and salvation history.

With the background of these studies and with the recongnition of these key issues we embark upon our examination of Matthew's structure.

Chapter 3

THE STRUCTURE OF MATTHEW:
REPETITION OF COMPARISON

We come now to the point where we apply the structural principles delineated in Chapter 1 to the text of Matthew's Gospel. In Chapters 3 through 7, our aim is to demonstrate that the Gospel is constructed according to four major structural elements: repetition of comparision, repetition of contrast, repetition of particularization and climax, and climax with inclusio. We shall devote one chapter to each of these major structural elements, and we shall conclude our examination of Matthew's structure with a brief discussion concerning the relationship between the discourses and the broad narrative framework of the Gospel.

In this chapter, our concern is to deal with the first of these structural elements, namely, the repetition of comparision. The relationship between Jesus and the expectations for the disciples in Matthew is essentially that of comparision. Matthew sets the expectations for, or the role of, the disciples and the person of Jesus side by side in terms of their relation to God, manner of living, and mission.

A. *Comparison between the Mission of Jesus and the Mission of the Disciples*

The clearest analogy between Jesus and the disciples in Matthew's Gospel is that of their respective ministries. One notes, first of all, that the geographical sphere of ministry is the same; Galilee is the sphere where eschatological salvation is proffered, first to Israel and later to the Gentiles. Jesus embarks on his eschatological ministry having come from Judea to Galilee (4.12; compare 3.13), just as the disciples receive their missionary commissioning when they return to Galilee; in both cases Matthew employs the prepositional phrase 'unto Galilee'.

The comparison between the ministry of Jesus and that of his disciples is reflected also in the calling of the disciples (4.18-22). They are called not only to 'follow' Jesus, but also to be 'fishers of people' (4.19). This phrase points back to the general statement of the preaching of Jesus in 4.17 and points ahead to the summary of Jesus' Galilean ministry in 4.23-25. The calling of the four fishermen is sandwiched between these two statements regarding the ministry of Jesus. At the very outset, therefore, Matthew links the mission of Jesus to that of the disciples.

1. *Comparison Involving the Acts of Ministry*
In line with these general connections between the ministry of Jesus and that of the disciples, Matthew records that Jesus and the disciples perform generally the same acts of ministry.[1] Both Jesus and the disciples (eventually) teach,[2] and they teach the same thing: 'all that I have commanded you' (28.19). In ch. 10 Jesus gives his disciples the authority to perform the same eschatological works that he accomplishes. Jesus thus gives his disciples authority (10.1), even as he has been given authority (11.27; 28.18). This authority includes the ability to cast out spirits,[3] and, in an obvious verbal parallel to the healing activity of Jesus described in the overview statements 4.23 and 9.35, 'to heal every disease and every infirmity'. In response to Jesus' healing of the paralytic in 9.8, the crowds glorify God, 'who had given such authority to people', pointing to the authority to heal shared by Jesus and later the disciples.[4]

Not only are the disciples to heal, they are also to preach, even as Jesus has preached, that 'the kingdom of heaven is at hand' (10.7; cf. 4.17). Indeed, both they and he preach 'the gospel of the kingdom'.[5] And the Matthean Jesus describes the ministry of the disciples in a way that clearly mirrors his own activity in chs. 8-9, as we shall see in a more detailed examination below.

2. *Comparison Involving the Significance of Ministry*
The comparison between the ministry of Jesus and that of the disciples is indicated not only in terms of acts of ministry, that is, preaching, teaching, and healing, but also in terms of the significance of their respective ministries. Even as Jesus is sent (by God),[6] so the disciples are sent (by Jesus);[7] and both Jesus and the disciples may be 'received' in their ministries.[8] Both engage in itinerant missionary work (10.9-10; compare 8.20), and both withdraw from those who

reject the message.[9] Moreover, the rejection of the message of the disciples carries the same consequences expressed in the same language as those attending the rejection of Jesus' message: 'It will be more tolerable for the land of Sodom and Gomorrah on the day of judgment than for that city' (10.15; cf. 11.22-24; also 12.41-42). Indeed the disciples even share in Jesus' activity of eschatological judgment.[10]

This comparison between the significance of the ministry of Jesus and that of the ministry of the disciples is underscored by the correlation in the scope of their respective ministries. Even as the scope of Jesus' activity is limited to Israel, so is the initial activity of the disciples (prior to 28.16-20); and again Matthew points to the comparison by employing precisely the same phraseology: 'unto the lost sheep of the house of Israel' (10.5-6; 15.24).

3. Comparison Involving Persecutions Attending the Ministry
But sharing in the ministry of Jesus means also sharing in the persecutions that accompany that ministry. The persecutions which attend the messianic vocation of Jesus are foreshadowed already in the infancy narratives; both the authorities in the person of Herod and the Jews ('all Jerusalem with him') are troubled by the appearance of Jesus. And Herod takes definite measures against him (2.3, 13-23). The theme of the persecution of disciples runs throughout the Gospel, beginning already in the sermon on the mount (5.10-11; see also 13.21; 20.22-23), but it is concentrated especially in three passages (chs. 10; 24; 23.29-36).

In line with the persecutions Jesus experiences, he warns the disciples of severe persecutions even as he sends them out in ch. 10. He describes them as 'sheep in the midst of wolves' (10.16) and consequently advises them to 'beware of people' (10.17), describing the activity of these persecutors. They will deliver the disciples up to councils.[11] The term 'deliver up' (παραδίδωμι) is a technical term used for the execution of John the Baptist, but used especially for the trial and death of Jesus;[12] moreover, Matthew also narrates that Jesus is condemned before the council (26.59). These opponents will scourge the followers of Jesus in their synagogues (10.17; 23.34), even as later the Matthean Jesus predicts he will be scourged (20.19). Further, these adversaries will lead the disciples before governors and kings (10.18), in analogy to Jesus, who was pursued by King Herod (2.1, 3.9) and will be delivered over to Pilate the governor.[13]

Indeed, as Jesus is eventually killed by his opponents, so the disciples will be delivered up to death (10.21). Yet those who, like Jesus, 'endure to the end' will be saved (10.22; 24.9).

In fact, the first reference to crucifixion in Matthew's Gospel is not in relation to Jesus, but to the disciples. Jesus demands that the disciple 'take up his cross and follow me' (10.38; 16.24). And Jesus elsewhere predicts concerning the Christian messengers sent to the Jews, 'some they will crucify' (23.34). The Matthean Jesus is well aware, of course, that the cross is also to be his fate (20.19; 26.6).

Matthew underscores this link between the suffering of Jesus and that of his disciples by means of the oft-repeated phrases 'for my sake' and 'on account of my name'.[14] The comparison is also reinforced by the connection between cross-bearing and following: 'take up his cross and follow after me' (10.38; 16.24). Indeed, the comparison between Jesus and the disciples is made explicit in 10.24–25: a disciple is not above his teacher nor is a slave above his master, but rather 'It is enough for the disciple to be like his teacher and the slave to be like his master'.

B. *Comparison between the Ethical Behavior of Jesus and the Ethical Expectations for the Disciples*

Matthew also compares Jesus and the expectations for the disciples in terms of ethical behavior, or, perhaps better stated, manner of living. In other words, there is comparison between the expectations and instructions of Jesus to his disciples, on the one hand, and his own life and activities as these are narrated by Matthew, on the other.

The inner structure or dynamics of Matthean ethics is quite clear. The community is required to obey the law (5.17-20), but the law is understood not in terms of the letter of the Old Testament command, but in terms of the inner attitude of love, which is manifested in obedience to God and in concrete acts of well-doing toward others.[15] To act in accord with the principle of love is not only to fulfil the law and the prophets (5.17; 7.12; 22.36-40), but also to do 'the will of the Father' (7.21; 12.50; 21.31).[16]

In line with this structure of ethics, in Matthew's Gospel Jesus is the epitome of obedience to the will of God. Jesus submits to baptism, even though he has no need to confess sin, in order to 'fulfill all righteousness' (3.15). By overcoming the temptations of Satan,

Jesus Son of God remains obedient to the Father, in contrast to the disobedience of Israel during the desert wanderings.[17] Matthew employs the Old Testament fulfillment quotations in part to demonstrate the conformity of Jesus to the will of God as revealed in the scriptures (26.53-56). As Birger Gerhardsson (1979: 89) has put it, 'The whole of Jesus' ministry takes place "according to the scriptures". In everything he fulfils the demands of the law—with his whole heart and with his whole soul and with all his resources'.[18] Matthew most directly presents Jesus as one who submits to the will of God in his account of the prayer in Gethsemane: 'not my will, but thine be done' (26.36-46; cf. 16.22-23). Finally, the Matthean Jesus demonstrates that his life springs from love when he declares in 20.28 that 'the Son of man came not to be served but to serve and to give his life a ransom for many'.

Matthew compares the life of Jesus to the expectations for the disciples not only in these general terms, but also in terms of particular demands. Since it would be impossible to deal with each ethical demand in the Gospel, we limit ourselves to four examples.

Jesus declares that one of the characteristics of members in the eschatological community is 'meekness' (5.5), a term which Matthew connects with 'humility' or 'lowliness' (11.29); apparently, these terms are at least generally synonymous for Matthew. Jesus demands lowliness of his followers in 18.3-4 and 23.12. But Matthew presents Jesus as the prime model of meekness and lowliness. In 11.29 Jesus declares of himself, 'I am meek and lowly in heart', and Matthew reinforces Jesus' point of view when he interprets the triumphal entry with the prophetic words, 'Behold, your king is coming to you, humble and mounted on an ass' (21.5).

Closely related to lowliness and meekness is the notion of servanthood. The principle of servanthood relates to many instructions in Matthew, especially those in chs. 18 and 24-25.[19] In 20.26-28 this comparison between Jesus and the expectations for the disciples is brought out explicitly: 'Whoever would be great among you must be your servant, and whoever would be first among you must be your slave, even as the Son of man came not to be served but to serve'.

In addition to meekness and servanthood, mercy is also one of the essential characteristics of true discipleship. Not only is mercy found in the beatitudes (5.7), but it is also one of the fundamental elements of the will of God. Twice Jesus declares in the words of the prophet, 'I desire mercy and not sacrifice' (9.13; 12.7); and mercy is one of the triad of the 'weightier matters of the law', according to Jesus (23.23). In 18.33 the disciples are to be different from the wicked servant who refused to have mercy on his fellow servant. Again, in Matthew's Gospel, Jesus is the merciful one *par excellence*. The healings of Jesus are repeatedly presented as expressions of his mercy,[20] as are his feedings (14.14; 15.32), and his association with the oppressed and with the outcasts of society (9.13).

Finally, the comparison between Jesus and the disciples in terms of ethical behavior concerns also the element of faithfulness in the midst of persecutions. In light of the persecutions which attend the eschatological missionary enterprise, Jesus exhorts his disciples to 'watch' (25.13), an activity which Jesus also pursues as he contemplates his ultimate sacrifice for the sake of the kingdom (26.40-41). Indeed, Matthew stresses the close relationship between Jesus and the disciples at this point when he has Jesus say 'watch with me' (26.38).

C. *The Role of Filial Language in the Comparison between Jesus and the Disciples*

In addition to the elements of mission and ethical behaviour, the use of filial language in the Gospel of Matthew also points to the essential comparison between Jesus and the role of the disciples. Matthew indicates that both Jesus and the disciples are 'sons' of God and 'know' God as Father. Jesus' unique filial relationship to God as his Son is maintained by the care Matthew exercises in having Jesus consistently differentiate between 'my Father' and 'your Father'; the Matthean Jesus never speaks of 'our Father'.[21] Yet the fact remains that both Jesus and the disciples are identified, respectively, as 'Son' and 'sons' of the Father (for instance, 5.18; 20.23). Matthew interprets this language in terms of the relationship between Jesus and his disciples in two passages: in 12.50 the disciples are sons of the Father because of their filial relationship to Jesus, Son of God; and in 17.24-27 Jesus indicates explicitly that the privileges of Sonship which he enjoys belong in certain cases also to the disciples.

In connection with this shared use of filial language, we should also mention that in Matthew the disciples generally understand and are able to receive the revelation which Jesus communicates to them.[22] This understanding has the effect of emphasizing their continuity with Jesus rather than their distance from him. It is true, of course, that in certain cases Matthew contrasts the disciples to Jesus (for instance, 15.15-16; 16.22-23); but in each case the contrast involves the failure of the disciples to measure up to Jesus' expectations for the disciples. In other words, the contrast is made possible by the recurring comparison and focuses upon the dichotomy between what the disciples are called to be and to do and what they actually do. On balance, this does involve a certain element of contrast between Jesus and the disciples, a contrast which is examined below. In the final analysis, however, the stark contrast in the Gospel as a whole between Jesus and his disciples, on the one hand, and the opponents, on the other, underscores the essential continuity between Jesus and the disciples. It is to the recurring contrast between Jesus and his opponents that we now turn.

Chapter 4

THE STRUCTURE OF MATTHEW:
REPETITION OF CONTRAST

In addition to the repetition of comparison, the Gospel of Matthew is also structured according to the repetition of contrast. One of the clearest structural patterns in Matthew's Gospel is the recurring contrast between Jesus and his opponents, especially the religious leaders. Other minor recurring contrasts likewise appear, such as the dichotomy between those who approach Jesus in faith and those who approach him without faith, and the differences Matthew emphasizes between the disciples and their opponents. Moreover, we have indicated that there is also an element of contrast between Jesus and his disciples.

Yet the primary contrast is in fact between Jesus and his opponents, and these other contrasts generally underscore this primary one.[1] We will therefore devote the bulk of this discussion to the dichotomy between Jesus and his adversaries. Moreover, since we discuss in the next chapter the growing animosity toward Jesus which results in his crucifixion, the following sketch will not deal with the movement toward the crucifixion of Jesus, but will focus upon other elements in the dynamic between Jesus and his opponents.

A. *Introduction and General Portrait of the Contrast*
between Jesus and his Opponents

As we shall see in the next chapter, the figure of Jesus is presented to the reader at the outset of the Gospel in 1.1–4.16. There we learn that Jesus is the Christ (1.1, 16-18), the Son of David,[2] and especially the Son of God[3] by virtue of his conception by the Holy Spirit (1.18, 20). He is the climax to salvation history, as both the genealogy and fulfillment quotations demonstrate.[4] Moreover, Jesus' fulfillment of prophecy points also to his obedience to the will of his Father. It is

66

The Structure of Matthew's Gospel

against this background that Matthew presents the contrast between Jesus and his opponents.

Matthew prepares the reader for this contrast in 1.1–4.16. The reader first discovers negative reaction to Jesus in ch. 2, in the person of Herod. Matthew tells us that Herod and 'all Jerusalem with him' were troubled at the news of the wise men (2.3). Since Herod is constantly called 'king' by Matthew (2.1, 3, 9) and since the wise men inquire regarding the 'king of the Jews' (2.2), one can infer that Herod feared a rival to his throne. Consequently, Herod ascertains the time of the star 'secretly' from the wise men (2.7), which suggests stealth and deception (compare 26.3-5), and this deception turns into blatant lying when Herod states that he wishes to know the whereabouts of the child so that he may worship him (2.8). Although Herod has tricked the wise men, he is in a furious rage when he discovers that the wise men are not returning to him (2.16a). Finally, this fear, deception, and anger climax in his murder of innocent children (2.16b).

As will be seen in the next chapter, this segment is paradigmatic for Matthew's presentation of the enemies of Jesus. Here we shall mention only the chief characteristics of Herod. First of all, Herod's opposition grows out of a basic misunderstanding of the nature and mission of Jesus. Jesus is not the type of king who usurps political thrones; rather, he rules as savior from sin, which he effects by pouring out his blood (26.28; 1.21). His throne is the cross (27.37). Again, Herod acts out of envy and a desire to maintain authority and status. This motivation reflects, further, a self-obsession which will stop at nothing to promote the interests of the self. This orientation toward life and reality is exactly the opposite of that which Jesus espouses when he declares, for example, that 'the Son of man came not to be served, but to serve, and to give his life a ransom for many' (20.28). Jesus gives his life on behalf of others; Herod takes lives for the sake of his own interests.

The contrast between Jesus and his opponents in 1.1–4.16 continues in the pericope regarding the baptism of John (3.1-17). This pericope presents a programmatic contrast between Jesus and the Pharisees and Sadducees. John addresses these persons as a 'brood of vipers' (3.7), a term which Jesus also uses of them in 12.34 and 23.33. In Matthew, this phrase points to the imminent judgment that awaits the Pharisees because of the great guilt they have incurred.

These Pharisees and Sadducees depend, not upon God's grace, but upon their racial descent from Abraham (3.9a). This racial pride rejects the need for faith and grace and hence for repentance. Therefore, their hypocrisy is in view here, since they come to John's baptism of repentance, but apparently fail to produce the fruit of repentance (3.8-10). This dependence upon descent from Abraham robs God of his sovereignty (3.9b) and reflects arrogance and pride, implying that they are worthy of special treatment and are superior to Gentiles. As it stands, these religious leaders are liable to eschatological wrath (3.7); they are the chaff which the coming one will burn (3.12).

In stark contrast to his attitude toward the Pharisees and Sadducees, John hesitates to baptize Jesus not because of Jesus' hypocrisy or stubbornness, but because John himself needs to be baptized by Jesus. Jesus has no need of confession of sin or of a baptism of repentance. Thus, John baptizes Jesus only after the latter declares that such is necessary to 'fulfill all righteousness' (3.15). The notion of obedience is once again taken up immediately after the baptism in the story of the temptation of Jesus (4.1-11).

Here, then, at the beginnning of the Gospel (1.1-4.16) the lines are clearly drawn and the configuration of the contrast between Jesus and his adversaries is established. The opposing characteristics set forth here, such as righteousness and obedience in the case of Jesus, and disobedience and hypocrisy in the case of the opponents, are carried out and expanded throughout the remainder of the Gospel. We now turn to Matthew's presentation of this contrast in 4.17-28.20.

As was demonstrated in the preceding chapter, Jesus is throughout Matthew the model of the obedient Son. In contrast to this portrait of Jesus, Matthew presents the opponents of Jesus as those who disobey the will of God. In the sermon on the mount, Jesus declares that unless his hearers assume a righteousness exceeding that of the scribes and Pharisees they cannot enter the kingdom (5.20). In the parable of the two sons (21.28-32), Jesus indicates that the chief priests and elders are stubborn and disobedient, since they have refused to believe the message John proclaimed. Here obedience is linked to acceptance of the eschatological kerygma (3.2); to put confidence in the message is to obey. Faith in the message of John (and of Jesus) is the 'will of the Father', which these religious leaders fail to do. The sinfulness and disobedience of Jesus' opponents is put most succinctly by Jesus when he declares that he is about to be delivered into the hands of the 'sinners' (26.45).

B. *Specific Analysis of the Contrast between*
Jesus and his Opponents

Not only does Matthew describe the guilt of these adversaries in general terms, he analyzes and expands upon their moral failures throughout the course of his narrative. The religious opponents are most often described in terms of hypocrisy. The 'hypocrites' of ch. 6 refers to these religious leaders, since the term 'hypocrite' is used by Matthew almost exclusively to refer to the opponents of Jesus,[5] and since the contexts surrounding this term in ch. 6 point to the type of activities which characterize the religious 'elite'. Here hypocrisy is understood as a dichotomy between act and motive. Although the acts are ostensibly directed toward God, the motives center on appearances before humans: 'that they may be praised by people' (6.2, 5, 16). The hypocrisy of the chief priests and elders is underscored in the parable of the two sons in 21.28-32; the disobedient son says that he will go out and work in the vineyard, but does not act on his speech. Jesus' charges of hypocrisy, however, come to full expression in ch. 23. The scribes and Pharisees 'preach but do not practice' (23.3). They know how to bind heavy burdens on the shoulders of others, but they fail to fulfill even the basic principles of the law (23.4). Jesus attacks their hypocrisy head-on in his woes concerning the inside and outside of the cup (23.25-26) and the whitewashed tombs (23.27-28). In contrast to the hypocrisy of these persons, Matthew presents Jesus as one whose words and actions are in total accord; this correlation between the words and actions of Jesus was examined at some length in the preceding chapter.

But Jesus' opponents are guilty of much more than hypocrisy. In line with the pattern begun by Herod, the opponents of Jesus deliver him up out of 'envy' (27.18). They fear for their status, authority, and position and are apparently jealous of the popularity Jesus enjoys with the crowds.[6] Moreover, they are guilty of most of the sins that Jesus declares in 15.17-20 defile a person: evil thoughts (cf. 9.4), murder,[7] adultery (cf. the metaphorical use in 12.38; 16.4), theft (cf. 21.13), false witness (cf. 26.60-61), and slander.[8] They are also guilty of extortion and self-indulgence (23.25).

These opponents are capable of such sins because they are in collusion with Satan. As J.M. Lotman (1975) has pointed out, in all the Gospels, and especially Matthew, there are only two positions: the right, which is the way of God; and the wrong, which is the way of the devil. There is ultimately no middle ground. Throughout the Gospel, these opponents are related to Satan even as Jesus is related to God. Like the devil (4.1-11), they ask for a sign (12.38; 16.1-5). Several times Matthew records that the opponents tried to 'test' or 'tempt' him.[9] Indeed, this term is used in Matthew only of Satan and of these opponents. Even as Jesus is Son of God, so the Matthean Jesus dubs them 'sons of Gehennah' (23.15). This connection between Jesus' adversaries and Satan is clearly indicated in the mockery surrounding the cross; they demand a sign: 'come down from the cross' (27.42), 'save yourself' (27.40), in order to prove 'if you are the Son of God'.[10] Furthermore, Matthew drives home this connection by means of irony: twice the Pharisees accuse Jesus of casting out demons by Beezebul (9.34; 12.24), and yet Matthew plainly shows that it is not Jesus but the religious opponents themselves who are in league with the devil.

If the opponents of Jesus are children of Satan, they are also understood by Matthew to form a unity of evil. As Rolf Walker has pointed out (1967: 38-74; also Hummel, 1963), Matthew does not, on the whole, distinguish between the various sects and groups among the opponents of Jesus; he presents them all in essentially the same way as a 'unity of evil'. This presentation of Israel as a unity of evil stands behind the progressively broadening opposition to Jesus. Throughout the bulk of the narrative, the crowds, while not accepting Jesus as the Christ, at least cling to him, often marvel at his authority in word and deed,[11] and even serve as a buffer between Jesus and the religious leaders (21.46; 26.4-5); yet at the end of the narrative they cry out for his crucifixion (27.15-20).

This unity of evil, however, applies not only to the various sects and groups which Matthew presents, but also to the whole history of Israel. Throughout its history, Israel has consistently rejected and even murdered the messengers whom Yahweh had sent to it. This fate has befallen the prophets and John the Baptist (5.12; 17.10-12; 23.29-36), and is now about to strike Jesus and the disciples. This pattern is expressed most forcefully in the parables of the wicked tenants and of the wedding feast (21.33–22.10). The syndrome reaches its climax in the murder of God's Son (21.37-39). These actions on the part of Israel reflect its insistence on securing the kingdom on its own terms rather than on God's terms, that is, through the Son (21.39, 41). Yet, since they have not repented and believed, they are not able to produce the fruit of the kingdom (21.41, 43). The result is twofold: loss of kingdom (21.43); and loss of city (22.7).

Thus, the opponents' rejection and murder of Jesus are understood as a rejection of the purposes of God. As a result of this lawlessness, these adversaries must depend upon trickery to accomplish their homicidal objectives, a recourse which reveals the unjustness of their actions and a tacit admission of their own guilt (26.5; compare 21.41). They know that they must depend upon false testimony to put Jesus to death (26.59-60). Ironically, they accuse Jesus of blasphemy for claiming to be the Son of God, when in fact they are the ones who blaspheme (26.63-66; compare 27.39). Though their proceedings are shrouded in a cloak of legality, it is an act of murder, for Jesus is innocent (27.4, 24) and indeed righteous (27.19). Yet even the death of Jesus does not ameliorate their hostilities toward the anointed Son of God, nor their subterfuge, as the bribing of the guards and the spreading of false rumors regarding the empty tomb indicate (28.11-15). Their guilt is compounded by their refusal to repent, even at the greatest revelation in salvation history (11.20-24; 12.38-42; 21.28-32). Even though the Gentile soldiers can confess the divine Sonship of Jesus on the basis of the witness God bears through the events surrounding the crucifixion (27.51-54), the opposition continues to view Jesus as an imposter (27.63). As a result, these opponents will receive a greater condemnation than even the most wicked of Gentile cities (11.21, 24; 12.41-42). Indeed, the Jesus whom they now condemn will be their judge (3.11-12; 25.31-46).[12]

Matthew not only analyzes the nature and severity of the disobedience and guilt of Jesus' opponents, but he also indicates the basis of their wrongdoing. They fail to understand the eschatological significance of the ministry of Jesus. 'This generation' is blind to the meaning of the mighty works Jesus performs (11.19b). The reason for this blindness is lack of revelation from the Father; he has hidden these things from them (11:26). Because they do not know the Son, they cannot know the Father, since the Father is revealed by the Son (11.27). In addition, those who are on the outside are unable to see, hear, and understand because 'their heart has grown dull, and their ears are heavy of hearing, and their eyes they have closed' (13.15).

This blindness has occurred because of their own stubbornness and refusal to repent (11.20-24; 12.38-42, 45).

Matthew goes further. He links the failure of the opponents to fulfill the will of God with their inability to determine what that will is. As opposed to Jesus, who is the true interpreter of the mind and will of God,[13] they do not know the will of God. Jesus teaches the will of God as one with authority, 'not as their scribes' (7.29). Jesus orders them to 'Go and learn what this means, "I will have mercy and not sacrifice"' (9.13; 12.2), thus pointing to their ignorant state. In another passage Jesus declares 'if you had known what this means . . . you would not have condemned the guiltless' (12.7).

This confusion regarding the will of God is connected with a dependence upon the tradition of the elders, which in many ways contradicts the will of God expressed in the Old Testament (15.1-9; 23.16-22). Consequently, these opponents are 'blind guides' who lead their followers into the pit with them (15.14) and who make their converts worse than they themselves (23.16). This confusion regarding the will and mind of God stems in part from hypocrisy (ch. 6; 15.17), and in part from an ignorance of the scriptures and lack of faith in the power of God (22.29). This false understanding of the will of God leads to legislative hair-splitting, which reveals the emptiness of their teaching (23.16-22; 5.34-36), and an emphais upon minor concerns with a lack of attention to the most significant demands (23.23-24). The emphasis is upon ritual purity rather than inward purity (23.25-28; 15.1-9). Their emphases place ceremonial cleanness and sabbath observance above the welfare of persons (9.10-13; 12.9-14), a complete inversion of Jesus' true interpretation of the law, which places love of God and of neighbor at the center (5.43-48; 7.12; 22.34-40).

Chapter 5

THE STRUCTURE OF MATTHEW:
REPETITION OF PARTICULARIZATION AND CLIMAX
WITH PREPARATION AND CAUSATION

Thus far, we have examined the structure of Matthew's Gospel according to the repetition of comparison and the repetition of contrast. We move on now to the third major structural relationship operative within the Gospel, namely, the repetition of particularization and climax with preparation and causation. By this phrase we mean (a) that 1.1, 4.17, and 16.21 are general headings which are expanded in the material that follows in each case; (b) that each of these sections (1.1–4.16; 4.17–16.20; 16.21–28.20) builds toward its respective climax; and (c) that 1.1–4.16 establishes the background for 4.17–28.20, while 4.17–16.20 provides the cause or basis for 16.21–28.20.

A. *The Preparation for Jesus Messiah,*
Son of God (1.1–4.16)

Four structural elements bind this material together into a discrete unit: particularization, repetition, climax, and contrast. We shall examine each of these structural elements in turn. Because repetition and climax are closely related in 1.1–4.16, these two elements will be presented together.

1. *Particularization of 1.1*
The first of these structural relationships involves a movement from the general statement, or 'superscription', of 1.1 to its expansion throughout 1.2–4.16: 'The book of the origin (βίβλος γενέσεως) of Jesus Christ, the Son of David, the Son of Abraham'.

There is little agreement regarding the precise function of 1.1. Three views have been put forward. First, many scholrs contend that 1.1 serves as the heading for only the genealogy (vv. 2-17), or at most for the genealogy and the infancy narratives (chs. 1–2).[1] McNeile (1938: 1) argues that γένεσις in 1.18 means 'birth' and heads up the infancy narrative, whereas in 1.1 the term is used with a different meaning. Hence, according to McNeile, Matthew sets the infancy narrative off from the genealogy. Marshall Johnson, in turn, maintains that γένεσις is generally employed as a 'technical formula', pointing to genealogical lists as such and probably carried such connotations for Matthew.

But Johnson nowhere provides evidence for either the general technical use of this formula or for Matthew's understanding of this term as technical. In fact, the evidence points in the opposite direction. The headings to the Old Testament genealogies always place the name of the progenitor in the genitive, never the name of the progeny;[2] the Matthean usage is inexplicable under the hypothesis that Matthew felt bound by a fixed, technical sense. Moreover, the notion that this term is used differently in 1.18 than in 1.1. flies in the face of clear evidence from the Gospel. The reference to γένεσις in 1.18 is linked to 1.1. by means of 1.17 and 1.16 , and by means of content. Krister Stendahl has demonstrated that 'Christ', 'Son of David', and 'Son of Abraham' are all taken up in the narrative materials of chs. 1–2. On the contrary, the phrase 'book of the origin' has almost certainly been taken over from the LXX of Gen. 2.4a and 5.1b, where it applies not merely to a genealogy, but also to narrative material (compare Gen. 2.4–4.26; 5.1–6.8).[3]

Second, other scholars argue that Mt. 1.1 is a title not to the genealogy or the genealogy and the infancy narratives, but rather that it serves as the title for the entire Gospel.[4] Klostermann contends that γένεσις was used to refer not only to genealogies, but also to histories (for instance, Gen. 6.9; 37.2). The examples Klostermann cites, however, are not analogous to Mt. 1.1, since they contain no mention of 'book' (βίβλος). Gaechter argues that the superscription does not belong to the genealogy at all, since the Old Testament genealogies typically begin with the name of the progenitor and not the final progeny. One may respond, however, that Matthew's change can be traced to his desire to employ chiasm in order to portray Jesus as the goal and ultimate fulfillment of salvation history: Mt. 1.1 speaks of Jesus as the Christ (cf. 1.16), the Son of David (cf. 1.6), and the Son of Abraham (cf. 1.2). Beare holds that Matthew intends to echo the title to the book of Genesis in the LXX. Yet this view fails to take into account the fact that γένεσις there is not immediately followed by a genealogy as it is in Matthew; it is highly unlikely that Matthew would have deliberately created such confusion. Many of the scholars who hold that Mt. 1.1 is a superscription to the Gospel (such as Klostermann [1971: 1] and Grundmann [1981: 61]) translate γένεσις as 'history'. But, as Kingsbury has indicated (1975: 10), this translation is discordant with the use of the word in 1.18, which, as we have already pointed out, is closely tied to 1.1. Hubert Frankemölle (1974: 363) maintains that 1.1 should be regarded as the title of the Gospel because the phrase is consistently used in such a way in documents associated with Jewish apocalypticism and Qumran. It is, however, difficult to determine how greatly Matthew was influenced by this usage, whereas almost all scholars recognize that Matthew drew upon the phrase as found in Gen. 2.4a and 5.1b. There is firm evidence, therefore, that Matthew was acquainted with the use of the phrase that applied to only a portion of a document.

Third, in contrast to those scholars who argue that 1.1 belongs to the genealogy or infancy narratives alone, or that it is the title to the entire Gospel, still other scholars, most notably Krentz (1964: 411) and Kingsbury (1975: 10), contend that Mt. 1.1 serves as a superscription for 1.1–4.16. This is the position that best commends itself, for the following reasons. To begin with, the expression 'book of the origin' in 1.1 is clearly a reference to the same expression in the book of Genesis. Although both Gen. 2.4a and 5.1b are usually cited as background, both the wording and the context of Gen. 5.1b stand closer to Mt. 1.1 than does Gen. 2.4a. The latter passage is not followed by a genealogy, and indeed it is not clear whether Gen. 2.4a originally belonged with the preceding or the following account of creation. The phrase in Gen. 5.1b introduces a genealogy (5.1-32) and the following narrative material (6.1-8). This section of Genesis closes with another superscription introducing the next division. Therefore, the use of the phrase in Gen. 5.1b introduces a section of both genealogical and narrative material within a book. Furthermore, as Krentz (1964: 411) has pointed out, Gen. 5.1–6.8 closes with the statement that Noah has found favor with the Lord; the narrative section thus has to do with Noah's personal history down to the time when he began to serve as 'an agent of salvation'. Similarly, Matthew begins the next division of his Gospel with a superscription (4.17), and all the material found within 1.1-4.16 has to do with the personal history of Jesus before his public ministry to Israel.

In addition, we contend that 1.1 serves as the heading for the first major division of the Gospel because the themes of 'Christ', 'Son of David', and 'Son of Abraham', which are included in 1.1 and are of special concern within the genealogy, are expanded or particularized, throughout 1.1–4.16. The fulfillment quotations which cluster in this material point to Jesus as the Christ who forms the climax of and gives meaning to salvation history.[5] Herod inquires of the chief priests and scribes of the people where the Christ is to be born (2.4). And John the Baptist refers to Jesus as 'the coming one' (3.11), meaning the Christ (cf. 11.2).

This expansion obtains not only for 'Christ', but also for 'Son of David'. In 1.20, 25, Joseph son of David adopts Jesus by giving him his name, thus showing how it is that Jesus, who according to the genealogy was not the natural son of Joseph, could still be called 'Son of David '. In 1.6 Matthew breaks the pattern of the genealogy by calling David 'the king'; accordingly, when the wise men search for the 'king of the Jews' (2.1), the phrase tactitly points to Jesus as the Son of David. The status of Jesus as Son of David is also indicated by the reference to Bethlehem, the city of David, in 2.5-6. Finally, the words from heaven at the baptism announcing that Jesus is 'my beloved Son' allude to Ps. 2.7, which has to do with the enthronement of David's son as king; thus, Matthew again points to Jesus as the scion of King David.

As in the case of 'Christ', and 'Son of David', the title 'Son of Abraham' in 1.1 is also expanded throughout 1.1–4.16. The majority of commentators agree that this reference to Son of Abraham anticipates the universalism of the Gospel.[6] Grundmann (1981: 62) posits that Abraham and David are singled out in the genealogy because they received promises of progeny in the Old Testament. The promise to Abraham was that 'in you will all the families of the earth be blessed' (Gen. 12.3), and more specifically in connection with the promise of offspring, 'and by your descendants shall all the nations of the earth bless themselves' (Gen. 22.18). Moreover, it has often been observed that one of the functions of the Gentile women in this genealogy from Abraham is to point to the universalism which would come in Christ, the Son of Abraham.[7] In addition, this universalistic theme is related directly to Abraham and his descendents elsewhere in the Gospel (8.11). And Matthew's proclivity for bracketing the Gospel with common themes at the beginning and end has suggested to many commentators that 'Son of Abraham' corresponds to the universal missionary charge of 28.18-20.[8]

When the universalistic character of 'Son of Abraham' is kept in mind, one can see that the reference to the coming of the wise men points to Jesus as the Son of Abraham who draws Gentiles to his worship (2.1-12). Moreover, John the Baptist makes explicit reference to sonship to Abraham (3.9) when he warns the Pharisees and Sadducees not to presume to say 'we have Abraham as our father', since God was able to raise up children to Abraham from stones (another probable anticipation of universalism). And the universalistic fulfillment quotation of 4.14-16 also points to Jesus as Son of Abraham. Matthew thus forms a bracket around this first main section of his Gospel; even as the universalism implicit in 'Son of Abraham' is echoed at the end of the Gospel, so 'Son of Abraham' in 1.1 also corresponds to the blessing to the Gentiles promised at the end of this first main division.

2. *Repetition of Major Themes, and Climax (3.17)*

In addition to the particularization of 1.1 throughout 1.2-4.16, this unit is also bound together by the repetition of three distinctive themes. In the first place, all the events narrated in 1.1-4.16 take place prior to the beginning of the public ministry of Jesus. The first reference to the ministry of Jesus is found in 4.17, which summarizes his proclamation to Israel.

With the exception of Jesus himself, none of the major characters or groups of characters in 4.17-28.20 appears on the scene before 4.17. The disciples are mentioned for the first time in 4.18-22, and the crowds appear in 4.23-25. The religious opponents (Pharisees and Sadducees) are introduced in 3.7-10, but they are not yet portrayed as opponents specifically of Jesus. In fact, in this pericope they do not speak at all, and do not come into contact with Jesus.

In addition to this absence of major characters in 1.1-4.16, the activities in which Jesus is primarily engaged throughout 4.17-28.20 are not mentioned here in 1.1-4.16. Jesus neither preaches, teaches, heals, casts out demons, nor says anything regarding his passion. In fact, Jesus says very little in this part of Matthew, and when Jesus does speak it is never on his own initiative, but only in response to the speech of others, narrated either implicitly (3.15) or explicitly (4.4, 6, 10).

The work of John the Baptist in ch. 3 also indicates the anterior nature of 1.1–4.16. The mission of John is to '*prepare* the way of the Lord' (3.3; 11.10), and his preaching points towards the one who is to come after him (3.11). In Matthew's Gospel John is the forerunner of the Messiah and of the work of the Messiah (17.10-13), which explains why Jesus begins his public ministry only after he has heard of the arrest of John the Baptist (4.12).

In addition to the repetition of preliminary matters, there is also a repetition here in 1.1–4.16 of fulfillment quotations. Although Matthew employs such quotations throughout his Gospel, nowhere else does he cluster them so closely together. Many scholars have noted that there are five formula quotations in the infancy narratives,[9] but 3.1–4.16 contains two additional quotations (3.3; 4.14-16). Hence, in 1.1–4.16 Matthew has inserted seven such passages. Matthew's penchant for numerical arrangements is well known, and he is especially fond of threes and sevens: seven petitions in the Lord's prayer (6.9-13), seven parables in ch. 13; seven woes in ch. 23. As Krentz (1964: 412-13) has argued, Matthew seems to employ the number seven in order to indicate completeness or sufficiency: seven demons in 12.45; seven loaves and baskets in 15.34, 37; and seven brothers in 22.27. Even the three series of fourteen names in the genealogy *may* indicate that the number seven has been doubled each time. The seventh fulfillment quotation thus serves to indicate that the time of preparation is complete.

In addition to the repetition of preliminary matters and the repetition of fulfillment quotations in 1.1–4.16, we note that there is here, finally, a recurring emphasis upon the person of Jesus. It is of course true that Matthew deals with the person and identity of Jesus throughout the whole of his Gospel. But here in 1.1–4.16 Matthew is concerned to establish a picture of Jesus for the reader which is presupposed throughout the narrative concerning Jesus' work and passion. In 1.1–4.16 Matthew presents the person of Jesus directly to the reader; in 4.17–16.20 Jesus is revealed primarily in terms of his public pronouncements; and in 16.21–28.20 he is presented primarily in terms of his passion. As we shall see shortly, this repetition is linked to the third major structural relationship in this unit, namely, climax; we shall consequently deal with these two relationships together.

Matthew's 'book' begins with an affirmation regarding the person of Jesus from Matthew himself. He declares that Jesus is 'Christ', 'Son of David', and 'Son of Abraham'. Matthew substantiates this threefold claim by presenting the genealogy of Jesus (1.2-17), where he emphasizes Jesus' lineage from Abraham and David (1.17), and the messiahship of Jesus, which he sets forth by showing that Jesus brings to its culmination the divinely ordered flow of salvation history; Jesus stands as the last generation of three groups of fourteen (1.17).

The testimony of the angel is introduced in 1.18-25. By addressing Joseph as 'son of David' (1.20) and commanding him to give Jesus his name and so adopting him, the angel affirms that Jesus is Son of David. Moreover, he declares that Jesus has been conceived by the Holy Spirit (1.20), a claim made by Matthew himself in 1.18. Thus, the angel is a reliable character: his testimony agrees with that of Matthew (Jesus is conceived by the Holy Spirit; Jesus is Son of David); and what the angel says comes to pass in the flow of the narrative. Mary does bear a son (1.21, 25), the prediction regarding Herod's murderous plans is proved all too accurate (2.13-16), and when the angel alerts Joseph that Herod has died, Joseph finds it to be true (2.19-22). Matthew coalesces his own point of view with that of God when he interprets the angelic message as signifying that Jesus is Emmanuel, God with us (1.22-23).

When the wise men arrive in Jerusalem from the east they inquire regarding 'the king of the Jews' (2.2). As was noted above, the fact that Matthew has taken pains already in the genealogy to call David 'the king' (1.6) indicates that the reference to the king of the Jews also points to Jesus as the Son of David. The designation 'king of the Jews' does not point to an authoritarian and tyrannical figure such as Herod. On the contrary, this ruler is defined by the word from Micah quoted in Mt. 2.6: 'he will *shepherd* my people Israel' (author's translation). He is thus the gentle and loving ruler of his people, who saves them from their sins (1.21). Again, the point of view of the wise men is reliable, not only because it agrees with that of Matthew and the angel, but also because these wise men obey the dream and thus preserve the life of Jesus.[10]

The next witness to the person of Jesus to appear on the scene is John the Baptist. He declares that Jesus is the Christ, the coming one, who is mightier than himself (3.11) and who far outstrips him in majesty. John is not worthy even to carry his sandals. John announces that Jesus, as the Christ, is the one who will bring eschatological salvation and judgment (3.11-12). John is also a reliable witness: he preaches the same message as Jesus and the disciples (3.2; 4.17; 10.7); he fulfills Old Testament prophecy (3.3; cf. 11.7-15), standing in the succession of Elijah (3.4; cf. 2 Kgs 1.8; Mt. 17.10-13); he proclaims the message of God without fear (3.7-10; 14.1-12); and his point of view agrees with that of Matthew, the angel, and the wise men.

The next and last testimony to Jesus in this succession of reliable witnesses comes directly from God himself; in 3.17 the heavenly voice declares, 'this is my beloved Son, in whom I am well pleased'. This declaration stands as the climax to 1.1-4.16 for three reasons. To begin with, it is here God himself who witnesses to Jesus, as opposed to mere mortals and angels in 1.1-3.12. Further, this statement announces that Jesus is far more than Son of Abraham or Son of David or even Messiah: he is God's own Son. Although the formal expression 'Son of God' does not appear here, the sense and substance of the remark is that Jesus is the Son of God. There is general agreement among scholars that when Matthew uses such terms as 'Son', 'my Son', 'his Son', and 'Son of God', he is referring to the one comprehensive category of Son of God. Finally, this statement stands as the culmination of several hints and allusions to the status of Jesus as Son of God.

Although Matthew does not call Jesus 'Son of God' in 1.1, there is an allusion to his divine origin already in the genealogy. In 1.16 Matthew breaks the pattern of the genealogy; instead of saying that 'Joseph was the father of Jesus', he states: 'Joseph the husband of Mary of whom Jesus was born'. The passive voice 'was born' (ἐγεννήθη) is a circumlocution for divine activity, which in turn points ahead to the passive 'was conceived' (γεννηθέν) of 1.20. Thus, Matthew suggests both that Jesus is not the natural son of Joseph and that he is the Son of God.

This notion of Son of God appears also in 1.18-25. Here Matthew takes pains to show that Jesus is not the product of a union between Joseph and Mary. Twice the text tells us that the child was conceived by the Holy Spirit (1.18-20). Through the words of the prophet, Mary is called a 'virgin' (1.23). Moreover, when Joseph discovers that Mary is pregnant he resolves to divorce her, though he is a righteous man (1.19); he thus knows that the child is not his. And even after Joseph takes Mary as his wife, he does not have sexual contact with her until she has borne Jesus (1.25).

Matthew also introduces the term 'son' into this section. The angel predicts that Mary will bear a 'son' (1.21), a prediction whose fulfillment is duly narrated by Matthew in 1.25, where the term is repeated. The most significant reference to 'son' in this passage, however, is found in the prophetic quotation of 1.23: 'a virgin shall conceive and bear a son'. Rudolf Pesch (1967: 410) has observed that in the introduction to this quotation and in the introduction to the one other formula quotation in Matthew which mentions 'son' (2.15), Matthew has altered his usual wording; in these two introductory statements he has added 'by the Lord'. Hence, the introduction to 1.23 reads: 'all this took place to fulfil what was spoken *by the Lord* through the prophet'. Pesch argues that Matthew has inserted this prepositional phrase into these two passages in order to indicate that God is here speaking about his own Son. Yet Matthew presents this as only an indirect statement by God, since it is not expressed directly, but comes 'through the prophet'.[11]

The concept of 'Son of God' is present also in ch. 2. As Kingsbury (1975: 43-44) has pointed out, 2.7-23 consistently speaks of Jesus as 'the child'.[12] In this way Matthew underscores the fact indicated already in ch. 1 that Jesus is not Joseph's biological son. Moreover, Matthew breaks this pattern of referring to Jesus as 'the child' in 2.15, where in a scriptural quotation the Lord once again speaks through the prophet of his Son: 'Out of Egypt have I called my Son'. Hence, the reader is given to understand that the term 'the child' of ch. 2 actually points to Jesus as Son of God.

All these indications of divine Sonship lead up to the declaration of 3.17. This climax is underscored by the presence of a double 'and behold' (καὶ ἰδού), which in Matthew is used to indicate that something of special significance is about to be said or done (for instance, 12.42; 28.9-10). Up to this point in the narrative, the divine Sonship of Jesus has been expressed through circumlocutions, metaphors, or statements made by God indirectly through his prophets. Now God himself announces in unambiguous terms that Jesus is his Son. Matthew establishes this climactic construction in order to show that Jesus is to be understood primarily in terms of Son of God and in order to allow God to be the first to proclaim his Sonship openly; in Matthew, the confession that Jesus is Son of God comes only through divine revelation (compare 16.16).

The declaration itself is drawn from two Old Testament passages. Isaiah 42.1 speaks of the Servant of Yahweh, while Ps. 2.7 is a coronation hymn that was used at the enthronement of kings of Judah. Thus, Jesus Son of God is at the same time the king in the lineage of David. Yet the meaning of 'Son of God' in this verse must be determined more directly from the climactic development leading up to 3.17 than from the Old Testament passages standing behind the declaration. Hence, Jesus is Son of God in the sense that he has his origin in God (1.18, 20). Furthermore, the significance of the divine Sonship of Jesus is explicated in the temptation narrative which immediately follows (4.1-11). Three times Jesus is tempted by Satan in his capacity as Son of God (4.3, 6). Whereas Israel as God's Son abandoned faith and yielded to temptation in the wilderness, Jesus as God's Son remains obedient to his Father. Therefore, Jesus is the Son who perfectly obeys the will of his Father.

We have seen that Matthew presents a series of reliable witnesses to disclose the true identity of Jesus to the reader. Jesus is the Christ, Son of Abraham, Son of David, Emmanuel, King of the Jews, Shepherd, Coming One, and most significantly, Son of God. Indeed, this clear disclosure of the identity of Jesus raises another, closely related issue: How should persons react to this Jesus, Son of God?

3. *Contrast between Divergent Responses to the Person of Jesus*
To answer this question, we turn to the fourth major structural relationship in 1.1-4.16: contrast. Matthew presents a definite contrast between those who accept Jesus as the Christ and those who reject him. This presentation is found specifically in the pericope of the wise men (ch. 2), but it is also closely related to the contrast between God and Satan in 3.13-4.11.

Since we have already dealt with the wise men in our chapter on the repetition of contrast, we need only make a few brief comments here. We indicated above that the wise men are reliable witnesses to the person of Jesus; they share the point of view of Matthew, the angel, John the Baptist, and God. They are exemplary, however, not only in the way in which they speak of Jesus, confessing him to be the king of the Jews, that is, Christ (2.2; cf. 2.5), but also in the way they respond to Jesus. They seek this Christ (2.2), and when they have found him they rejoice (2.10), worship (2.2, 11a), and offer him gifts (2.11b). The contrast with Herod is stark. He is troubled at the news of the birth of the king (2.3) and resorts to deception (2.7), lying (2.8), and murder (2.16) in order to be rid of the threat of this Christ. Matthew allows no middle ground here: the wise men worship; Herod seeks to kill him. In this way Matthew establishes the clear lines of demarcation between proper and illegitimate responses to Jesus.

But Matthew goes further. In aligning themselves with Jesus, the wise men also align themselves with God, who declares that Jesus is his Son (3.17). Herod, whose attempts to destroy Jesus would result in God's salvation-historical purpose coming to nothing, aligns himself with Satan, who also stands opposed to Jesus (4.1-11). These contrasting reactions to Jesus are thus related to the cosmological struggle between God and Satan. Yet this cosmological struggle is not a battle between equals, for God is superior to Satan, as the victory of Jesus, Son of God, over Satan's temptations makes clear. Moreover, God has the final eschatological word, since at the end Jesus, Son of God, will exercise eschatological judgment. Thus, those who align themselves with Jesus and hence with God are the 'wheat' that Jesus will gather into his barn, whereas those who reject Jesus are the 'chaff' that is cast into the fire (3.12). The response to Jesus thus has both cosmological and eschatological implications.

We conclude, then, that these four major structural relationships, namely, particularization, repetition, climax, and contrast, bind 1.1-4.16 together into a unified whole. But what of those scholars who divide the material differently and reject the unity of 1.1-4.16?

4. Examination of Other Views Regarding the Structure of 1.1-4.16
Many commentators see a major structural break at 3.1. They argue that there is a significant lapse of time between chs. 1-2 (Jesus as infant) and chs. 3-4 (Jesus as adult). Moreover, they contend that chs. 1-2 are private in nature, whereas in chs. 3-4 both John and Jesus assume public roles.[13]

Although it is true that a significant lapse of time exists between 2.23 and 3.1, this does not outweigh the consideration that the whole of 1.1-4.16 has to do with events preceding the public ministry of Jesus. Moreover, the δέ in 3.1 connects the account of the ministry of John the Baptist to the infancy narratives, and this connective stands over against the asyndetic character of the phrase 'From that time Jesus began' in 4.17. In addition, the phrase 'in those days' (3.1) reinforces the connection between 3.1 and the preceding. This phrase is a rather loose connective which indicates inner continuity with the preceding, a continuity which transcends the lapse of time; it is used, for example, in Exod. 2.11 (LXX), where it bridges forty years in the life of Moses.[14]

Furthermore, although it is true that John assumes a public role in ch. 3, it is by no means clear that Jesus functions publicly in these chapters. Since the temptation in the wilderness is obviously private, the question surrounds the nature of the baptism of Jesus by John. The observations that (a) Matthew sets the pericope regarding the baptism of Jesus (3.11-17) off from the account of the preaching of John (3.1-10) by means of 'then' (τότε), that (b) there is no reference made in 3.11-17 to either the crowds or the Pharisees and Sadduces, and that (c) Matthew exercises carefulness to restrict the sighting of the dove to Jesus alone (3.16) all point to the conclusion that the baptism of Jesus is also a private matter.

Other scholars discern a major structural break between 4.11 and 4.12, maintaining that the setlement of Jesus in Galilee marks the beginning of his public ministry.[15] Yet these commentators fail to recognize that 'now' (δέ) links 4.12 to the preceding and that the absence of Jesus' name in 4.12 forces the reader back to infer the subject from 4.10. Moreover, the mention of John the Baptist points back to ch. 3. Finally, the notation of the settling of Jesus in Galilee linked with the formula quotation of 4.12-16 corresponds in terms of both form and content to 2.22-23 (see Kingsbury, 1975: 14-16).

Matthew 1.1-4.16 thus stands as a unified whole, providing the background for 4.17-28.20. It prepares the reader for all that follows (a) by presenting the true and proper understanding of the person of Jesus, (b) by setting forth in stark contrast the two essential reactions to the person of Jesus, and (c) by anticipating the rejection of Jesus by the Jews and the consequent universal appeal of the Gospel.

B. *The Proclamation of Jesus to Israel (4.17-16.20)*

We have just shown that the first major division of Matthew's Gospel concludes at 4.16. Our argument now is that 4.17-16.20 forms the second major unit in the Gospel. We contend that Matthew has drawn this material together into a coherent whole distinct both from that which precedes and that which follows by means of three structural relationships: particularization, causation, and climax.

1. *Particularization of 4.17*
As was seen above, 1.1 serves as the general heading for 1.1-4.16. This observation implies that the succeeding division or divisions of Matthew's Gospel will also begin with a general statement; and that is, we contend, exactly what one finds in 4.17 and, later, in 16.21. Matthew 4.17 announces, 'From that time Jesus began to preach and to say, "Repent, for the kingdom of heaven is at hand"'.

The history of the investigation into this passage could be written in short compass; scholars have generally ignored it. Pierre Bonnard does not even mention it, and most of the commentators who do take notice of the verse say very little about it.[16] Many commentators remark that the formula indicates a turning point in the ministry of Jesus, but for reasons usually left unexplained they fail to draw structural implications from this observation.[17] Exceptions to this rule are Ernst Lohmeyer, Krentz, and Kingsbury. One should note, however, that even materials published after the work of Krentz and Kingsbury generally give this passage short shrift.

Yet 4.17 is worthy of note in many ways. For one thing, 4.17 is parallel in form to 16.21: 'From that time Jesus began to show his disciples that it was necessary for him to go to Jerusalem and to suffer many things from the elders and chief priests and scribes, and to be killed, and on the third day to be raised'. Both passages contain the preposition 'from' + the adverb 'that time' + the phrase 'Jesus began' + the infinitive ('to preach and to say' in 4.17; 'to show' in 16.21) + a summary of content of the message (direct discourse in 4.17; object clause introduced by 'that' in 16.21).

This parallelism is all the more significant when one considers the unique literary character of the formula. The phrase 'from that time' (ἀπὸ τότε) occurs on only two additional occasions in the New Testament: Mt. 26.16; Lk. 16.16. Yet the phrase in 4.17 and 16.21 is utterly distinctive; in the other two passages it is neither linked with Jesus, nor does it contain any reference to 'begin'.

In addition to the parallelsim between 4.17 and 16.21, another feature that distinguishes the use of the phrase 'from that time' in 4.17 and 16.21 from that found in 26.16 is its asyndetic character. Matthew 26.16 is connected to its preceding context by means of 'and' (καί), but no such connective is found in 4.17 and 16.21. The asyndeton is all the more remarkable when one examines the liberal use of connectives in the material surroundig each of these verses. The asyndetic character of the phrase 'from that time' in 4.17 and 16.21, then, distinguishes the use of the phrase in these two passages from that of 26.16 and underscores the formulaic character of this phrase at 4.17 and 16.21.

Although there are differences between the use of the phrase 'from that time' in 4.17 and 16.21, and in 26.16, the meaning of the phrase is generally the same in all the passages where it is used; it marks the beginning of a new period of time. In 26.16 it indicates a turning

point in the life of Judas, and in Lk. 16.16 it points to the distinction
between the period of the law and prophets and the time of
eschatological proclamation of the kingdom. The meaning corresponds
to its use in LXX; in Ps. 92.2 it indicates the beginning of the new
age.

The use of 'began' (ἄρχομαι) is as instructive as the phrase 'from
that time' in determining the significance and meaning of 4.17 and
16.21. In his article, 'Pleonastic ἄρχομαι in the New Testament', J.W.
Hunkin (1924: 393, 395) demonstrates that there are numerous cases
in which the New Testament writers employ ἄρχομαι in its 'regular'
sense, meaning 'to begin', or 'to proceed'. Of the twelve occurrences
in Matthew, Hunkin considers five to mean distinctly 'begin',
including 4.17. Although he labels the seven other occurrences as
'doubtful', he goes on to state, 'In St Matthew's class (b) above, the
doubtful cases, hardly any of them are very doubtful', as over against
Luke. Hence, in the opinion of Hunkin there is no such thing as
pleonastic ἄρχομαι in Matthew. Gerhard Delling (*TDNT*, I: 479)
agrees with Hunkin's assessment of 4.17 and 16.21 when he observes
that ἄρχομαι always has a pregnant meaning with the phrase 'from
that time'. And Nigel Turner (Moulton, *et al.* 1976: IV, 32) contends
that Matthew does not like the pleonastic ἄρχομαι and avoids its use.
One may conclude, then, that ἄρχομαι in conjunction with 'from
that time' expresses the beginning of a new stage in the life of
Jesus.

Before we leave this discussion of the formulaic character of the
phrase 'from that time Jesus began' in 4.17 and 16.21, we should
mention that some scholars wish to connect 4.17 with the preceding.
Fenton (1963: 51-52) for example, notes that the phrase 'Repent, for
the kingdom of heaven is at hand' appears in the mouth of John the
Baptist in 3.2. He judges that Matthew constructs an inclusio
between these two passages. But Fenton fails to take sufficient
account of the asyndetic character of 4.17, the preparatory nature of
1.1-4.16, and the parallel between 4.17 and 16.21, the latter clearly
indicating a new beginning. This phrase announcing the nearness of
the kingdom appears also as the substance of the proclamation of the
disciples in 10.7; it thus serves not as inclusio with 3.2, but as a
salvation-historical link, uniting the ministries of John the Baptist,
Jesus, and the disciples in the time of fulfillment. Eduard Schweizer
(1975: 75) connects 4.17 to the fulfillment quotation of 4.15-16 since
'the quotation as combined with Jesus' announcement shows that it

is in his preaching that light shines on those who dwell in darkness'. Not only does Schweizer ignore the asyndetic character of 4.17, but he also fails to recognize that 4.17 is a summary of the ministry of Jesus to *Israel* (4.23-25; 9.35), whereas 4.15-16 prepares the reader for something other than this ministry to Israel; indeed, the references to 'light' and 'darkness' in the passage have to do with the eventual participation of the Gentiles in the eschatological benefits.

But if, in fact, 4.17 and 16.21 serve as a parallel formula in Matthew's Gospel, do they also serve as general headings to their respective divisions, particularized in the following materials? The answer to this question as regards 16.21 must await our discussion of the section 16.21-28.20. In the case of 4.17, the answer is in the affirmative. The theme of 4.17, namely, that Jesus publicly presents himself (to Israel), announcing the kingdom of heaven and consequently calling Israel to repentance, provides the framework for 4.17-16.20. This division falls into two major sections. In the first (4.17-11.1), Jesus goes about Galilee teaching, preaching the gospel of the kingdom, and healing (4.23; 9.35; 11.1). After he calls his first four disciples, Jesus ascends the mountain and with authority proclaims the character and requirements of participation within the kingdom. Having come down from the mountain Jesus travels around the Sea of Galilee, performing ten mighty acts (chs. 8–9). In ch. 10, Jesus sends his disciples out to Israel on a mission modelled on his own, namely, a ministry of preaching and healing, but not of teaching. Jesus warns the disciples, however, that they can expect a generally negative response to their ministry; indeed, they will be persecuted even unto death (10.16-39). This motif of rejection prepares for the second section: 11.2-16.20. In this material, Jesus' proclamation of the kingdom and call to repentance meet with rejection by Israel as a whole. John the Baptist questions the messianic status of Jesus (11.2-6); the cities where his mightiest works were performed refuse to repent (11.16-24); and the religious leaders set themselves in solid opposition against him (ch. 12). Although the crowds do not reject Jesus, neither do they accept him; and even his own family apparently refuses to believe in him (12.46-50). In response to this lack of acceptance of his eschatological ministry, Jesus moves away from those who are on the outside and toward his disciples, the only group that accepts his eschatological ministry (11.25-30; 12.46-50). Jesus turns away from the crowds by speaking to them in parables which they are unable to understand

(13.1-35), and he withdraws time and again from the religious opponents. Yet even during this period, Jesus does not totally abandon his ministry to Israel. Although he no longer teaches or preaches to them, he continues to manifest himself as Israel's Messiah by means of his healings[18] and his feedings of the crowds (14.13-21; 15.32-39). At the same time, Jesus moves toward his disciples, revealing to them the mysteries of the kingdom of heaven (13.36-52; 15.10-21; 16.5-12) and finally drawing from them the confession that he is the Christ, the Son of God (16.13-20).

This brief survey of 4.17–16.20 reveals that the theme of Jesus' proclamation of the kingdom and call to repentance (4.17) is expanded by means of the framework: proclamation of the kingdom of God leading to rejection by Israel as a whole, but acceptance by the disciples. We turn now to a more detailed investigation of the structure of this division by means of an examination of the causation and climax found here.

2. Causation: Movement from the Proclamation to the Response to the Proclamation

The two major sections within 4.17–16.20 are determined by the structural phenomenon of causation. 4.17–11.1 is the cause: Jesus presents himself to Israel by means of teaching, preaching, and healing (4.23–9.35) and by means of sending out his disciples to perform eschatological ministry to Israel analogous to his own (9.35–11.1). 11.2–16.20 is the effect: the response, both positive and negative, to the proclamation of Jesus to Israel.[19]

We turn first to the causal material, that is, to the proclamation of Jesus to Israel in 4.17–11.1. This material is bound together by the repetition of statements presenting an overview of Jesus' ministry throughout Galilee, found in 4.23; 9.35; 11.1. These statements provide the reader with the general orientation according to which he or she is to understand all the material in 4.17–11.1.

The first two overview statements are parallel in both form and content. Indeed, their parallelism and their strategic positions have led most scholars to identify them as a classic example of inclusio. In both passages, Matthew records that Jesus went about all the country 'teaching in their synagogues and preaching the gospel of the kingdom, and healing every disease and every infirmity'. The third overview statement is partially different in form and content. It mentions only teaching and preaching, omitting any reference to healing: 'And it happened when Jesus finished instructing his twelve disciples he went on from there to teach and preach in their cities'.

The differences between 11.1 and the two other overview statements (4.23 and 9.35) may be explained in the following way. While Matthew uses the three passages to draw 4.23–11.1 together ino one unit, he constructs the inclusio around 4.23–9.35 in order to bind this material together as a sub-unit within 4.17–11.1.

Thus, 4.17–11.1 contains two sub-units. The first of these sub-units, enclosed by 4.23 and 9.35, presents two major activities of the ministry of Jesus: his teaching (chs. 5–7), and his mighty acts (chs. 8–9). Yet 4.23 and 9.35 function not only as inclusio, but also as particularization, since specific examples of two of the three activities mentioned in these verses are given: teaching (chs. 5–7), and healing (chs. 8–9).

As regards teaching, the particularization of this element in 4.23–9.35 does not refer simply to one teaching episode within the itinerant ministry of Jesus, since 4.23 and 9.35 state that he taught in their synagogues, whereas in 5.1 Jesus is said to teach on the mountain. Chapters 5–7 are rather an expansion of the reference to Jesus' activity of teaching as a whole. The mountain is mentioned because it is the place of revelation (cf. 17.1-8; 28.16-20). As regards healing, while chs. 8–9 do tell of mighty acts other than healings (8.23-27; 9.18-26), healings constitute by far the bulk of these miracles, and all the acts Jesus performs in public are healings. The third activity mentioned in 4.23 and 9.35, namely, preaching, is not mentioned in chs. 5–9, because the substance of Jesus' preaching of the gospel of the kingdom has already been given in 4.17.[20] The teaching and healing found here are thus performed in the context of the proclamation of Jesus that the kingdom of heaven is at hand, reinforcing their eschatological and proclamatory nature (see also 11.2-6).

In addition to the expansion of the general statements in 4.23–9.35, there are five other points of importance in chs. 5–9. First, Matthew wishes to emphasize the public nature of the activities of Jesus. The overview passages describe Jesus as being in public, as do the repeated references to the crowds[21] and to the spreading news of his mighty acts (8.34; 9.6). Second, Matthew is concerned to indicate that Jesus here presents himself exclusively to the people of Israel. He teaches 'in their synagogues' (4.23; 9.35), and he heals all kinds of sicknesses 'among the people' (4.23).[22] Third, Matthew underscores the eschatological nature of the ministry of Jesus by references to Galilee,[23] to the gospel of the kingdom (4.23; 9.35), and to the kingdom of heaven.[24] Fourth, Matthew is interested in calling attention to the authority of Jesus, thus closely linking the person of Jesus with his acts of ministry (7.28; 9.7). Fifth, integrally related to the authority of Jesus is the response of the people: the crowds are astonished (7.28; 9.7, 33), while the Pharisees assert that Jesus is associated with the devil (9.34). This reaction to Jesus and his authority foreshadows 11.2–16.20.

To sum up: In 4.23–9.35 Matthew presents Jesus as one who performs an eschatological ministry of teaching and healing in Galilee to all Israel within the context of his proclamation that the kingdom of heaven is at hand. These acts point to the transcendent authority of Jesus and draw forth reactions of two types: amazement; and the accusation that Jesus is in league with the devil.

Matthew 4.17–9.35 is linked to 9.35–11.1 by means of comparison: a clear analogy is drawn between the ministry of Jesus and that of his disciples. Matthew accomplishes this comparison by means of several devices. In the first place, Matthew positions ch. 10 between two statements giving an overview of the ministry of Jesus in Galilee (9.35; 11.1). These statements do not form an inclusio as do the overview statements 4.23 and 9.35; nevertheless, they provide the context according to which ch. 10 is to be understood.

Matthew also accomplishes this comparison between 4.17–9.35 and 9.35–11.1 by means of the transitional character of 9.35. This verse not only concludes the material in 4.23–9.35, but it also introduces the material in ch. 10. Matthew 9.36 is linked to 9.35 by means of the connective 'and' (δέ) and by the circumstance that the subject (Jesus) is not expressly named in v. 36; the reader is forced to go back to the reference to Jesus in 9.35a. The reference to the crowds in 9.36 also points back to the mention of the crowds in 9.33. These connections between 9.35 and 9.36 link the whole missionary discourse to 9.35, since there is no doubt that 9.36-38 belongs with ch. 10. This conclusion is supported both by the continuity of content (laborers sent out to minister to the people), by the repetition of terms, such as 'worker' (9.37-38; 10.10) and 'sheep' (9.36; 10.6, 16), and by the continuity of audience: the disciples (9.39; ch. 10).

Finally, Matthew achieves his comparison between 4.17–9.35 and 9.35–11.1 by employing a number of phraseological and substantive parallels intended to form an analogy between the mission of Jesus and the mission of the disciples. Because we dealt with some of these elements in our earlier discussion on the repetition of comparison, we will mention them only briefly here. In ch. 10, Jesus gives his disciples authority to perform the same eschatological work that he has been doing. Accordingly, he gives his disciples authority to cast out spirits (10.1; cf. 8.16; 9.32-34) and, in an obvious verbal parallel to his healing activity as described in 4.23 and 9.35, to 'heal every disease and every infirmity'. The disciples are to preach, even as Jesus has preached, that 'the kingdom of heaven is at hand' (10.7; cf. 4.17). And Jesus speaks of the ministry of the disciples in a way that mirrors his own actions in chs. 8-9 (10.8): 'heal the sick' (see 8.5-17; 9.1-8, 18-31), 'raise the dead' (9.18-26), 'cleanse lepers' (8.1-4), 'cast out demons'.[25] Indeed, whereas 4.23 records that Jesus went about 'all Galilee', 9.35 says that he went about 'the cities and villages', two terms which Matthew uses repeatedly to speak of the mission of the disciples in ch. 10.[26] The only significant element of discontinuity between the description of the ministry of Jesus in 4.17-9.35 and that of the disciples in 9.35-11.1 concerns the element of teaching. The disciples are not yet given authority to teach; that will come only in 28.19-20, after they have come to understand the nature of the messianic calling.

Not only does the description of the disciples point backwards to the activity of Jesus in chs. 8-9, but this description of the disciples also points ahead to the rejection of Jesus by 'this generation' in chs. 11-16. Thus, although the theme of rejection is introduced already in chs. 5-9, here in ch. 10 rejection becomes much more significant and explicit. The mention of repudiation in ch. 10 deals with the rejection of the disciples and their message, but the clear comparison between the ministries of Jesus and of the disciples in this chapter indicates that it points to the rejection of Jesus as well. Matthew thus constructs the comparison between Jesus and the disciples in part because he wishes to use the theme of the rejection of the disciples to anticipate that of Jesus.

Matthew therefore establishes a double connection between Jesus and the disciples. Statements regarding the mission of the disciples point back to the ministry of Jesus in chs. 5-9; statements having to do with the rejection of the disciples point ahead to the rejection of Jesus in chs. 11-16.

Moving now from the cause of 4.17-11.1 (proclamation to Israel) to the effect of 11.1-16.20 (responses to this proclamation), we see that Matthew begins his catalogue of responses in 11.2-16.20 by reintroducing the person of John the Baptist (11.2; cf. 4.12), who hears in prison of Jesus' deeds and asks by means of his disciples, 'Are you he who is to come, or shall we look for another?' (11.3). The proclamation of John regarding the coming one in ch. 3 was full of apocalyptic fire, but included no predictions of such deeds of healing as Matthew records in chs. 8-9. This disappointment in his expectation led John to uncertainty regarding the messianic mission of Jesus.[27] The question from John implies not rejection, but doubt.

This encounter with the disciples of John leads to Jesus' litany against 'this generation'. This generation has rejected the message of John, which portends the rejection of Jesus as well, since John was the forerunner and herald of the Messiah (11.9-15). The people are stubborn and inclined not to believe; they have rejected John because of his asceticism, while they have rejected Jesus because of his lack of asceticism (11.16-19).

The accusations of Jesus against the people intensify with the woes of 11.20-24. His mighty works have proclamatory value, but the stubbornness of the people has robbed them of their witnessing power. Jesus' call to repentance has fallen on deaf ears (11.20-21; cf. 4.17). Indeed, the hardness of their hearts has kept the people from understanding the true meaning of the events. The guilt of the people and the depth of their stubbornness are indicated by the contrast between their rebellion and that of the most notorious Gentile cities; their guilt and punishment far surpass that of Tyre and Sidon, or even Sodom (11.22-24).

The climax to ch. 11 comes in vv. 25-31. Here Jesus gives one reason for his rejection by the greatest part of Israel: it is due to the will of God, who has withheld his revelation from Israel. Here, too, Matthew presents a contrast between the 'babes' (that is, the disciples), who enjoy the revelation from above, and the 'wise and understanding' (that is, 'this generation'), who reject Jesus.

Matthew 11.25-31 not only brings to climax the litany that Jesus speaks against Israel in ch. 11, but also connects Jesus' pronouncement of rejection (11.7-24) with actual examples of this rejection. The religious opponents are on the attack in ch. 12. They accuse first the disciples (12.2) and then Jesus himself (12.9-13) of breaking the law. Finally, they plot to destroy Jesus (12.14). Indeed, they accuse Jesus directly of casting out demons by the prince of demons (12.24). In response, Jesus indicates that they are separate from him; not only are they not with him, they are against him (12.30). Their lives are at cross-purposes with his own. Indeed, they not only speak against him, but Jesus warns them that they are in danger of blaspheming against the Holy Spirit (12.32).

Chapter 13 begins a new sub-section. Jesus responds to the rejection of 'this generation' by turning away from the crowds and turning toward his disciples. In the first discourse (chs. 5–7), the crowds were present at the beginning and at the end; here they are present at the beginning, but not at the end. In 13.1-2, their presence is stressed, but at 13.36 Matthew reports that Jesus 'left the crowds and went into the house, and his disciples came to him'. This change in locale and audience represents a change of focus in the ministry of Jesus.

Jesus speaks to the crowds in parables because the secrets of the kingdom of heaven have not been granted to them (13.11). They are dull of hearing, and in them the dire prophecy from Isaiah is fulfilled (13.14-15). In stark contrast to them, the disciples have eyes that see and ears that hear (13.36). To the disciples God has given the mysteries of the kingdom (13.11).

Jesus continues to meet with rejection by all segments of Israel throughout the sub-section chs. 14–16. Jesus is repudiated in his home town of Nazareth: the response to both his teaching and mighty works is unbelief (13.53-58). Herod's murder of John reflects the fact that 'this generation' has rejected Jesus (14.1-12). Throughout this section, the encounters that Jesus has with the religious leaders remain at the level of acrimony and accusation (15.1-20; 16.1-4). In response to their strident opposition, Jesus continually withdraws from them (14.13; 15.21; 16.4). And Jesus is no longer said to preach or teach in any positive sense; yet he graciously continues to present himself as the Messiah of Israel through healing (14.34-36; 15.29-31) and feedings (14.13-21; 15.32-39). In contrast to Israel as a whole, throughout chs. 14–16 the disciples continue with Jesus as Jesus instructs them and reveals himself to them,[28] finally drawing from them the confession that he is the Christ, the Son of God (16.13-20).

3. *Climax: The Confession of Peter*
This discussion of the causal movement within 4.17–16.20 leads naturally into the third major structural feature binding this material

together, namely, climax. The contrasting responses to Jesus by the people and by the disciples come to a high point of intensity and clarification when Jesus asks his disciples the questions that stand behind all the material in these chapters: 'Who do people say the Son of man is?' (16.13); and 'Who do you say that I am?' (16.15).

We have noted that the proclamation of Jesus to Israel produces a number of responses. Already in 7.28 the crowds respond with astonishment to his teaching. In 9.33 the crowds marvel at his mighty works, while the Pharisees attribute his exorcisms to collaboration with Beelzebul (9.34). Yet these are only adumbrations of the full presentation of responses which the reader encounters in chs. 11-16. Not only does Matthew deal with these responses in a fuller and more systematic manner in these latter chapters, he also places these responses in chs. 11-16 within the context of the question of Jesus' identity.

Matthew orients chs. 11-16 to the issue of the identity of Jesus by means of three questions which appear in the course of the narrative (see Kingsbury, 1984). The question of Jesus' identity is raised at the very beginning of this material by John the Baptist (11.2-6). As we stated earlier, on the basis of reports regarding the deeds of Jesus, John is no longer sure of the messianic status of Jesus and consequently sends his disciples to ask Jesus if he is in fact the Christ. In 12.23 the people respond to a healing which Jesus has performed by asking, 'Can this be the Son of David?', a question phrased in such a way that it indicates that a negative answer is expected. And in 13.54 the Nazarene townspeople ask, 'Is this not the carpenter's son?' All these questions suggest doubt, reflecting the generally negative character of the reactions in this section.

In addition to these three questions, two assertions are made. The first comes from the mouth of Herod Antipas. In his opinion, Jesus is able to perform great miracles because he is John the Baptist redivivus. Since John is generally held to be a prophet (14.5; cf. 11.9; 21.6), and since John has clearly mirrored the demeanor of Elijah,[29] the notion that Jesus is John raised from the dead would also imply that he is a prophet, and perhaps even Elijah. This assertion is representative of those who see and hear of the mighty deeds of Jesus, yet fail to accept him.

The other assertion is found at the conclusion of the second boat scene in 14.33. Having seen Jesus walking on the water, his disciples worship and cry out, 'You are the Son of God'. This forms the answer to the question raised by the disciples in the first boat scene: 'What kind of person is this, that even the winds and sea obey him?' (8.27). At the culmination of this section, Matthew juxtaposes these two views and contrasts them. Whereas all previous references to the identity of Jesus came in response to his mighty deeds, here Jesus asks his disciples explicitly the question of his identity. The first question has to do with the opinion of the people (οἱ ἄνθρωποι). According to them, Jesus is John the Baptist, or Elijah, or Jeremiah, or one of the prophets. The bottom line to all these answers is that Jesus is a prophet. All these answers are wrong, for John the Baptist, who functioned as Elijah, was the forerunner of Jesus; and Jeremiah and the prophets bear witness to Jesus.[30] The second question has to do with the opinion of the disciples. Peter, speaking for the group, declares, 'You are the Christ, the Son of the living God' (16.16). This affirmation is not the opinion of humans (cf. 16.13); it is revealed by God himself (16.17). It is entirely the right answer, for Jesus responds with a blessing (16.17), and it agrees with God's point of view as expressed in 3.17. The reference to 3.17 also indicates that even as the first major division of the Gospel culminates with the declaration from God that Jesus is his Son, so this second major division comes to a climax with that same declaration from the mouth of the disciples.

The proclamation of Jesus to Israel, then, issues on the one hand in the rejection of Jesus by the people as a whole, and results on the other hand in bringing the point of view of the disciples into line with God's point if view. Yet the disciples are to tell no one that Jesus is the Christ, because they have not yet learned the true role of the Messiah and the meaning of discipleship to this Messiah. They have confessed him as Son of God on the basis of his mighty acts (14.33); now it is necessary for them to learn that messiahship involves much more than the performance of miracles. This necessity points ahead to the next major division. The recognition that Jesus is Messiah leads naturally and logically into a period of instruction regarding the nature and meaning of this messiahship and its implications for the followers of Jesus. This movement from the recognition of messiah-ship to education in meaning regarding this messiahship is what we mean by causation between 4.17–16.20 and 16.21–28.20.

C. *The Passion and Resurrection of Jesus Messiah, Son of God (16.21-28.20)*

The last main division of Matthew's Gospel concerns the journey of Jesus to Jerusalem and his suffering, death, and resurrection. Our contention is that this material forms a unity around the structural principles of particularization, climax, repetition of comparison, and repetition of contrast.

1. *Particularization of 16.21*

In 16.21 Matthew declares: 'From that time Jesus began to show his disciples that it was necessary for him to go to Jerusalem and suffer many things from the elders and chief priests and scribes, and be killed, and on the third day be raised'. This verse contains two basic elements: first, journey of Jesus to Jerusalem to suffer, die, and be raised; and second, the presentation Jesus makes to his disciples of the necessity for such an undertaking. The first, namely, the journey to Jerusalem and the passion and resurrection, is expanded or particularized, throughout 16.21-28.20 by means of climax. The second, namely, the presentation Jesus makes to his disciples of this necessity, is expanded or particularized, by means of the repetition of comparison and the repetition of contrast. Of course, since this narrative is unified, these repetitions are closely related to the climax. For purposes of analysis, however, we will deal with these structural elements separately, while at the same time being careful to demonstrate their relationship.

2. *Climax: The Death and Resurrection of Jesus*

We begin with climax, by which we mean the movement towards the suffering, death, and resurrection of Jesus in Jerusalem and ultimately his missionary commissioning in 28.16-20. Prior to 16.21, the death and resurrection of Jesus are adumbrated by hints and oblique references. In 9.3 certain scribes accuse Jesus within their own minds of blasphemy, after Jesus declares the sins of the paralytic forgiven. In 9.15 Jesus speaks of the time when the bridegroom will be taken away. In his list of the apostles, Matthew alerts the reader to the fact that Judas Iscariot was the one 'who betrayed him' (10.4). In 10.38 Jesus demands that the disciples take up their cross and follow him. In 12.14 the Pharisees begin to plot in order to destroy Jesus. And Jesus alludes to his death and resurrection in 12.39-40 when he declares that the 'Son of man will be three days and three nights in

the heart of the earth'. Yet only in 16.21 does Matthew directly and
explicitly introduce the theme of the passion and resurrection, and it
is here for the first time that Jesus instructs his disciples regarding
his passion and resurrection.[31]

In line with this theme of the passion and resurrection of Jesus,
16.21–28.20 is unified by means of the journey to Jerusalem.
Matthew alerts the reader to this journey already in 16.21, where he
tells us that Jesus shows his disciples that he must go to Jerusalem.
The reference to 'go' is significant, for by it Matthew gives notice
that Jesus will continue his travels through Galilee (17.22) to
Capernaum (17.24), then away from Galilee to Judea beyond the
Jordan (19.1), on to Jericho (20.29), until he and his disciples reach
the environs of Jerusalem in 21.1 and Jerusalem itself in 21.10.

In addition to the geographical framework, Matthew employs
another device to tie 16.21–20.34 to the events of the passion and
resurrection in Jerusalem, namely, the repetition of predictions
regarding the passion of Jesus. Three of these predictions are closely
related in form and content, and function as the counterpart to the
three overview statements in 4.17–11.1. The first is the general
statement of 16.21; the second, somewhat abridged, appears at 17.22–
23; the third, and by all means the most complete, prediction comes
at 20.17-19. Indeed, this last passage provides an outline of events
which will transpire at Jerusalem: (1) Jesus will be delivered over to
the chief priests and scribes (cf. 26.14-25, 47-55); (2) the latter will
condemn him to death (cf. 26.47-68); (3) the chief priests and scribes
will also deliver Jesus to the Gentiles to be mocked and scourged and
crucified (cf. ch. 27); and (4) Jesus will be raised on the third day (cf.
ch. 28). These passages prepare the reader for the events surrounding
the passion and resurrection of Jesus and summarize the salient
features of that passion.

This repetition of summary predictions is closely related to the
geographical framework, since each of these predictions includes a
reference to the journey to Jerusalem. The journey motif is expressed
in the first two passion predictions by Matthew (16.21; 17.22), but in
the third passion prediction both Matthew and Jesus draw attention
to the relationship between the journey of Jesus to Jerusalem and his
passion and resurrection (20.17-18). Mathew has therefore constructed
a pattern of prediction and fulfillment which undergirds the motif of
the journey of Jesus to Jerusalem and provides that journey with its
theological meaning.[32]

The climax towards the death and resurrection of Jesus is indicated not only by the journey to Jerusalem with its passion predictions, but also by the movement of the narrative. The flow of the story throughout 16.21–28.20 moves steadily toward the cross (ch. 27) and the missionary commissioning (ch. 28). After Peter's confession at Caesarea Philippi (16.16), Jesus charges his disciples to tell no one that he is the Christ (16.20). Although the disciples now know who Jesus is, they are not yet ready to 'go and make disciples of all nations' (28.19). They must first learn the true purpose of the messianic mission: suffering, death, and resurrection. This Jesus sets out to do in 16.21–28.20.

The first thing Jesus tells his disciples in 16.21–28.20 is that the Messiah must suffer (16.21). Peter immediately rejects this notion, and Jesus in turn reprimands him (16.22-23). Six days later, Jesus and the three disciples ascend the mount where Jesus is transfigured before them, and a heavenly voice from the cloud declares, 'This is my beloved Son with whom I am well pleased; listen to him' (17.5). Thus God, in the same words he uttered at the baptism (3.17), confirms Peter's confession that Jesus is in fact his Son (cf. 16.16). Yet God does not simply repeat the words spoken at the baptism, but adds the command 'listen to him'. The disciples need that word, for they do not yet understand or accept the truth which Peter has just repudiated, namely, that the mission of Jesus is to suffer and die. The point at which the disciples will finally grasp this truth is indicated in Jesus' command to silence regarding the transfiguration: after his resurrection (17.9).

The theme of imminent suffering is picked up again when, on that same occasion, Jesus alerts his disciples that, in analogy to John the Baptist, he too will suffer (17.12); and when Jesus comes down from the mountain and encounters the inability of the disciples to cast out the demon, Jesus again alludes to his imminent end when he asks, 'How long am I to be with you? How long am I to bear with you?' (17.17). Jesus yet again picks up the theme in his response to the request of James and John for positions of glory in the kingdom (20.20-24): although he cannot promise them such favors, he does assure them that they will drink of his 'cup', an obvious reference, in light of the following material, to his suffering and death.[33] These references in 16.21–20.34 to the approaching death and resurrection of Jesus reach their high point in the declaration Jesus makes just before entering Jerusalem regarding the purpose of his coming: to give his life as a ransom for many (20.28).

Once Jesus reaches Jerusalem events move steadily toward the cross. Although the crowds hail him as 'Son of David' (21.9), as far as they are concerned he is only the 'prophet Jesus' (21.11), showing that they still do not recognize his messianic character (cf. 16.14). In fact, however, Jesus is much more than Son of David. At the end of the section 21.1–22.45, Jesus asks the Pharisees the question regarding the Son of David: If the Messiah is the Son of David, how is it that David calls him lord? (22.43). Although Jesus leaves the question hanging, the reader knows the answer; Jesus is Son of David insofar as he stands in the lineage of David,[34] but he is also David's lord since he is Son of God and therefore superior to David (2.15; 3.17; 17.5). Therefore, the true identity of Jesus remains lost to Israel as a whole. This ignorance regarding Jesus' identity points ahead to his condemnation by Israel as a whole in ch. 27.

If the crowds do not recognize the true identity of Jesus, the religious leaders in Jerusalem place themselves solidly against him. These constant confrontations between Jesus and his opponents in Jerusalem also propel the movement toward the cross. From the very beginning of his sojourn in Jerusalem, Jesus clashes violently with the religious leaders. In the midst of the shouting throngs, Jesus enters the temple and drives out those who are buying and selling (21.12), accusing them of turning God's house of prayer into a den of robbers (21.13). For their part, when the chief priests and scribes see the mighty acts of healing that Jesus performs in the temple and the children calling out to him as 'Son of David', they are indignant (21.15). In response to all these events, the religious leaders ask Jesus the fundamental question of the nature and source of his authority (21.23). When Jesus, in response to this question, links his authority to that of John the Baptist, the reader recalls that Jesus is aligned to John not only in terms of authority, but also in terms of rejection and suffering (21.23-27; cf. 17.10-13).

The opposition between Jesus and the religious leaders continues when, on the heels of this pericope regarding the authority of John, Jesus proclaims his parables against Israel to 'the chief priests and elders of the people', who are members of the Sanhedrin (21.23; cf. 26.57-68). In the parable of the two sons, Jesus condemns the religious leaders for failing to repent at the preaching of John the Baptist, likening them to disobedient children (21.28-32). In the parable of the vineyard, Jesus portrays the guilt of Israel throughout salvation history, likening God to the owner of the vineyard and the religious leaders to the wicked tenants. Jesus is the 'son' whom the wicked servants kill (21.38-39), but who, according to the scripture, is destined to become head of the corner, pointing to his vindication by God in the resurrection. This parable fulfils a dual function in the climactic development. On one level, Jesus points ahead to his death and resurrection, thus continuing the prediction-fulfillment pattern throughout this material; on the other level, the parable serves to intensify the animosity the religious leaders feel toward Jesus, thus making them all the more determined to destroy him. The parable of the wedding feast also underscores the guilt and condemnation of Israel. The people of Israel are called 'murderers' (22.7); God himself will destroy their city (22.7); and they fail to participate, because of their unworthiness, in the eschatological banquet (22.8-9).

In response to these blistering attacks by Jesus, the religious leaders themselves engage in a battle of words; they ask Jesus a series of questions to entrap him in his talk (22.15-40). In each case they are woefully unsuccessful and unable to respond to his answers. Being entirely ignorant of the true nature of Jesus, they are unable to answer the question regarding the Son of David which he places before them; after that point, Matthew tells us, they ask him no more questions (22.46).

The direct attacks between Jesus and the religious leaders in Jerusalem, which point to the death of Jesus at the hands of these opponents, come to a climax in Jesus' litany regarding the guilt of Israel in ch. 23. Here the sinfulness of Israel, which stands behind the attacks of the religious leaders against Jesus and explains their plots to kill the Son of God, is clearly set forth as are the dire consequences of their murderous actions. In a series of seven woes, Jesus charges the scribes and Pharisees with hypocrisy of the highest order. This chapter sets forth the character and motives which stand behind the opponents of Jesus and have caused them to condemn the innocent (cf. 12.7) and murder the prophets (23.31).

After Jesus speaks to his disciples regarding the necessity of their faithfulness in the midst of tribulation (chs. 24–25) in light of his own faithfulness in the context of his cross (chs. 26–28), Jesus resumes the predictions regarding his passion. In 26.2 Jesus reminds his disciples of the earlier predictions of his crucifixion. The chief priest and elders of the people gather together in the palace of the high priest to plot the death of Jesus (26.3-4); and Jesus is anointed beforehand for his burial (26.6-13). All these episodes look ahead to the cross with increasing intensity.

Up to this point, the text has not indicated precisely how Jesus will be delivered over to his enemies (see 20.17-19). The reader knows that Jesus will be crucified during the passover (26.2), yet the leadership seems unwilling to risk an uprising (26.5; cf. 21.46). At this point, Judas offers to betray Jesus, thus providing the leaders with a golden opportunity to arrest him (26.15).

The passover which Jesus eats with his disciples looks ahead to the cross and interprets it. Jesus declares in 26.18, 'my time is at hand', and, knowing the machinations of Judas, he asserts, 'one of you will betray me' (26.33; cf. 26.24). Jesus also predicts that all the disciples will fall away, including Peter, who will deny him three times (26.31, 34). Yet, in the midst of this prediction, Jesus looks beyond the failure of the disciples to their reunion with him in Galilee after the resurrection (26.32). Meanwhile, Jesus interprets the meaning of his imminent death in terms of a covenant established with his blood which will bring about the forgiveness of sins 'for many' (26.28).

From this point, events move very quickly toward the cross. Jesus confronts the reality of his own death with deep sorrow in the Garden of Gesthemane (26.36-46). His desire is that the cup of suffering would pass from him; that is his prayer (26.39). But the reader knows that it is the will of God for Jesus to suffer and die in Jerusalem (δεῖ, 16.21), and Jesus submits to the will of God (26.42). Immediately Judas, his betrayer, appears, and in accordance with the fulfillment of scripture Jesus is arrested and stands trial before the Sanhedrin. Thus, the prediction repeatedly made by Jesus that he will be delivered over to the chief priests and elders and scribes is realized (16.21; 20.18). Moreover, in realization of the prediction Jesus made at the last supper, all the disciples forsake Jesus (26.56), and Peter denies him three times (26.69-75).

At the trial before the Sanhedrin, the high priest asks Jesus if he is the Christ, the Son of God (26.63; cf. 21.33-43). As long as the false witnesses were giving their perjured testimony, Jesus remains silent (27.57-62); but now when he is confronted with the truth of his divine Sonship, Jesus breaks his silence and answers in the affirmative, 'So you have said' (26.64).[35] And because of that answer Jesus is condemned to death for blasphemy.

On the basis of this charge of blasphemy, Jesus is delivered over to Pilate; thus, another prediction of Jesus is fulfilled (27.1-2; cf. 20.19). The focus of the trial before Pilate is whether Jesus is the 'king of the Jews'.[36] Jesus affirms that he is (27.11). Yet, despite the insurrectionist overtones of this affirmation in the ears of Pilate and the religious leaders (27.12), the real meaning of the kingship of Jesus is understood in terms of his role as the one who submits to suffering and death in order to give his life as 'ransom for many' (27.32-54; see 20.28).

As we indicated above, the mockeries of the passers-by and the religious leaders around the cross resemble in both phraseology and substance the temptations by Satan in ch. 4 (27.41-44); they call upon Jesus to demonstrate his divine Sonship by means of a sign. Jesus refuses to yield to these appeals, and with a loud cry he dies (27.50). Thus, the predictions that Jesus made regarding his death come to fulfillment;[37] moreover, his death culminates the process of handing over to the chief priests and elders, handing over to the Gentiles, being mocked, scourged, and crucified.

The signs come not from Jesus, but from God (note recurring use of the passive voice); by means of the supernatural portents surrounding the death of Jesus, God himself bears witness that Jesus was his Son (27.45-55; cf. 27.41-44). In response to these signs, the Roman soldiers cry out, 'Truly this man was the Son of God!' (27.54). Thus, in contrast to the Jewish leaders and passers-by (21.45-46; 26.57-68; 27.39-44), the soldiers rightly interpret the events surrounding the death of Jesus and vindicate Jesus' claim to be the Son of God (cf. 21.37-38; 26.63-64).

In light of the climactic development to this point, what is the significance of the fact that Jesus dies here as Son of God?

First, Jesus dies as the obedient Son. We have observed that the words of the passers-by and religious leaders echo the temptation of Jesus in the wilderness (4.1-11). In both cases Jesus is tempted to demonstrate his Sonship through signs; in both cases Jesus refuses to yield to the temptation, choosing rather to express his Sonship by means of obedience. Indeed, Jesus dies as one who puts his trust in God (27.43). This obedience is indicated already in the Garden of Gethsemane when Jesus, contemplating his imminent death, prays, 'Father . . . thy will be done' (26.42).

Second, because Jesus dies as obedient Son, his death has power to save from sin. It is at the cross that Jesus pours out his blood for the forgiveness of sins (26.28), thus giving his life a ransom for many (20.28) and saving his people from their sins (1.20-21).

Third, in response to the death of Jesus, Son of God, God himself rends the veil of the temple (27.51), indicating that the temple is about to be destroyed (26.61; 27.40),[38] and that Israel's cultic system will be brought to an end. Jesus now replaces the temple as the dwelling place of God among his people (1.23; 28.20).

Fourth, the circumstance that it is precisely Gentile guards who confess Jesus to be the Son of God indicates that in fact his death brings salvation and forgiveness of sins not only to Jews, but also to the 'many' (20.28; 26.28), that is, to Gentiles.

Fifth, in contradistinction to the command to silence regarding Peter's confession of Jesus as Son of God in 16.16, there is no command to silence here. As Kingsbury (1984) has indicated, the reason for this difference is clear: these guards make the confession as they face the cross; they confess Jesus as Son of God in recognition of his suffering and death.

Sixth, this initial climax to the third main division of Matthew's Gospel ends with the affirmation that Jesus is the Son of God, as did the first and second divisions. The point of view of the Roman guards agrees with that of God (3.17) and Peter (the disciples, 16.16).

The cross is not, of course, the end. The narrative moves on to its ultimate climax in 28.16-20. The predictions of Jesus, which have not failed yet, included not only death but also resurrection. Indeed, there is mention of Jesus' resurrection in the middle of the account of the crucifixion (27.53). The women who follow Jesus from Galilee witness his death (27.55-56), and they form the link between the crucifixion and resurrection narratives. Three days after the burial of Jesus (27.57-61) and the sealing of the tomb (27.62-66), the women visit the burial site and encounter the angel who announces to them the resurrection of Jesus (28.1-7). The angel describes the resurrected Jesus as the crucified one, the perfect tense pointing to the fact that the risen Lord is one with the crucified Jesus. In accord with the predictions of Jesus to his disciples (26.32), the angel declares that Jesus will go before his 'brothers' into Galilee (28.10). The ultimate climax to this division and, as we shall see, to the Gospel as a whole comes with the fulfillment of this promise in 28.16-20. Here the resurrected and exalted Christ appears to his disciples with the command to make disciples of all nations. In contrast to the instructions of Jesus to tell no one that he is the Christ (16.20), the disciples, now in the presence of the cricified and risen Lord, are sent out to proclaim freely the messianic claims of the Son of God. The events of the last major division of Matthew's Gospel have taught them the true meaning and significance of the messiahship of Jesus and prepared them for their evangelistic task. This concern regarding the understanding of the disciples leads us into the presentation Jesus makes to his disciples of the necessity of his death in 16.21-28.20.

3. *Repetition of Comparison between the Cross of Jesus and the Cross of the Disciples*

We mentioned above that 16.21 is expanded in the third main division not only by climax, but also by the repetition of comparison and the repetition of contrast. By repetition of comparison we mean the ongoing correspondence between what Jesus does and what the disciples are to do. Just as Jesus orients his life around the cross, so the disciples are to orient their lives around their cross. We noted earlier that there is repetition of comparison between Jesus and the expectations for the disciples in the Gospel as a whole. In 16.21-28.20, however, the emphasis on the cross causes the comparison to take on a distinctive form. Because of this distinctive form, comparison becomes an element which binds 16.21-28.20 together into a discrete unit.

As we observed above, Mt. 16.21 contains a dual focus. It speaks not only of the journey of Jesus to Jerusalem and his passion, but it also speaks of the presentation Jesus makes to the disciples of the necessity for this journey with its passion and resurrection. We note that Matthew does not say that Jesus 'taught' or 'instructed' his disciples regarding his passion, but rather that he 'showed' (δείκνυμι) them. Although some commentators, such as M.J. Lagrange (1948: 330) and Heinrich Schlier (*TDNT*, II: 25), have argued that there is no difference at all between δείκνυμι and instructing or teaching, the evidence points in the opposite direction. A glance at the concordance reveals that, in the New Testament, the word never means simply 'teach'. Rather, this term means 'present' or 'show', which may include verbal description, but in the New Testament always includes more than simply speech. The term is used in Mt. 4.8, where the devil presents Jesus with a panoramic vision of the kingdoms of the world; and in Mt. 8.4 Jesus instructs the former leper to show himself to the priest, thus demonstrating his cleansing. If we place 'show' in 16.21 within the context of the flow of the narrative throughout 16.21-28.20, it becomes evident that Jesus shows his disciples the necessity of his passion not only by what he says, but also by what he does, especially by himself undertaking the journey to Jerusalem.[39]

In addition to these observations regarding 'show', we note as well that Jesus does not show his disciples his passion *per se*, but rather the necessity (δεῖ) of his passion. This necessity represents no blind, impersonal fate nor an accident of history that must be played out, as the word sometimes indicated in classical Greek usage (Grundmann *TDNT*, II: 22). An examination of its usage in Matthew reveals that it is employed only after 16.21 and that it points to the will and purpose of God,[40] especially the will of God as prophesied in the Old Testament that the Messiah must suffer (26.54). Thus, Jesus demonstrates to his disciples both by what he says and by what he does that it is the will of God for him to suffer and die.

But this 'necessity' does not make the journey of Jesus to the cross automatic. Matthew portrays Jesus as struggling with the will of God over his messianic role. Jesus is tempted by Satan to demonstrate his messiahship, or his divine Sonship, by means of signs (4.1-11). In analogy to the temptations of Jesus in the wilderness, Peter assumes the role of Satan in 16.23; when Peter rebukes Jesus for declaring that he must go to Jerusalem to suffer and die, Jesus responds with the same phraseology he employs with the tempter in 4.10: 'Get behind me, Satan'; and he declares that Peter is a hindrance or cause of stumbling to him.[41] Moreover, in the Garden of Gethsemane Jesus struggles with his own desire to avoid the cup of suffering, although he yields to the will of God (26.36-47). And finally, the mockery of the crowd and religious leaders around the cross echoes, as we have seen, the temptations of 4.1-11. Despite these struggles and temptations, Jesus remains true to the will of God, choosing the purpose and design of God for his mission over against his own wishes. Therefore, Matthew presents Jesus throughout 16.21-28.20 as faithful and obedient to the will of God, which means for him the way of the cross and suffering.

Yet the obedience to God's will by way of the cross which Jesus undertakes in 16.21-28.20 involves not only suffering, but also the elements of humility and self-denial in the service of others. Accordingly, Jesus enters Jerusalem as the king who is 'humble' (21.4), and in the passion narrative the kingship of Jesus is defined, not in terms of worldly rule, but in terms of pouring out his blood 'for the forgiveness of sins' (27.27-54; cf. 26.28). His messianic calling is 'to serve and to give his life a ransom for many' (20.28).

To sum up: for Jesus, acceptance of the way of the cross involves faithfulness to the will of God, which means both endurance of the pain and suffering of the cross and an attitude of humility and self-sacrificial service for others.

The expectations of discipleship in 16.21–28.20 are presented in the same terms as this portrait of Jesus. The paradigmatic statement regarding discipleship comes almost immediately after the general statement of 16.21. In 16.24 Jesus tells his disciples, 'If anyone would come after me, let him deny himself, take up his cross, and follow me'. 'To deny oneself', as Heinrich Schlier (*TDNT*, I: 469) has put it, means to say no to the self, or to reject a claim upon the self. It thus involves the element of self-surrender. 'To take up one's cross', in the context of 16.21–28.20, means to emulate Jesus in the way of the cross; this emulation, as we have just seen, involves faithfulness to the will of God, especially in terms of endurance of suffering for the sake of the kingdom and an attitude of humility and of selfless service for others.

This acceptance of suffering and service by the disciples in analogy to Jesus stands behind the instructions which Jesus gives to his disciples throughout this section. His followers are not to insist on their own prerogatives when these prerogatives cause offense to others (17.24-27; 18.5-14); rather, they are to humble themselves like little children (18.1-4; 19.13-15). The disciples are not to orient their lives around response to personal hurt, but they are to forgive others freely (18.21-35). They are not to insist on exercising authority over others, but are rather to act as servants and slaves to others (20.25-28). Even as Jesus was faithful to the will and calling of God for him, so they are to obey faithfully the will of God as Jesus has interpreted it for them.[42]

This faithfulness of the disciples in accord with Jesus' faithfulness stands over against the unfaithfulness of the religious leaders; indeed, their unfaithfulness serves as a foil to the faithfulness which is expected of the disciples. Since the disciples are aligned with Jesus, who himself stands over against unrepentant Israel and especially the religious leaders, the disciples are to be like Jesus by being unlike those opponents. In chs. 21–23 these opponents are portrayed as being utterly unfaithful to the calling and covenant of God. Like disobedient children, they fail to do the will of the Father who has called them (21.28-32). Although the kingdom has been theirs, they have failed to deliver its fruit (21.43). Consequently, the kingdom will be taken away from them (21.43), and they will suffer the judgment of God: loss of city (22.7), and hell (23.33). The disciples must be careful to remain faithful to God so that they will not be found unworthy to partake of the eschatological banquet (22.11-14), even as Israel as a whole has been pronounced unworthy (22.1-10). The actions of the disciples also stand under the judgment of God (chs. 24-25). Unlike the religious leaders, who insist on high-sounding titles and places of honor (23.1-7), the disciples are to assume the humility and servanthood of Christ (23.8-12).

4. *Repetition of Contrast between Jesus and the Disciples*

In the context of this recurring comparison between Jesus and the expectations for discipleship, however, we find that throughout 16.21–28.20 the disciples themselves fail to meet these expectations. The upshot is a recurring contrast between Jesus and the portrait of what the disciples are to be, on the one hand, and the twelve disciples, on the other. This contrast focuses on the unwillingness, or slowness, of the disciples to assume their cross, that is, to follow Jesus in the way of humility, self-sacrifice, and suffering.

This recurring contrast between Jesus and the disciples appears already at the beginning of this division of Matthew's Gospel. Immediately after the first passion prediction (16.21), Peter strongly censures Jesus for declaring that the Christ must suffer and die (16.22-23). In light of Peter's rejection of this prediction and the slowness of the disciples to accept Jesus' teaching of the cross, the heavenly voice in 17.5 declares not only 'This is my beloved Son, with whom I am well pleased', as in 3.17, but adds the words 'listen to him'. Yet the disciples still do not understand that the kingdom belongs to children (19.13-15); and even after Jesus gives his most comprehensive passion prediction, James and John seek the highest seats in the kingdom (20.20-23), and the other ten are indignant because they themselves wanted a fair shake at these positions of honor (20.24). And finally, the falling away of the disciples and Peter's denial in the face of sharing the suffering of Jesus reveal that the disciples have not entirely committed themselves to the cross of Christ (26.30-35, 56, 69-75).

This problem of the slowness of the disciples to accept the cross of discipleship can be met only by Jesus' promise that he will go before them into Galilee (26.32) and by the word of demand and encouragement from the mouth of the exalted Christ (28.16-20). In the end, therefore, Jesus not only places the demands of the cross upon his disciples, but he himself provides them with the help and strength to meet these demands.

5. *Summary of 16.21-28.20*

In this study of 16.21-28.20, we have argued that 16.21 encapsulates the major themes in the material that follows. The mention of Jesus' journey to Jerusalem and his passion is expanded or particularized by means of climax, which uses the geographical framework and the pattern of prediction and fulfillment to move the reader on to the events of the death and resurrection of Jesus. The mention of Jesus' showing his disciples the necessity for his suffering is expanded or particularized by means of a recurring comparison between his acceptance of the cross and the demand that the disciples accept their cross as well. Along with this recurring comparison, there is a recurring contrast between what is demanded of the disciples and the faulty performance of the twelve. Yet this is not the last word, for at the climax of the section 16.21-28.20 and of the Gospel as a whole the disciples are given strength to fulfill the demands by means of the powerful word of command and promise from the exalted Christ. We turn now to an examination of the climactic nature of 28.16-20 vis-à-vis the Gospel of Matthew as a whole.

Chapter 6

THE STRUCTURE OF MATTHEW:
CLIMAX WITH INCLUSIO

The fourth major structural relationship binding the Gospel of
Matthew together is that of climax, found at 28.16-20. Here Jesus
appears to his disciples as the exalted and resurrected Christ, who
commissions them to make disciples of all nations. Moreover, the
promise of Jesus to be 'with us' (28.20) serves with 1.23 to bracket the
Gospel, thus indicating inclusio.

A. *The Structure and Form of 28.16-20*

A complete exegesis of 28.16-20 stands outside the purview of this
study. A brief discussion of the structure and form of the passage
will, however, serve the larger purpose of delineating the climactic
function of these verses.

1. *The Structure of 28.16-20*
The structure of 28.16-20 is relatively simple. The passage can be
divided into two sections, with vv. 16-17 forming the introduction to
the declarations of Jesus in vv. 18-20. The introduction provides the
setting in terms of characters (eleven disciples, Jesus), locale (Galilee,
the mountain), occasion (command of Jesus), and situation (worship
and doubt).

We turn first to an examination of those elements found in the
introduction (vv. 16-17). The identity of the characters is clear. The
locations mentioned have distinct theological significance. The
phrase 'unto Galilee' echoes Matthew's statement in 4.12, where
Jesus is said to have withdrawn 'unto Galilee' just before he began
his public ministry; Galilee is therefore the sphere of eschatological
ministry for both Jesus and the disciples. In Matthew, the mountain
is the place of revelation (cf. 5.1; 17.1-8). Moreover, the command of

Jesus points back to the instruction Jesus gave his disciples through the women in 28.10.

Perhaps the most significant feature of the introductory material of vv. 16-17 has to do with the situation of worship and doubt. Verse 17 indicates that the existence of the post-Easter disciples is characterized by both worship and doubt. A great deal of ink has been spilled over the exact meaning of this statement. Many earlier commentators, such as Plummer (1909: 427) and McNeile (1938: 437), argued that 'those who doubted' were not the disciples, but others who were present with the eleven. Virtually all recent scholars have abandoned that interpretation, maintaining either that all worship and all doubt, or that only some of the eleven doubt.[1] Whichever of the latter two interpretations one accepts, Matthew's theological meaning is clear: the post-Easter disciples must confront the existence of doubt as they carry out the work of Christ in the world. As I.P. Ellis (1968: 575-77) demonstrates, the concept of 'doubt' (διστάζω) indicates not unbelief, but weak faith. In Matthew it is used in connection with 'little faith' (ὀλιγόπιστος; cf. 14.31-33) and stands over against 'great faith' (cf. 15.28). This doubt expresses a wavering, which hinders disciples from appropriating the full possibilities of endurance, power, and mission which are offered through Christ. Then, too, this situation of doubt in the midst of worshipping disciples suggests also an element of interrogation within the passage. The problem of doubt is answered by the declarations of Jesus in vv. 18b-20, and especially by his promise to be with them always (v. 20b).

Turning from the introductory verses (vv. 16-17) to the declarations of Jesus (vv. 18-20), we find that these declarations can, in turn, be divided into two units. The proclamation of authority in v. 18b provides the basis for (causation) both the commision of vv. 19-20a and the promise of enduring presence in v. 20b. With regard to the proclamation of v. 18b, the authority which is given to Jesus (by God) is inclusive in scope, and this inclusiveness is emphasized by repetition: 'all authority', 'in heaven and earth'. This inclusiveness of the authority of Jesus corresponds to the inclusive scope of the missionary charge in vv. 19-20a.

With regard to the commissioning of vv. 19-20a, we find that this commission is expressed by means of a finite verb, 'make disciples' (μαθητεύσατε), with three accompanying participles. In spite of Bruce Malina (1970: 89-90), the participle 'having gone' or 'go' (πορευθέντες) does explicitly contribute to the message of these verses; Anton Vögtle (1964: 285) suggests that this participle is used both here and in ch. 10 in order to emphasize the contrast between the exclusive mission of ch. 10 and the inclusive mission here. Malina is correct, however, when he indicates that this is a circumstantial participle, expressing the circumstances which surround or attend the activity of making disciples. The participles 'baptizing' (βαπτίζοντες) and 'teaching' (διδάσκοντες) are generally identified by scholars as instrumental participles, indicating the ways in which disciples are to be made.[2]

The commands of 28.19-20a are followed by the declaration of 28.20b, which promises the presence of Christ with the disciples as they carry out the mission of 28.19-20a and thus substantiates the command. The disciples are encouraged to fulfill the instructions of vv. 19-20a because of the knowledge that Jesus continues to be with them.

2. *The Form of 28.16-20*

The form (*Gattung*) of 28.16-20 has been a center of controversy among scholars for many years. Several suggestions have been advanced.[3] Martin Dibelius (1959: 282-85) identified the passage as a 'myth', emphasizing its relation to 11.25-30 and pointing to its lack of historical connections. This proposal overlooks many of the non-mythological elements in the passage and Matthew's attempt to relate the exalted Christ of 28.18-20 to the earthly Jesus. Rudolf Bultmann (1958: 619) classified the passage as a 'cult legend', emphasizing baptism to the virtual exclusion of other elements.

More significant than the proposals by Dibelius and Bultmann is the hypothesis put forward by Otto Michel (1983: 36-37) and Joachim Jeremias (1958: 38-39) of an enthronement hymn based on Dan. 7.13-14. They contend that Matthew composed an enthronement hymn in analogy to other such hymns found in the New Testament[4] in order to teach that, in his resurrection, Jesus fulfilled the enthronement of the Son of man pictured in Daniel.

A number of problems with this proposal have surfaced. First, the Danielic passage points to world conquest, whereas evangelism, and not conquest, is at issue in Mt. 28.18-20. Second, in the Danielic passage the kingdom is eternal, whereas the kingdom of the Son of man in Matthew is not eternal, but will, at the eschaton, become the kingdom of the Father (13.41-43). Third, the expression 'all authority in heaven and on earth' in Matthew includes the unseen as well as the seen; this goes far beyond the entirely mundane nature of the Danielic statement. Fourth, specific enemies are in view in Daniel; there is a transfer of authority from these particular leaders and powers to the Son of man. But Matthew has in view no specific holders of authority from whom dominion is taken. Fifth, there is no universalism in Daniel 7; the Gentile rulers are destroyed. By contrast, Mt. 28.18 forms the presupposition for the universalism of vv. 19-20a. Sixth, although the expression 'all nations' (πάντα τὰ ἔθνη) appears in both passages, the sense is different. In Daniel, Israel is excluded, whereas in Matthew Israel is included.[5] Seventh, in Matthew the emphasis is not upon the appearance of the resurrected one, but upon his speech, that is, what he says. Eighth, the analogy to the enthronement hymns in the New Testament is weak. In Matthew 28 the exalted Christ himself speaks, not the community (cf. 1 Tim. 3.16; Heb. 1.5-14; Phil. 2.9-11), and the emphasis in the Matthean passage is upon making disciples rather than upon the exaltation *per se*. Finally and most significantly, in 28.16-20 Matthew presents Jesus not as Son of man, but as Son of God, as is indicated in the baptismal formula: 'baptizing them in the name of the Father and of the Son' (v. 19). These objections point to the conclusion that Mt. 28.18-20 is not an enthronement hymn and is not meant to present Jesus as the fulfillment of Dan. 7.13-14.

In addition to the proposals which identify the genre of 28.16-20 as that of a 'myth', a 'cult legend', or an 'enthronement hymn', another proposal for the genre of this passage has been advanced by Trilling (1968: 48) and Lohmeyer (1956: 416), who find in 28.18-20a a threefold pattern of revelatory word, command, and promise. Yet, as both must concede, these three elements do not appear together in any Old Testament passage.

Frankemölle (1974: 43-61), for his part, sees the passage as a covenant formula (*Bundesformel*) along Old Testament lines, with a fivefold schema arranged around the concept of 'God with us' (*Mitsein*). Yet, as Gerhard Friedrich (1983: 158-59) observes, the 'God with us' concept in the Old Testament is not particularly related to covenant formulae, and the fivefold schema of Frankemölle fits the structure of 28.18-20 in only the most general way.

Malina (1970-71: 88-91) sees Mt. 28.18-20 as a combination of the royal decrees (especially 2 Chron. 26.23) and the Old Testament prophetic proof pattern. But this synthesis weakens his case, since it is a tacit admission that neither genre can account for all the data; and the individual parallels Malina attempts to draw have many points of discontinuity with Mt. 28.16-20.

Yet the theory which has enjoyed the greatest following in recent years is that advanced by Benjamin J. Hubbard (1974: 62-72). Hubbard sees the formal pattern of 28.16-20 along the lines of Old Testament commissions. These commissions contain seven elements:

1. Introduction (= Mt. 28.16)
2. Confrontation (= Mt. 28.17a, 18)
3. Reaction (= Mt. 28.17b)
4. Commission (= Mt. 28.19-20a)
5. Protest (Mt. 28.20b)
6. Reassurance (missing in Matthew)
7. Conclusion (missing in Matthew)

According to Hubbard, Matthew has taken over this schema and expanded it, especially in the commission section.

There are, however, also problems with this proposal. For one thing, Hubbard tends to read Old Testament passages in the light of Mt. 28.16-20. He is especially prone to expand some protests and conclusions into full-fledged commissions. Furthermore, the individual examples Hubbard cites often do not support his outline. For instance, the commissioning of Joseph (by Pharaoh) (Gen. 41.39) has no confrontation. Indeed, the commission itself is sometimes missing except for very small notices or promises which Hubbard confuses with commands.[6] Finally, there are also problems with the use Hubbard makes of the New Testament. For instance, Lk. 24.36-53 lacks a commission; and in Mt. 28.16-20 itself the series of statements does not correspond to the schema Hubbard puts forward. In this passage the reaction precedes the confrontation, with the result that Hubbard is forced to reverse the phrases in vv. 17 and 18.[7]

It is clear from this survey that Mt. 28.16-20 does not fit any one existing form, or *Gattung*, entirely. In recent years scholars have become increasingly sensitive to the problem of placing this passage within a formal category and with Vögtle (1964) and Kingsbury (1974) have emphasized more and more the role of the Matthean composition in the passage. Our contention is that its meaning is to be determined by its structural relationship to the Gospel as a whole rather than by a putative allusion to one or more Old Testament passages or forms.

We wish to make three additional observations regarding the passage as a whole before we examine the major themes which come to a climax in these verses. The first observation is that there is a certain supra-historical aura pervading the passage. The relationship between 28.16-20 and the immediately preceding context is in many ways choppy and discontinuous. As Bornkamm (1964: 171-72) has shown, there is no interest in historical details. The mountain is the place of revelation rather than a distinct geographical location. There is no mention of the manner or appearance of Jesus. Matthew records nothing of Jesus' removal from them. There is no mention of the fright or joy of the disciples or of their recognition of Jesus. The doubt of the disciples is answered not by the appearance of the exalted Christ, but rather by his word; and this word is not a farewell speech, since Jesus does not in fact depart.

The meaning of this supra-historical dimension is found in Matthew's conception of Jesus as one who endures forever with his disciples, the church. The Matthean Jesus continues to dwell in the midst of his community in the time of the implied reader just as truly as he 'dwells' with his disciples in the days of his earthly ministry. And Jesus continues to instruct and address his community now, just as he teaches his disciples on the Galilean hillside. For this reason, Matthew leaves the culmination of his Gospel open-ended.

The second observation regarding 28.16-20 is that Matthew is here concerned to establish continuity between the earthly Jesus and the exalted Christ. He accomplishes this connection by assimilating in many ways throughout his Gospel the earthly Jesus to the living Lord of the church.[8] But Matthew also forms this connection by means of a number of literary devices in 28.16-20. Examples of these devices include the connection between 28.17 and 14.31-33 and between 28.18 and 11.25-27, the presence of 'authority' in 28.18, which recalls the indications throughout the Gospel that Jesus is the one who possesses transcendent authority, and the reference to Jesus as Son of God (28.19; cf. 3.17; 17.5). Thus, the earthly Jesus who taught his disciples in Galilee and travelled with them to Jerusalem is one with the exalted Christ who continues to dwell with his disciples, teaching and guiding them as they seek to fulfill the charge Jesus has given them.

The third observation regarding 28.16-20 is that the command of the exalted Christ expresses the enlargement of the ministry of the disciples over against their somewhat restricted activities in the

Gospel as a whole. Here, for the first time, the disciples are given authority not only to preach and to heal (ch. 10), but also to teach. Further, we noted above that after the confession of Peter, Jesus instructs his disciples to tell no one that he is the Christ (16.20); and later Jesus tells the three disciples that they are to say nothing of the transfiguration until he has been raised from the dead (17.9). Now in 28.16-20 the disciples are commanded to announce publicly the messianic status of Jesus.

B. *The Major Themes which Move toward Climax in 28.16-20*

We now turn to examine three major themes in the Gospel as a whole which move toward the climax of 28.16-20: the authority of Jesus, universalism, and the presence of Jesus with his community.[9]

1. *The Notion of the Authority of Jesus which Comes to Climax in 28.16-20*

The notion of authority, which is so prominent in 28.16-20, pervades Matthew's Gospel as a whole. Virtually no paragraph escapes the expression of Jesus' authority. Indeed, the Gospel begins with an arresting statement of majesty (1.1), and this initial declaration of authority forms an artistic parallel to the climactic statement at the end of the Gospel.

Matthew expresses the authority of Jesus in many and diverse ways. One of the most useful tools Matthew employs is that of the titles of majesty. These titles are employed throughout the book in order to shape and refine the reader's perception of Jesus. Among the minor titles of majesty are 'the coming one';[10] 'shepherd', indicating, in line with its Old Testament use, the authority of Jesus to rule over the eschatological people of God;[11] 'servant' (12.18); 'Son of Abraham' (1.1); and 'Emmanuel' at 1.21, where Matthew adds its interpretation, 'God with us'.

Other titles, which are used much more frequently throughout the course of Mathew's Gospel, may be regarded as major titles. The most general of these major titles is 'Christ', indicating the royal Messiah in the line of David, who culminates Israel's history and who ultimately determines salvation or condemnation for persons.[12] Closely related to 'Christ' is the title 'king', pointing to the rulership Jesus exercises over his people. For Matthew, Jesus fulfills this royal vocation by suffering in order to atone for sins.[13] In addition to 'king', the title 'Son of David' is also closely related to 'Christ'. 'Son of David' designates Jesus as the royal Messiah from the line of David who has been sent to Israel; it emphasizes the blessing and healing which has come specifically to Israel through its Messiah. As such, 'Son of David' is tied in Matthew to Jesus' healing ministry.[14] The title 'Lord' (Κύριος) when applied to Jesus, and not to God, always functions to attribute divine status and authority to Jesus.[15] Still, the foremost title in Matthew is 'Son of God', which points to the unique filial relationship Jesus has to God, his Father.[16]

In contradistinction to such titles as 'Lord', and 'Son of God', 'Son of man' is a public rather than a confessional title. By this distinction between public and confessional, we mean that Jesus uses 'Son of man' to speak of himself as he interacts with persons in general, especially his opponents, yet Jesus is never confessed as 'Son of man'. The title 'Son of man', however, also points to the authority of Jesus: as Son of man Jesus is raised from the dead and will be vindicated at the parousia when he comes to judge all persons.[17]

In addition to these christological titles, terms denoting human respect are also predicated of Jesus. The people hold him to be a 'prophet' (16.14; 21.11, 46) and Jesus once obliquely refers to himself as such (13.57). This is not a christological title in Matthew, since it is presented as the wrong answer to the question of Jesus' identity over against the true confession that Jesus is the 'Christ, the Son of the living God' (16.13-16). Yet its use indicates that even those without faith accord a particular status to Jesus.

In addition to 'prophet', another term signifying human respect is that of 'teacher'. Jesus is consistently addressed by opponents, those without faith, and Judas as 'teacher' or 'rabbi'.[18] Again, although it is clear that this is not a christological title, it nevertheless points to a modicum of esteem toward Jesus, even by his opponents.[19]

The reader encounters the authority of Jesus not only through titles of majesty, but also at the very beginning of the Gospel in the form of the genealogy (1.1-17). Here Jesus stands as the climax to the history of salvation, which, according to Matthew, begins with Abraham (1.1, 2, 17) and moves on through the history of David (1.1, 6, 17). Matthew thus indicates that God is in control of history, that salvation history is teleological, and that Jesus as the culmination of this history gives meaning and purpose to salvation history. Indeed, the references to Gentiles within the genealogy (1.3, 5-6) and to the deportation to Babylon (1.11, 17) suggest at the outset that Jesus has implications not only for the history of Israel, but also for the history of all humankind. The notion that Jesus is the climax of salvation history stands behind Matthew's understanding of Jesus' fulfillment of the Old Testament and especially his use of fulfillment quotations.[20] This notion is explicitly indicated elsewhere in the Gospel (for instance, 9.14-17).

A third way in which Matthew underscores the authority of Jesus is found in his description of Jesus' birth and infancy. Jesus is conceived by the Holy Spirit, and he will exercise his authority to save his people from their sins. Indeed, he is 'God with us' (1.20-23).[21] The authority of Jesus, in this passage, is from God, and Jesus participates in this authority to such an extent that, where he is, God is also present to help and deliver.

This divine origin of Jesus is related to Jesus' authority; and this divine origin, indicated in his conception by the Holy Spirit, is supported by two additional emphases found in the birth narratives. For one thing, the events surrounding the birth of Jesus occur in order to fulfil the scriptures. Furthermore, the divine origin of Jesus is supported by means of the recurring phenomena of revelations from the angel of the Lord.[22] In each case, these revelations are designed to protect Jesus from mortal danger; the life that is conceived by the Holy Spirit is also preserved by direct intervention from Heaven.

The authority of Jesus is demonstrated not only by the account of Jesus' birth, but also by the story of the wise men. The birth of Jesus is an event so decisive that it is reflected even in creation: the wise men see his star (2.2, 7). The activity of the wise men underscores the authority of Jesus. They have come to worship him (2.2); and when they finally discover the child, they fall down and worship (2.11). This response of the wise men is crucial, both because it represents the profound acknowledgement of transcendent authority and because this response of worship appears several times in Matthew's story.[23] The term 'worship' designates the recognition of divine authority. As Heinrich Greeven (*TDNT*, VI: 763) has pointed out, the object of 'worship' in the New Testament is always understood to have divine status. What is true for the New Testament as a whole is certainly, in this case, true also for Matthew. The decisive weight of 'worship' for Matthew is set forth in 4.10: 'You shall worship the Lord your God and him only shall you serve'.

Furthermore, the verb 'to fall down' is often employed in the New

Testament in combination with 'worship' to reinforce the notion of divine status. Again, this general New Testament usage appears specifically in Matthew's Gospel (also at 4.9; 18.26); and 'to fall down' frequently occurs in the Gospel alone or with verbs of supplication (17.6; 18.29; 26.39) to indicate abasement in the presence of majesty.[24]

But the wise men do not simply fall down in worship. Their recognition of the transcendent authority of Jesus is reflected in their presentation of gifts to Jesus. The term 'present', both in Matthew (5.23-24; 8.4) and in the LXX,[25] often has to do with offerings presented to God. And 'gift' is used elsewhere in Matthew exclusively for offerings to God.[26]

If Matthew points to the authority of Jesus by means of the infancy narratives, he does so also in the pericope dealing with John's witness to Jesus and the baptism of Jesus (3.1-17). John associates the coming of the kingdom with the coming of Jesus and emphasizes the authority of Jesus as eschatological judge (3.8-11).[27] Further, the authority of Jesus is superior to that of John. John is the forerunner, while Jesus is the one to whom he points, the fulfillment (3.3, 11). John baptizes with water unto repentance, whereas Jesus will baptize with the Holy Spirit and fire (3.11-12). John has need to be baptized by Jesus and agrees to baptize Jesus only after Jesus persuades him that such is necessary to fulfil all righteousness (3.14-15). Finally, when John baptizes Jesus, the Holy Spirit comes upon Jesus, empowering him for eschatological ministry in Israel (3.16); and God attests directly that Jesus is his Son (3.17). The divine Sonship of Jesus and his anointing for eschatological ministry are confirmed by the authority Jesus exercises over Satan in the temptations (4.1-11).

Yet Jesus has authority not only over Satan, but also over persons. Jesus possesses the authority to call the four fishermen to discipleship to himself (4.19-21; cf. 9.9) and to make them 'fishers of people' (4.19). The authority of Jesus is demonstrated by their ready acceptance of his call (4.20, 22, 9.9), a call which, indeed, involves forsaking 'all things' (cf. 19.27).

The authority of Jesus is expressed not only in his encounter with Satan and in the calling of his disciples, but also in his public ministry. Jesus exercises authority to 'teach in their synagogues' and to 'preach the gospel of the kingdom' (4.23; 9.35; 11.1) and to 'heal every disease and every infirmity' (4.23; 9.35; cf. chs. 8-9).

The authority of Jesus to teach is substantiated by the many references to his specific instructions, especially in the sermon on the mount (chs. 5-7). There Jesus has authority to proclaim eschatological blessings (for instance, 5.3-11), to speak regarding heavenly rewards (5.12; 6.1-16), to speak of God to his hearers as 'your heavenly Father' (5.16-48; 6.1-32; 7.11) to 'fulfill' the law and the prophets (5.17-48); to declare the basis for status in the kingdom (5.19); to declare the righteousness of the scribes and Pharisees inadequate for entrance into the kingdom (5.20); to place his teaching above the letter of the law, that is, to declare the true meaning and interpretation of the law, even though this means the abrogation of the letter of the law in some places;[28] to instruct regarding piety (6.2-18); to declare God's evaluation of acts (6.1-17); to declare what God knows (6.8, 32);[29] to declare how God will judge (6.14-16); to declare how God will react to those who seek his kingdom and his righteousness (6.25-34); to pronounce the sum of the law and the prophets (7.12; also 22.34-40); to declare the basis of eschatological judgment (7.19-20; 12.36); and to speak of God as 'my Father' (7.21; 10.33; and often). Most of these elements are repeated throughout the Gospel. Moreover, response to the instructions of Jesus has ultimate eschatological implications, as indicated by the contrast of 7.24-27 (also 21.23-32). The first explicit mention of 'authority' in Matthew's Gospel appears within the response of the crowds to the sermon: 'The crowds were amazed at his teaching, for he taught as one who had authority and not as their scribes' (7.27-29).

Even as the authority of Jesus to teach is expanded in the sermon on the mount, so his authority to heal is spelled out in chs. 8-9. A number of specific elements within these chapters emphasize this authority. The centurion compares the authority he experiences to that which Jesus possesses; even as the centurion can command his slave to perform some duty in another location, so Jesus can effect a far-off healing by simply saying the word (8.9). Moreover, the authority to heal the paralytic points beyond the miracle itself to the authority Jesus possesses on earth to forgive sins (9.7). Finally, Jesus has power not only to heal the sick, but also to raise the dead (9.18-26; 11.5).

Matthew underscores the authority of Jesus in his healing ministry throughout the Gospel. These stories point to the immediacy of the healings[30] the ease with which Jesus performs these mighty acts: usually with a touch or a word;[31] and the inclusiveness of the healings, as indicated by the 'all' in the summary statement of 8.16.

The crowds respond that 'nothing like this was ever seen in Israel', and even the Pharisees tacitly acknowledge his authority when they murmur that 'he casts out demons by the prince of demons' (9.32-34). Jesus gives authority to preach and heal to his disciples (ch. 10), thus showing that he has authority to dispense authority.

Jesus indicates the basis of his authority to preach, teach, and heal in 11.25-30. In anticipation of the climactic statement of 28.18-20, Jesus declares in 11.27 that 'all things have been delivered to me by my Father, and no one knows the Father except the Son and whosover the Son wishes to reveal him'. Jesus can reveal the Father because 'all things' have been delivered to him. The reference to 'all things' thus points specifically to the knowledge Jesus possesses of the Father and to his consequent ability to reveal the Father.[32] Yet the expression 'all things' is not limited to this knowledge or revelation, but rather takes up the notion of full authority as the basis of this revelation.[33]

In line with the unique relationship Jesus has to his Father (11.25-30), he has authority to 'give rest' (11.29). As 'Lord of the sabbath' (12.8), he possesses the authority to heal on the sabbath, thus interpreting its true function (12.9-14). Jesus can do these things because he is greater than the temple (12.6), than Jonah (12.41), and Solomon (12.24).

Not only does Jesus have authority to preach, teach, and heal, but he also exercises authority over the church, the eschatological people of God. Jesus has authority to build his church (16.18), to hand over the keys of the kingdom (16.19), and to instruct his disciples regarding community life and discipline within the church (ch. 18).

In addition to the expression of Jesus' authority within his ministry and in his relation to the church, this authority is also indicated by references to Jesus' transcendent knowledge. Throughout the Gospel of Matthew, the predictions that Jesus makes are fulfilled.[34] This transcendent knowledge is demonstrated also by the ability of Jesus to discern the thoughts of others (for instance, 9.4) and to know of events at which he was not present (17.24-27). Moreover, Jesus has the ability to declare the eschatological future (19.28; chs. 24-25).

The final events of the Gospel revolve around the authority of Jesus. Opposition to Jesus from the religious leaders arises precisely at the question of this authority. The first explicit mention of opposition appears in a passage where the authority of Jesus to forgive sins is met with the response that he is blaspheming (9.3). The first notice that the Jewish leaders were plotting Jesus' death comes at the end of a pericope dealing with the authority of Jesus over the sabbath (12.14). And Jesus is condemned to death on the charge of blasphemy, because he assumes the authority of the Son of God (and Son of man) who sits at the right hand of God until he comes at the last day as eschatological judge (26.63-68).[35] As part of the climax of the Gospel, the authority of Jesus over the power of death immediately prepares the way for his climactic statement of authority in 28.18.

All these expressions of authority lead up to Jesus' declaration of all authority in heaven and earth at 28.18. Although the 'authority' mentioned there binds up all these elements of authority found throughout the Gospel, the authority of the risen and exalted Christ goes far beyond the sum of all these elements, since the exalted Christ is no longer limited by his earthly existence. It is no longer a matter of receiving authority from heaven for activity on earth (9.8); the exalted Christ extends the authority the Father has given him to the entire range of the universe: 'in heaven and on earth'.

This discussion of Jesus' authority has indicated the significance of the theme in Mathew's Gospel, the nature of this authority, the essential continuity between the expression of authority in the Gospel as a whole and that found in 28.16-20, along with the discontinuity which gives 28.16-20 its climactic character. This discontinuity involves the inclusive and universal exercise of that authority which was described throughout the Gospel in terms of Jesus' earthly existence.

2. The Notion of Universalism which Comes to Climax in 28.16-20
The tension between particularism and universalism in Matthew's Gospel has long been recognized. Along with the overarching limitation of the ministry of Jesus and his disciples to the Jews, subtle references to the fuller scope of the kingdom and its benefits also appear.

Jesus instructs his disciples to 'go nowhere among the Gentiles', but to go rather 'to the lost sheep of the house of Israel' (10.5-6), a limitation which Jesus places upon himself in the face of pleas from the Canaanite woman (15.24). Moreover, throughout the Gospel the references Jesus makes to Gentiles are negative.[36]

Yet the pointers to a universal extension of the ministry and blessings of the Gospel are unmistakable. We will briefly trace this notion through the Gospel. We have discussed above the universalistic implications of the title 'Son of Abraham' (1.1-2, 17). In addition, Matthew breaks the pattern of the genealogy at several points in order to mention Gentile women who stand as progenitors of the Messiah (1.3, 5a, 5b, 6). Close on the heels of the genealogy appear the wise men from the east, who function as prototypes of disciples. They seek the king of the Jews (2.2), and when they find him they rejoice greatly (2.10), worship, and present to him offerings (2.11). Indeed, these wise men are contrasted not only to Herod, but to 'all Jerusalem', who are troubled when they hear of the birth of Jesus (2.3). Yet the first clear reference to the inclusion of the Gentiles comes in the formula quotation which Matthew employs to set the geographical stage for the ministry of Jesus (4.14-16).

The universalism encountered in 1.1-4.16 is found also in Matthew's account of the ministry of Jesus. A hint that the mission of the disciples will lead to the evangelization of the Gentiles appears in the first words Jesus speaks to the disciples: 'I will make you fishers of people' (4.19). Jesus' first discourse contains similar indications; Jesus tells his disciples that they are the 'salt of the *earth*' and the 'light of the *world*' (5.13-14).

This universalism is found not only in the sermon on the mount, but also in the account of Jesus' mighty works in chs. 8-9. The second healing recorded in Matthew is that of the centurion's servant (8.5-13). Jesus 'marvels' at the faith of the centurion and contrasts this faith with the relative unbelief encountered in Israel (8.10). This contrast in turn leads to a crucial passage in which Jesus declares that many Gentiles will share the eschatological banquet with Abraham, Isaac, and Jacob, while the 'sons of the kingdom' (that is, the Jews) will be expelled into outer darkness (8.11-12).

We mentioned above that Jesus instructs his disciples in ch. 10 to restrict their missionary activity to the Jews. In the same chapter, however, Jesus predicts that the disciples will be dragged before public officials 'to bear testimony before them and the Gentiles' (10.18) and that they will be hated 'by all' for Jesus' sake (10.22). The Jewish repudiation of the ministry of Jesus leads Jesus to declare that such Gentile cities as Tyre, Sidon, and Sodom will face less severe judgment than the Jewish cities which have experienced such privileged revelation (11.20-24). Indeed, Nineveh and the queen of the south will arise at the day of judgment and condemn 'this generation', because those Gentiles were receptive to the revelation of God in their day, while these Jews fail to respond to the much greater revelation expressed in the ministry of Jesus (12.41-42; cf. 12.6). Within this context of the Jewish rejection of the ministry of Jesus, Matthew places the prophecy from Second Isaiah which speaks of the Servant who will 'proclaim justice to the Gentiles' and in whose name the Gentiles will hope (12.17-21).

Reference to the broader appeal of the Gospel is present also in the parables of the kingdom in ch. 13. Subtle indications are expressed in the reference to the extensive growth of the mustard plant (13.31-32) and in the likeness of the kingdom to a net 'which was thrown into the sea and gathered fish of every kind' (13.47). A much clearer indication of universalism appears, however, in the interpretation of the parable of the tares: the field where the servants of the household sow good seed is 'the world' (13.38).[37]

The indications of universalism found in these parables is picked up again in ch. 15. As the particularism of ch. 10 gives way to the witness the disciples will bear to the Gentiles, so the initial refusal of Jesus to heal the daughter of the Canaanite women is followed by an acquiescence to her plea (15.21-28).

The next indication of universalism is found in the parables against Israel. The notion that the Gentiles will receive the invitation of the Gospel in consequence of the rejection of Israel is made explicit in the parables of 21.28–22.14. Although the first of these parables (21.28-32) relates more to moral and religious outcasts than to Gentiles, the latter two parables indicate clearly that a change in those who possess the kingdom is about to occur. In connection with the parable of the vineyard, Jesus expressly states that 'the kingdom of God will be taken away from you and given to a nation (ἔθνος) producing its fruits' (21.43). In the parable of the marriage feast, those who were originally invited are found unworthy, with the result that the servants are instructed to search along the highways for those who would take their places (22.9).

Matthew next picks up the theme of universalism in chs. 24–25. The future missionary activity of the disciples among the Gentiles is even more clearly presented in the eschatological discourse of chs. 24–25 than in the missionary discourse of ch. 10. Jesus predicts that they will be hated by 'all nations' (πάντων τῶν ἐθνῶν, 24.9), that 'the gospel of the kingdom will be preached throughout the whole world, as a testimony to all nations' before the end (24.14), and that at the end he will gather his elect 'from the four winds, from one end of heaven to the other' (24.41). The sheep and the goats assembled before Jesus at the judgment are identified as 'all the nations' (25.31-46). The indications of universalism grow more intense in Matthew's passion narrative. In his response to the anointing at Bethany, Jesus declares that the woman's act will be told 'wherever the gospel is preached in the whole world' (26.13). Jesus interprets the meaning of his approaching death in terms of the blood of the covenant, which is poured out for *many* for the forgiveness of sins (26.28; see also 20.28). And this interpretation of the death of Jesus is expressed in more concrete form when the Roman soldiers, facing the cross and beholding the supernatural events surrounding the death of Jesus, cry out, 'Truly, this man was the Son of God!' (27.54).

Here again, a major theme running throughout Matthew's Gospel reaches its high point in the commissioning of 28.16-20. In this climactic passage for the first time the universalism of the Gospel is clearly and unambiguously set forth. Here universalism is made explicit and binding. Indeed, this universalism could come to full expression only in 28.16-20, since it is linked to the universal authority of the exalted Christ.

3. *Climax with Inclusio: The Notion of 'God (or Jesus) with us' which Comes to a Climax in 28.16-20*

As we indicated in the title to this chapter, the climax (28.16-20) is bound up with another structural feature, namely, *inclusio*. In the last verse of the Gospel, Jesus promises to be 'with you' (μεθ᾽ ὑμῶν), that is with his disciples, until 'the end of the age' (28.20). This promise corresponds to the word of the angel to Joseph in 1.21-23, where, according to the prophetic declaration, 'they will call his name Emmanuel', which Matthew expressly interprets as 'God with us' (μεθ᾽ ἡμῶν ὁ θεός).

We judge that this recurrence is in fact inclusio, for the following reasons. To begin with, both 1.23 and 28.20 assume crucial positions in Matthew's Gospel, standing as they do near the beginning and at the very end of the Gospel. Furthermore, Matthew interprets Jesus' name with the translation 'God with us' in 1.23. In addition, Matthew is fond of inclusio and uses it frequently throughout his Gospel (for instance, 19.30 and 20.16). Finally, the content of both passages points to their importance in Matthew's theology and purpose. 1.21-23 has to do with the naming of Jesus, a process that is highlighted by the special attention given to the event itself, by the reference to the command of the angel, by the fact that the naming overshadows the birth itself, and by the general concern Matthew demonstrates throughout the Gospel for naming and address. Regarding 28.20, we have argued above that this passage summarizes the major themes of Matthew's Gospel; and the promise of Jesus to be with his community 'always, to the close of the age', indicates directly the role of Jesus in the time of the implied reader.

But the phrase, 'I am with you', of 28.20 represents more than inclusio. It is also a part of the climax of 28.16-20. This conclusion follows from the observation that the 'with-you (or us)' theme recurs throughout the Gospel and comes to a point of intensity at 28.20. The presence of this theme in the Gospel as a whole and its development toward 28.20 will now be examined.

Matthew 1.23 stands in the context of the miraculous conception of Jesus by the Holy Spirit (1.18, 20) and in a section in which Matthew presents Jesus as Son of God.[38] The notion of sonship is present even within the formula quotation, and that in two ways: the prophetic passage declares that a virgin will 'bear a *son*' (1.23; cf. v. 21); and Matthew, contrary to his usual custom, expressly adds the prepositional phrase, 'by the Lord', to his introductory fulfillment notice. He does this only once more, in 2.15, a passage which refers to 'my son'. This observation indicates that Jesus functions as God with us because of his unique filial relationship of Sonship to God (cf. 11.25-27).

We note also that the passage is different from Isa. 7.14 (LXX), to which it points, in one significant particular. Whereas Isaiah reads, 'you shall call his name' (καλέσεις), Matthew has, 'they shall call his name' (καλέσουσιν). Certainly Frankemölle (1974: 16-18) is correct when he argues that this reference to 'they' points to 'his people' of 1.21, that is, to those whom Jesus will save from their sins. Thus, the community of the believing ones, the church (16.18-20; 18.18-20), calls Jesus 'God with us'. This observation indicates that God has come to dwell with his people in the person of his Son, Jesus Christ.

In reality, however, two names are ascribed to Jesus in this passage: 'Jesus', and 'Emmanuel'. There is a twofold connection between these names. For one thing, the names appear in statements that are parallel in wording (1.21; cf. 1.23). For another thing, the prophecy regarding Emmanuel (v. 23) is fulfilled in the Jesus-naming, and especially in Jesus' role as savior from sin (v. 22). Moreover, when Joseph finally names the child in v. 25 he calls him 'Jesus', not 'Emmanuel'. The upshot from all this is that 'Jesus' is to be the child's personal name, whereas 'Emmanuel' will be the description of his role. 'Emmanuel', or 'God with us', is part of Matthew's theological definition for the name 'Jesus'. Conversely, 'Emmanuel', or 'God with us', is defined in terms of Jesus' role as savior from sin. The Old Testament concept of the presence of God with his people indicated that God was present to help or deliver in the face of obstacles (for instance Deut. 20.4; Judg. 6.16; Josh. 1.9). Here Matthew declares that God is present in Jesus to provide deliverance from sin for his people.

To sum up: in his Son, Jesus Messiah, God dwells with his people in order to save them from their sins.

After 1.23, this theme of 'God with us' appears next in 18.20. In the middle of his community discourse, Jesus declares that 'where two or three are gathered together in my name, there am I in the midst of them' (ἐν μέσῳ αὐτῶν). Although the majority of scholars believe that this passage corresponds to 1.23 and 28.20,[39] Trilling (1968: 42) has argued that the phrase 'in the midst of them' connotes a static presence of the exalted One in the worship of his community, over against the dynamic presence of Jesus to help the church in its worldwide mission, as in 28.20. In response to Trilling, Frankemölle (1974: 32-33) has demonstrated that the two expressions are used interchangeably with no difference in meaning.

Here Matthew presents Jesus as the one who is present in the midst of his community. The precise function of Jesus as he is thus present is not immediately clear, but the context suggests that this presence concerns especially the help Jesus provides the church as it prays and as it struggles to meet the demands of internal discipline.

But Jesus is not only present with his disciples in their earthly existence, as in ch. 18; his presence is extended forward in time. During the last supper, Jesus indicates that his disciples will experience his presence in the eschatological kingdom (26.29). Furthermore, Jesus is not only present with his disciples as they encounter difficulties within the community, as in ch. 18, but his presence is extended outward: in 26.38, 40 Matthew indicates that Jesus is with the disciples in their suffering. Although here, as often, it is difficult to determine whether 'with' is used merely to provide local meaning or if Matthew weighs it with theological significance.

However, when this passage is viewed in light of Matthew's overall picture of discipleship it is quite clear that theological intention is present. There is no specific indication of local presence involved, and in Matthew the disciples are constantly portrayed as following in the persecution and suffering which Jesus experiences. Here, therefore, 'with' points to the unity of suffering between Jesus and his disciples and to the presence of the crucified Lord in the midst of his suffering church in order to help them to do the will of God (26.39, 42) by 'enduring to the end' (10.22; 24.13). All these references to the presence of Jesus in the midst of his community (1.23; 18.20; 26.29) lead up to the climactic declaration of 28.20. As the disciples confront their universal mission, Jesus promises to be with them always. In other words, the post-Easter existence of the church is characterized above all by the continual presence of Jesus. This presence is described in terms of its power and potential; it is the presence of the exalted Lord who has been given all authority in heaven and on earth (28.20). It is described also in terms of its extent (and here the recurrence indicates emphasis): Jesus will be with them always, even to the end of the age. The focus here is not so much on the end as on the enduring, continuing presence of Jesus. Indeed, the end of history is defined as that point when Jesus is no longer with his community.

In summary, in his Son, Jesus Messiah, God has drawn near to his people to grant them eschatological salvation. The presence of God in the person of Jesus delivers them from their sins, helps them in prayer and enables them to carry out the demanded responsibilities of church discipline, points ahead to their fellowship with the exalted Lord in the heavenly kingdom, sustains them as they face persecutions and sufferings, and ultimately grants them the power to carry on the task of discipling all nations, that is, the mission of continuing the redemptive work of Jesus in the world. As the climax of 28.20 shows, all these challenges which confront the eschatological community can be met with full courage as the disciples recognize and appropriate the possibilities of the presence of Jesus in their midst.

C. *Summary of Climax*

Let us now summarize our study of the climax of 28.16-20. The passage itself contains an introduction (vv. 16-18a) and a declaration (18b-20), in which Jesus, Son of God, announces his universal authority, commands his disciples to undertake a universal mission of discipling, and promises to be with his disciples as they pursue their mission. There is, however, no agreement on the form or genre of the passage; since no proposal commends itself, we conclude that 28.16-20 is to be understood not in terms of a putative allusion to an Old Testament form or passage, but in terms of its role as the climax to the Gospel. In line with the divisional climaxes of 3.17, 16.16, and 27.54, 28.16-20 presents Jesus as Son of God. 28.16-20 functions as the climax to Matthew's Gospel in the following ways.

To begin with, the activity of the disciples is expanded in 28.16-20; they are now given authority to teach (as well as to preach and to heal; cf. ch. 10), and they are now instructed to announce publicly the messiahship of Jesus, in contrast to the earlier prohibition (cf. 16.20). Furthermore, this passage summarizes several major themes found in the Gospel as a whole. In addition, Mt. 28.16-20 deals with these major themes in terms both of continuity and discontinuity. Not only does this climactic passage include the major themes as they are presented throughout Matthew, it also pushes them beyond their earlier descriptions. At some points, this forward movement involves contrast (as in the case of the disciples, and universalism); at other points, it involves expanding the meaning these concepts carried within the course of the Gospel (as in the case of the authority of Jesus, and 'with you'). Again, this passage describes the final appearance and word of the resurrected and exalted Christ to his disciples. Finally, the observation that in Matthew Jesus never departs, but continues to be present and to speak as the book closes, indicates the relevance of these themes and their development toward 28.16-20.

Chapter 7

THE STRUCTURE OF MATTHEW: RELATIONSHIP BETWEEN GREAT DISCOURSES AND NARRATIVE FRAMEWORK

Since we have urged that Matthew is structured according to the threefold division (1.1–4.16; 4.17–16.20; 16.21–28.20), it is now necessary for us to discuss the role of the five major discourses in the Gospel.

A. *Observations regarding the Relationship between the Narrative and the Discourses in Matthew*

The first observation having to do with the relationship between the narrative and the discourses in Matthew is that the formula which is repeated at the end of the discourses is transitional in nature. The formula consists of a temporal clause, introduced with the temporal particle, 'when' (τότε), followed by the main clause. Thus, the temporal clause functions as the subordinate clause in relation to the main part of the sentence. In each case, the subordinate clause points back to the discourse, while the main clause points ahead to the material that follows. This observation led Streeter (1925: 262) to say regarding this formula, 'its emphasis is not on "Here endeth", but on "Here beginneth"'. It is, therefore, incorrect to speak of these formulae as 'concluding' in the sense of terminative. They do not function to separate, but rather to connect, the discourses with what follows.[1]

Second, not only are the discourses integrated into the material that follows in each case, but the lack of clear, decisive beginnings to the discourses indicates that these discourses are also integrated into the material that precedes. O. Lamar Cope (1976: 15) has observed that there is no distinct and uniform formula for beginning a discourse in Matthew's Gospel. Keegan (1982: 416) who himself adopts the fivefold schema of Bacon, has recently drawn attention to the total lack of unanimity which exists regarding the point where the various discourses begin. He notes that there is a span of nine verses (9.35–10.5) over which commentators identify the beginning of the missionary discourse, and that the sermon on the mount is said to begin at 4.23, 25; or 5.1, the community discourse at 17.22, 24; or 18.1, and the eschatological discourse at 23.1; 24.1; or 24.3. These observations imply that the discourses are closely related in each case to the preceding material and that the preceding material flows naturally into the discourse.

Third, the notion that the discourses are integrated into the flow of the surrounding narrative is indicated also by an examination of the contexts of each of the discourses. The sermon on the mount (chs. 5–7) is placed in the context of the proclamation of Jesus that the kingdom of heaven is at hand (4.17), a theme emphasized in the sermon itself (for instance, 5.10; 6.10). The calling of the disciples (4.18-22) and the mention of the crowds which followed Jesus (4.23-25) prepare for the sermon by providing its audience (5.1-2; 7.28). In terms of the material that follows the sermon, we have observed that the sermon is joined to chs. 8–9 by means of the inclusio of 4.23 and 9.35 and by means of the initial presentation of Jesus as one who exercises authority in his teaching (chs. 5–7) and in his mighty acts (chs. 8–9).

Moving on from the sermon on the mount to the missionary discourse, one finds that ch. 10 is related to chs. 8–9 by means of the comparison between the ministry of Jesus in chs. 8–9 and the ministry of the disciples in ch. 10. On the other hand, ch. 10 prepares for the rejection of Jesus by Israel as a whole in chs. 11–16. Jesus' description of the persecution of the disciples as they carry on their mission adumbrates his own rejection and persecution.

In the same way as the sermon on the mount and the missionary discourse, the parables of the kingdom (ch. 13) are also related to the surrounding context. Chapter 13 stands in the midst of the rejection of Jesus by Israel as a whole. The repudiation by all segments of Israel, except the disciples (11.25-27), which is related in chs. 11–12, explains why Jesus turns away from the crowds and turns toward his disciples in ch. 13. The following material (chs. 14–16) gives concrete examples of this dual turning: Jesus has less to do with the crowds and repeatedly withdraws from his opponents, while at the same time Jesus reveals himself to his disciples, finally drawing from them the confession that he is the Christ, the Son of God.

The integration of content between the discourses and the

surrounding narrative material obtains also for ch. 18. We have observed that ch. 18 is bound up with the overarching theme of the cross and self-denial which pervades 16.21–28.20; ch. 18 describes concrete expressions of humility and self-denial within the life of the community. In addition, specific references in ch. 18 are echoed in the surrounding material. The theme of avoiding offense (18.1-14) points back to the pericope regarding payment of the temple tax in 17.24-27. The reference to childlikeness (18.1-5) is picked up later in 19.13-15; and the reference to greatness in the kingdom (18.1) is repeated in 20.26-27 and in 23.11.

In line with the other major discourses in the Gospel, the eschatological discourse (chs. 24–25) is closely related to its context. In contrast to the Jewish leaders (chs. 21–23), the disciples are to be faithful to their calling, lest they, like these religious leaders, also fall under judgment. The positive example of faithfulness to the will of God, even in the midst of suffering and persecution, is found in the majestic obedience of Jesus, which he displays during his passion (chs. 26–28).

Thus, the individual discourses are closely related, in each case, to their narrative contexts. We should also note, however, that the overarching structural themes in the Gospel as a whole, such as repetition of comparison, repetition of contrast, and climax, draw from both the narrative framework and the large discourses.

Fourth, not only are the discourses integrated into the narrative framework, but it is also true that there is no alternation between narrative and discourse material in Matthew. There is much 'discourse' in the so-called narrative sections;[2] and there are even narrative elements within the great discourses (for instance, 13.10, 34-36, 51-52). The distinction between narrative and discourse in Matthew is further eroded by the consideration that, just as in the case of the discourses, the narrative material frequently contains *paraenetic* value for the post-Easter church. Bornkamm and Held (Bornkamm, *et al*.; 1963: 52-57, 165-299) for instance, have demonstrated this *paraenesis* in the narrative material in their studies on the boat scenes at 8.23-27 and 14.22-33.

Fifth, since we have indicated that the discourses are integrated into the flow of the narrative and that there is no alternation between narrative and discourse material in Matthew's Gospel, we should say something about the existence of the five great discourses in the Gospel. The explanation for the existence of these large discourses is found in Matthew's general tendency to group like material, and in the tendency within Judaism to group material into units of five (five books of Moses, five books of Psalms, five divisions in the *Megilloth* and the *Pirqe Aboth*).[3] There is no reason to think that the number five relates to one body of material, such as the Pentateuch. In the absence of such evidence, it is reasonable to assume that Matthew is following a literary rather than a theological lead.

Sixth, although we have argued that the discourses are integrated into the flow of the narrative and that Matthew does not load the fact that there are *five* discourses with theological weight, it is still true that the five great discourses are explicitly noted by Matthew in the transitional statements; by this means, he draws attention to them. This conclusion is supported by (1) their similarity in form; (2) the content of the statements, that is, the fact that on two occasions they indicate the character of the discourse (11.1 = Jesus instructing his twelve disciples; 13.53 = Jesus finishes these parables); (3) the last statement speaks of Jesus finishing 'all' these teachings (26.1), thus indicating that the discourses have come to an end. The 'all' here refers not only to chs. 24–25, but to all the discourses. This inclusive use of 'all' in 26.1 is supported by the following considerations. Only here in 26.1 is 'all' added to the otherwise uniform formulae. Further, this statement regarding the end of the discourses of Jesus relates to the gradual cessation of Jesus' ministry in light of his coming passion; thus, Matthew records in 22.46 that from that time on no one dared ask Jesus any questions, the Jewish leaders leave the scene of Jesus' ministry at the end of ch. 22, and the crowds no longer follow him after ch. 23.

Thus, on the one hand, Matthew draws attention to the five great discourses, but, on the other hand, these discourses are part of the flow of the narrative. The question, therefore, surrounds the function of these five great discourses.

B. *The Function of the Great Discourses*

Our examination of the structure of Matthew's Gospel has shown that Matthew is essentially a story about Jesus. As such, within this story of Jesus the great discourses point to Jesus' activity of instructing and commanding the community of his disciples, with particular reference to issues relevant to the post-Easter existence of the church. Matthew places these discourses within the narrative, or better stated, he includes them as part of the story, in order to contribute to his picture of the role of Jesus as one who is present with his community, instructing and commanding not only the twelve during his earthly ministry, but also the post-Easter church (28.18-20). In other words, the existence of these five discourses underscores a major aspect of Jesus' presence with his community throughout history, that of speaking words of instruction and commandment.

In terms of literary structure, therefore, the discourses function to underscore the climax of 28.16-20. There the exalted Christ is pictured as continually present with his community 'to the end of the age', speaking words of instruction, encouragement, and commandment. It is at this climactic point that Christ charges his disciples to make disciples, by 'teaching them to observe all that I have commanded you' (see above, Chapter 6). The teachings and commands of Jesus to his disciples that have special bearing on the post-Easter existence of the church tend very definitely to be clustered in these five great discourses, as many scholars have observed.[4]

It is true that some commands that could be understood as having to do primarily with the post-Easter church are found outside the great discourses, such as 16.24 and 23.3, 8-12. Such cases are, however, very few in number and their position in the gospel may reflect other concerns of Matthew. 16.24, for instance, reflects Matthew's desire to place this paradigmatic call to cross-bearing at the beginning of the division 16.21-28.20, a division which focuses upon the comparison between the cross of Jesus and the cross of the disciples (see, above, pp. 104-107). And 23.3, 8-12 reflects Matthew's concern throughout chs. 21-25 to contrast the expectations for the disciples with the unfaithfulness of the religious leaders (see, above, pp. 106-107).

It is also true that some of the material in the discourses has specifically to do with the period of Jesus' earthly ministry, as, for instance, the commands to restrictive proclamation in ch. 10 (see 10.5-6, 23). These few references within the great discourses do not, however, contradict our claim that the focus of these discourses is clearly upon the post-Easter church (see, for example, 10.16-42, and observe that Matthew no where mentions that the twelve actually went out on a missionary journey during Jesus' earthly existence). Rather, this tension within the discourses between a few statements that relate to the time of the earthly Jesus and the bulk of statements that relate to the time of the exalted Christ actually serves Matthew's purpose of coalescing the earthly Jesus (and his relationship to his disciples) with the exalted Lord (and his relationship to his church).

It is further true that ch. 13 contains little in the way of explicit commands to the post-Easter community. Yet Kingsbury (1969) has demonstrated that the post-Easter church is especially in view in ch. 13, and that the main concern of the chapter is in fact *paraenesis* for this church. These parables thus involve instruction and implicit commands to the post-resurrection community. Of course, implicit commands relating to the post-Easter church are found frequently outside the five great discourses, as Bornkamm and Held have shown (Bornkamm, *et al.*, 1963: 52-58, 165-299). But it is with ch. 13, along with the other great discourses, that Matthew pauses from the movement of the story to give notice to the reader that this Jesus is one who gives instruction and commands that are particularly relevant for the ongoing life of the church.

These considerations indicate that the discourses play a primarily formal role in the climactic development toward 28.16-20. That is to say, although they are not the only passages in Matthew's Gospel that contain *paraenesis* relevant for the ongoing existence of the church, their very presence emphasizes Jesus' role as one who spoke and continues throughout history to speak words of instruction and command to the community of his disciples.

Chapter 8

OBSERVATIONS AND CONCLUSIONS

The purpose of this final chapter is to summarize our literary-critical investigation into the structure of Matthew's Gospel, and to provide a brief discussion of the theological implications which arise from our investigation of structure.

A. *Summary*

There is presently no consensus regarding the structure of Matthew's Gospel. To a large extent, the differences that exist among scholars regarding Matthean structure can be traced to differences of method, especially to various emphases in the application of redaction criticism to the text. Those scholars who focus upon the process of redaction (that is, upon changes or additions Matthew has made to received tradition) tend to view the structure of the Gospel differently from those who stress the product of redaction (that is, the final composition of the work).

The discipline of literary criticism offers a way past this impasse. This discipline focuses upon the final form of the text, and brings with it a special concern for the identification of rhetorical features that point toward the structure of the final text. Literary criticism is therefore uniquely qualified to aid biblical scholarship in discerning the literary structure of ancient texts.

The purpose of analyzing literary structure is to determine the major units and sub-units of any given book and to identify the structural relationships between and within these units. The rhetorical features which point to these structural relationships include such elements as repetition (recurrence), contrast, comparison, and climax (to mention only the most common rhetorical categories presented).

Before reapplying these rhetorical categories to the text of Matthew's Gospel, it was necessary to survey the history of research into its structure (Chapter 2). These structural investigations can be divided into three major groups: geographical or chronological, topical, and conceptual.

Most of the earlier structural investigations into Matthew's Gospel focused upon geographical or chronological elements. The early conservatives approached Matthew with these elements in mind because of their desire to reconstruct the life of Jesus from the Gospel of Matthew, while the early source critics adopted this approach because of their emphasis upon Matthew's use of Mark. According to the latter, Matthew took over the chronological account of the life of Jesus from the Gospel of Mark. The geographical-chronological structure stresses Matthew's presentation of Jesus as the prophesied and rejected Christ; coupled with this christology is a twofold view of salvation history: promise and fulfillment.

Most recent interpreters have rejected the geographical chronological division of the Gospel in favor of some sort of topical outline. Three major topical outlines have been advanced by scholars: the fivefold alternating pattern; the chiastic pattern; and the threefold division, with breaks at 4.17 and 16.21.

The first of these outlines focuses upon the alternation between narrative and discourse material in Matthew's Gospel. First advocated by Bacon, this outline understands the Gospel as comprised of five 'books', each book containing a narrative section followed by a discourse section, which is closed by the repeated formula, 'And it happened when Jesus finished these words' or the like. Matthew has added a 'preamble' (chs. 1–2) as well as an 'epilogue' (chs. 26–28). Moreover, Matthew has shaped his Gospel in order to conform to the five books of the Pentateuch, thus presenting Jesus as a new Moses who presents a new law to his church. Bacon and many other scholars who advocate this structure tend to emphasize the salvation-historical continuity between the law of the Old Testament and the law Jesus promulgates to his church.

Closely related to Bacon's fivefold schema are the topical outlines based upon the principle of chiasm (a-b-c-b'-a'). Such chiastic structures can generally be divided into two groups, according to the identification of the central passage which is held to be the turning point. This turning point has been located in the middle of ch. 13 and at ch. 11. The tendency of the chiastic outline is to emphasize the radical break in salvation history occasioned by the rejection of Jesus by Israel and his consequent turning to the disciples, or the church, and to the Gentiles.

Some scholars have detected problems with both Bacon's fivefold schema and outlines based on chiasm and have argued instead for a topical outline based upon the 'superscriptions' which can be found at 1.1; 4.17; 16.21. According to these scholars, the formula at the end of the discourses is simply transitional and cannot be pressed thematically, while the formula at 4.17 and 16.21 actually sums up the material that follows in each case. 1.1–4.16 deals with the person of Jesus Messiah; 4.17–16.20 deals with the proclamation of Jesus Messiah; and 16.21–28.20 deals with the death and resurrection of Jesus Messiah. Since each of these divisions comes to a climax with the presentation of Jesus as Son of God, this structural outline emphasizes the divine Sonship of Jesus. This outline also tends to view salvation history in two epochs: the time of prophecy, and the time of fulfillment.

We mentioned that three major views regarding the structure of Matthew's Gospel have been advanced. In addition to the geographical and topical outlines, there is also the conceptual view of Matthew's structure. The scholars who hold to this view define the structure of the Gospel according to a theme or a central idea around which Matthew has arranged his material. Most scholars who belong in this camp identify this central concept as Matthew's view of salvation history and argue that Matthew understands salvation history in three epochs: Israel-Jesus-the church. Accordingly, these salvation-historical studies emphasize ecclesiology over christology and see a radical salvation-historical break between the period of Jesus and the period of the church.

Within the context of this survey of scholarly research into the structure of Matthew's Gospel, the literary-rhetorical categories set forth in Chapter 1 can be applied to the text of the Gospel in order to determine its literary structure (Chapters 3 through 7). We contend that the Gospel of Matthew is structured according to the following compositional relationships: repetition of comparison; repetition of contrast; repetition of particularization and climax; and climax.

The first of these structural relationships is that of the repetition of comparison (Chapter 3). Throughout the Gospel, what Jesus says and does is compared to the expectations for the disciples. The clearest analogy between Jesus and the role expected of the disciples is that of their respective ministries. The geographical sphere of the ministries of Jesus and of the disciples is the same; they perform the same acts of ministry; and they share the same kinds of persecutions that accompany their ministries. Matthew also compares Jesus and the expectations for the disciples in terms of ethical behavior, or manner of living. Further, Matthew points to the essential comparison between Jesus and the role of the disciples by his use of filial language: even as Jesus is the Son of God, so the disciples are sons of God.

In addition to the repetition of comparison, Matthew also structures his Gospel according to the repetition of contrast, namely, between Jesus and his opponents, especially the religious leaders (Chapter 4). Throughout the Gospel, Jesus is presented as the obedient Son of God, who is entirely faithful to the will of his Father. His opponents, however, are entirely unfaithful to the will of God and therefore incur guilt. Even as Jesus is Son of God, so these opponents are in league with the devil. This opposition to Jesus is, in fact, opposition to the purpose of God; thus, their opposition to Jesus issues in their murder of the anointed Son of God.

The repetition of comparison and the repetition of contrast have to do with themes that are repeated throughout the Gospel and hence have no direct bearing upon divisions within the Gospel. The third major structural relationship, however, does have implications for marking off main divisions in the Gospel: repetition of particularization and repetition of climax, together with preparation and causation (Chapter 5). The phenomenon of repetition of particularization can be found in 1.1; 4.17; and 16.21. These passages function as general headings that are expanded or 'particularized', in the material that follows in each case. The repetition of climax occurs when each of these sections (1.1–4.16; 4.17–16.20; 16.21–28.20) builds toward its respective culmination. 'Preparation' refers to the circumstance that 1.1–4.16 establishes the background for 4.17–28.20, while 'causation' means that 4.17–16.20 provides the cause or basis for 16.21–28.20.

The first major division of the Gospel, then, is 1.1–4.16. This division sets forth the preparation for Jesus Messiah, Son of God, and is bound together by means of four structural relationships. The first of these relationships is a movement from the general statement of 1.1 to its expansion, or particularization, throughout 1.2–4.16. This division is also bound together by means of the repetition of three distinctive elements: events preceding the beginning of Jesus' public ministry; use of fulfillment quotations; and the person and identity of Jesus, presented directly to the reader. This recurring concern for the person of Jesus points to the third structural relationship binding 1.1–4.16 together, namely, climax. The many oblique, metaphorical, and indirect references to Jesus as Son of God come to a climax in the direct affirmation from God himself at the baptism of Jesus: 'This is my beloved Son, with whom I am well pleased' (3.17). The concern for the person of Jesus points also to the fourth and final structural element uniting 1.1–4.16, that of contrast. Matthew presents a definite contrast between those who accept Jesus as the Christ and those who reject him. The wise men are paradigmatic of those who accept Jesus, while Herod is paradigmatic of those who repudiate him.

Having established the background in 1.1–4.16 for the rest of his narrative, Matthew goes on to describe the proclamation of Jesus to Israel in 4.17–16.20. This second major unit of the Gospel is structured according to particularization, causation, and climax.

Even as 1.1 serves as a general statement that is particularized throughout 1.2–4.16, so 4.17 is particularized throughout 4.18–16.20. The unique, formulaic character of 4.17 is demonstrated by its parallelism with 16.21 and by its asyndetic construction. More significantly, the theme of 4.17, namely, that Jesus announces publicly to Israel the kingdom of heaven and calls Israel to repentance, provides the framework of 4.17–16.20; this framework involves messianic presentation of the kingdom of God leading to rejection by Israel as a whole, but acceptance by the disciples.

This framework points to the second structural relationship operative within 4.17–16.20, namely, causation. 4.17–11.1 is the cause: Jesus presents himself and the kingdom to Israel by means of teaching, preaching, and healing (4.23–9.35) and by means of sending out his disciples to perform eschatological ministry analogous to his own (9.35–11.1). 11.2–16.20 is the effect: the responses, both positive and negative, to Jesus' proclamation of the kingdom to Israel.

The causal movement within 4.17–16.20 leads into the third major structural feature binding this material together: climax. The contrasting responses to Jesus by the people and by the disciples come to a high point of intensity when Peter declares, in response to Jesus' question, that Jesus is the Son of God (16.16). Even as the first major division of the Gospel comes to a climax in the declaration from God that Jesus is his Son, so this second major division reaches its climax with the same declaration from the mouth of the disciples. The recognition of who Jesus is leads naturally and logically into a discussion of what he is about and its meaning for the disciples. This movement from recognition of who Jesus is to education in meaning regarding his mission is what is meant by causation between 4.17–16.20 and 16.21–28.20.

The last main division of Matthew's Gospel, then, concerns the meaning of the messiahship of Jesus in terms of his passion and resurrection (16.21–28.20). This material forms a unity around the structural principles of particularization, climax, repetition of comparison, and repetition of contrast.

As in the case of 1.1 and 4.17, 16.21 is a general statement which is particularized in the material that follows. This verse contains two elements: the journey to Jerusalem to suffer, die, and be raised; and the presentation Jesus makes to his disciples of the necessity for such an undertaking. The journey to Jerusalem with the passion and resurrection is particularized by means of climax; the presentation Jesus makes to his disciples is particularized by means of the repetition of comparison and the repetition of contrast.

The climax involves the movement towards the suffering, death, and resurrection of Jesus in Jerusalem and ultimately the missionary commissioning by Jesus in 28.16-20. This climactic movement is indicated by the repetition of predictions relating to the death and resurrection of Jesus, by the journey to Jerusalem, and by the flow of the narrative, which moves steadily toward the climactic events in chs. 26–28. In the climax of the cross, the passers-by tempt Jesus as the Son of God, and the Roman soldiers confess that Jesus is the Son of God (26.54). Thus, in accord with the climaxes to the preceding divisions (3.17; 16.16), this last major division also culminates with the declaration that Jesus is the Son of God. Moreover, in the climax of the missionary commissioning, Jesus refers to himself as the Son [of God] (28.19).

Matthew 16.21 is expanded not only by means of climax, but also by means of the repetition of comparison and the repetition of contrast. This repetition of comparison involves the ongoing correspondence between what Jesus does and what the disciples are to do: just as Jesus orients his life around the cross, so the disciples are to orient their lives around their cross. The repetition of contrast involves the dichotomy between Jesus and his expectations for the disciples, on the one hand, and the failure of the twelve to measure up to Jesus and to these expectations, on the other. The disciples are slow to accept their cross, and this failure can be met only by the promise of Jesus that he will go before them into Galilee (26.32) and by the word of demand and of encouragement from the exalted Christ (28.16-20). In the end, therefore, the problem of the failure of the disciples is answered by the climax to the division and to the Gospel at 28.16-20.

In addition to the repetition of comparison, repetition of contrast, and repetition of particularization and climax, Matthew employs a fourth structural relationship in order to bind his Gospel together. This fourth relationship is that of climax with inclusio, found at 28.16-20 (Chapter 6). The following considerations point to the climactic nature of 28.16-20. First, the ministry of the disciples is broadened in this passage over against the preceding material. Second, this passage summarizes several major themes in the Gospel. These themes include the authority of Jesus, universalism, the notion of the presence of Jesus with his community, and discipleship. Furthermore, not only does this climactic passage include these major themes as they are presented throughout the Gospel, but it also moves beyond these earlier descriptions by means of contrast and expansion of meaning. Third, 28.16-20 describes the last appearance and word of the exalted Christ to his disciples. Fourth, the fact that in Matthew's Gospel Jesus never departs, but continues to be present and to speak, indicates that this scene presents the activity of Jesus in the time of the implied reader.

Bound up with this climax is the element of *inclusio*. In the last verse of the Gospel, Jesus promises to be 'with you', that is, with his disciples, until 'the end of the age'. This promise corresponds to the word of the angel in 1.23: 'they will call his name Emmanuel', which Matthew interprets as 'God with us'. Thus, 1.23 and 28.20 form a bracket around the Gospel.

But the phrase, 'with you', at 28.20 represents more than inclusio; since the theme of God (or Jesus) with us recurs throughout the Gospel and comes to a point of intensity at 28.20, it is also part of the climax of 28.16-20. An examination of this theme in the Gospel indicates that its meaning is as follows: In his Son, Jesus Messiah, God has drawn near to his people to grant them eschatological salvation.

These conclusions regarding the structure of Matthew's Gospel

raise the question of the relationship between the five great
discourses and the narrative framework of the Gospel (Chapter 7).
We contend that Matthew draws attention to the five great
discourses, but that he also incorporates these discourses into the
flow of the narrative. The function of these five discourses within the
narrative framework is to point to Jesus' activity of instructing his
community, with special reference to the post-Easter existence of the
church. Thus, Matthew incorporates these discourses within his
story of Jesus in order to underscore the climax of 28.16-20, where
the exalted Christ is described as being continually present with his
community throughout history, speaking words of instruction and
commandment.

B. *Theological Implications*

The study of structure is not an end in itself. The reader, finally,
wants to know what implications the study of structure holds for
better understanding the content of a document. We can only touch
on the theological inferences from our study briefly. To draw out
implications at length would require a second volume. In line with
the types of theological inferences we drew in our survey of the
various structural approaches in Chapter 2, these implications deal
with christology and salvation history. It is at these two points that
the theological implications of the structure of Matthew's Gospel are
most apparent.

The general theological implications which will be put forward
have been discerned by certain other scholars who have dealt with
the Gospel of Matthew according to composition criticism or
redaction criticism (for instance, Kingsbury). Yet we have arrived at
these theological implications on the basis of a different method:
rhetorical analysis of the Gospel of Matthew. The strength of these
conclusions regarding Matthew's theology is that the two methods
have produced the same results. This observation underscores the
legitimacy of these theological conclusions for Matthew's Gospel.

1. *Theological Implications regarding Christology*
The structure of the Gospel provides clear indications regarding
christology. We have noted that the first main division of the Gospel
(1.1-4.16) prepares the reader for the rest of the Gospel by, among
other things, presenting directly the nature and identity of Jesus. By

means of a series of reliable witnesses, including Matthew himself, Jesus is identified as 'Christ', 'Son of David', 'Son of Abraham', and 'king'. These designations, first expressed here in 1.1-4.16, are elaborated throughout the rest of the Gospel. As 'Christ', Jesus is the anointed one in the line of David, who fulfills prophetic expectations (2.5-6), culminates Israel's history (1.1-17), and ultimately determines salvation or condemnation for persons (3.1-12). As 'King', Jesus stands in the line of David and exercises rulership over his people. Yet Jesus fulfills this rulership not according to the tyrannical practices of earthly rulers, but according to the prophecy from Micah, which speaks of the ruler who shepherds his people (2.5-6). For Matthew, Jesus fulfills this royal vocation by suffering in order to atone for sins (2.2; ch. 27). As 'Son of David', Jesus fulfills eschatological hopes associated with David by means of his ministry of healing (9.27; 12.23). Jesus is 'Son of Abraham' in the sense that he fulfills the promise of God to Abraham that in Abraham's descendants all the nations would find blessing.

Although Jesus fulfills expectations associated with these titles, he is presented above all in 1.1-4.16 as 'Son of God'. The primary nature of this christological category in the first main division is indicated by the fact that this division comes to a climax in the declaration from God that Jesus is, in fact, his Son (3.17). Here, God himself witnesses to the person of Jesus; and this statement stands as the culmination of several allusions and indirect references to Jesus as the Son of God. According to the climactic movement toward 3.17, Jesus is Son of God in the sense that he has his origin in God (1.18, 20). Moreover, one aspect of his divine Sonship is indicated in the story of the temptation which immediately follows the baptism (4.1-11); there, Jesus is tempted by Satan, yet he refuses to yield to these temptations, so that he is the Son who perfectly obeys the will of his Father.

The primary nature of the category of 'Son of God' is indicated not only by Matthew's direct presentation of Jesus in the first main division of his Gospel, but also by structural features found in the second and third main divisions. In the second main division (4.17-16.20), the contrasting responses to Jesus by the people and by the disciples (for instance, 14.1-12, 28-33) come to a climax with the confession from the disciples that Jesus is 'the Christ, the Son of the living God' (16.13-20). This confession from Peter, who speaks for all the disciples, is correct, since it comes not from humans (cf. 16.13), but is revealed by God himself (16.17), since it meets with a blessing from Jesus (16.17), and since it agrees with God's point of view expressed in 3.17.

Before leaving the second main division, we should note that part of the climactic development in this division toward Peter's confession at 16.16 is the declaration Jesus makes regarding his relationship to God in 11.25-30. There Jesus addresses God as 'Father' and refers to himself as 'the Son'. According to 11.26-27, the Father has delivered 'all things' to the Son; moreover, only the Father 'knows' the Son, and only the Son 'knows' the Father. This passage points to another meaning of the divine Sonship of Jesus: not only is Jesus the Son of God in the sense that he has his origin in God (1.21), or in the sense that he perfectly obeys the will of his Father (4.1-11), but he is also the Son of God in the sense that he enjoys a unique filial relationship with the Father.

As in the case of the first and second main divisions, the structure of the third main division (16.21-28.20) also points to the centrality of the christological category of Son of God. The climax of this third main division involves the death, resurrection, and missionary commissioning of Jesus. At both the cross and the Galilean commissioning, Jesus is presented primarily as Son of God. The passers-by and the religious leaders around the cross call out to Jesus to come down from the cross in order to prove 'if you are the Son of God' (27.43). Moreover, the Roman soldiers who face the cross confess that Jesus was the Son of God (27.54). Jesus thus dies as the obedient Son of God, who demonstrates his divine Sonship not by performing supernatural signs, but by suffering and dying in compliance with the will of his Father. The climactic movement towards the cross indicates, further, that by dying as the obedient Son of God, Jesus gives his life as a ransom for many (20.28), thus saving his people from their sins (1.21; 26.28).

If Jesus is presented as Son of God at the cross, he is also so presented at the Galilean commissioning (28.16-20); here Jesus refers to God as 'Father' and to himself as 'the Son' (28.19). As the Son of God, Jesus abides with his disciples until 'the end of the age' (28.20).

This reference to Jesus as the Son of God in 28.20 indicates, finally, that the divine Sonship of Jesus is linked to the inclusio which brackets the Gospel at 1.23 and 28.20. In his Son, Jesus Messiah, God has drawn near to dwell among his people.

This discussion regarding the implications of Matthew's structure for his christology has shown that Matthew applies to Jesus a number of christological titles, including 'Christ', 'Son of David', 'Son of Abraham', and 'king'; yet the primary christological title in the Gospel is that of 'Son of God'. This conclusion is supported by the centrality of this category in the first main division of the Gospel, which presents the person of Jesus, by its connection to the recurring climaxes in the Gospel (3.17; 16.13-20; 26-28), and by its connection to the inclusio having to do with the presence of God, or Jesus, with the eschatological community (1.23; 28.20). Jesus is the Son of God in the sense that he has his origin in God (1.21), in the sense that he perfectly obeys the will of his Father (4.1-11; ch. 27), and in the sense that he enjoys a unique filial relationship with the Father (11.25-30). The role of Jesus as Son of God is understood in terms of the presence of God with his end-time people: in the person of his Son, God has drawn near to dwell among his people (1.23; 28.20).

Before leaving this discussion of christology, we should make one more observation. The structural features that point to Jesus as the Son of God also indicate that christology is the central concern of Matthew's Gospel. The first main division of the Gospel, which introduces the reader to the narrative, concerns, above all, the presentation of the person of Jesus; and the climax to each major division of the Gospel (3.17; 16.13-20; 26-28) as well as the climax to the Gospel as a whole (chs. 26-28) all deal with the person of Jesus. Moreover, the general statements which are expanded in the three main divisions also concern Jesus (1.1; 4.17; 16.21). These considerations point to the central role of christology within the dynamics of Matthew's structure.

2. *Theological Implications regarding Salvation History*
The structure of Matthew's Gospel has implications not only for christology, but also for salvation history. It is clear, in the first place, that the coming of Jesus marks a radical turning point in salvation history. This turning point is indicated already in the first main division of the Gospel, which introduces the reader to the narrative (1.1-4.16). According to the genealogy, the birth of Jesus culminates the history of Israel; and the fulfillment quotations, found throughout the Gospel, but clustered especially in the first main division, indicate that Jesus is the fulfillment of Old Testament prophecy. The theme of the authority of Jesus, which reaches its climax in 28.16-20,

points in various ways to the salvation-historical fulfillment of Jesus. Jesus is the Christ, the Son of David, and especially the Son of God (1.1; 3.17); he will baptize with the Holy Spirit (3.11); he proclaims that the kingdom of heaven has arrived (4.17); he exercises an eschatological ministry in Israel of preaching, teaching, and healing (4.23; 9.35; 11.1); he has power over Satan (4.1-11) and over demons (12.28); and his death brings about the forgiveness of sins (1.21; 26.28). Finally, the inclusio of 1.23 and 28.20 indicates that in the person of Jesus Messiah, his Son, God has drawn near to dwell with his eschatological people.

The time of fulfillment involves not only the ministry of Jesus, but also that of John the Baptist. That John the Baptist is part of the time of fulfillment is indicated by the comparison between John and Jesus, a comparison that we have mentioned at various points in our study. John the Baptist and Jesus both come in fulfillment of prophecy (1.23; 3.2). John and Jesus alike suffer at the hands of this 'evil generation' (14.1-12; ch. 27); Matthew records that both John and Jesus are 'delivered up' (4.12; 27.2). And both John the Baptist and Jesus proclaim that 'the kingdom of heaven is at hand' (3.2; 4.17). Yet the time of fulfillment begins with the birth of Jesus, and not with the minstry of John, since Jeesus is designated 'Christ' at the time of his birth (1.1-17; 2.4), and since Jesus is 'Emmanuel' or 'God with us' from his birth (1.23).

If there is a radical salvation-historical break between the time of preparation before Jesus and the time of fulfillment with Jesus, there is no evidence of a salvation-historical break between the time of Jesus and the time of the church. Indeed, the evidence points in the opposite direction. There are three structural elements that indicate that the time of the earthly Jesus and the time of the exalted Christ (post-Easter church) together comprise the age of fulfillment.

The first structural element that indicates this involves the inclusio of 1.23 and 28.20. We have already noted that the reference to 'Emmanuel', or 'God with us', in 1.23 points to the fact that the time of fulfillment has dawned with the birth of Jesus. Thus, from the time of Jesus' birth, God dwells with his people in the person of Jesus. But the exalted Christ also promises to abide with his disciples, or his church, until 'the end of the age' (28.20). By this use of inclusio, Matthew emphasizes that the presence of Jesus with his community includes both his earthly existence with his disciples and his exalted existence with his post-Easter church; in both cases, Jesus abides with his people, and through this presence of Jesus, God also dwells with the eschatological community.

The second structural element that binds the time of Jesus to the time of the church in the age of fulfillment is the climax to the Gospel at 28.16-20. This is the only passage in the Gospel of Matthew that presents the exalted Christ as speaking to his church. As we noted in our discussion of climax, this passage evinces essential continuity between the person and declarations of the exalted Christ of ch. 28 and the person and declarations of the earthly Jesus of chs. 1-27. Matthew achieves this continuity by assimilating in various ways throughout the Gospel the earthly Jesus to the living Lord of the church. For instance, Jesus is repeatedly addressed as 'Lord' by persons who approach him in faith (for instance, 14.28; 15.22); and he is frequently worshiped (2.11; 14.33). Moreover, the speech of the earthly Jesus is often assimilated to that of the living Lord of the church (for instance, 18.20). But Matthew also establishes this continuity by means of a number of literary devices in 28.16-20. These devices include the connection between 28.17 and 14.31-33 and between 28.18 and 11.25-27, the reference to 'authority' in 28.18, which points to indications throughout the Gospel that Jesus possesses transcendent authority, and the reference to Jesus as Son of God (28.19), which recalls the status of Jesus as Son of God during his earthly existence (for instance, 3.17; 17.5). The earthly Jesus who taught his disciples in Capernaum and walked with them in Judea is one with the exalted Christ, and continues to speak and to be present with his disciples.

Even more significant than the inclusio and the climax in binding the time of the earthly Jesus to the time of the church is the repetition of comparison between Jesus and the expectations for the disciples. The ministry of the disciples, including their post-Easter ministry, is linked to the earthly ministry of Jesus by means of comparison. Galilee is the geographical sphere of ministry for both the earthly Jesus (4.12) and the post-Easter disciples (28.10, 16), Jesus and the disciples perform the same acts of ministry. Even as the earthly Jesus taught (for instance, 4.23; 5.1), so the post-Easter disciples are commanded to teach (28.19). Moreover, both Jesus and the disciples preach that 'the kingdom of heaven is at hand' (4.17; 10.7); and the post-Easter disciples, like the earthly Jesus, preach 'the gospel of the kingdom' (4.23; 24.14; 26.13). Finally, the persecutions that attend the eschatological ministries of Jesus and John the

Baptist also attend the eschatological ministries of the post-Easter disciples (10.16-39; 24.9-15). This comparison between the ministry of the earthly Jesus and that of the post-Easter disciples indicates that the time of the earthly Jesus and the time of the post-Easter church both belong to the eschatological age of fulfillment.

Yet within this age of fulfillment, the time of the earthly Jesus is central and pivotal. John the Baptist prepares the way for Jesus, and the ministry of the disciples flows from the ministry of Jesus. The ministry of the disciples is modelled after the ministry of Jesus, and hence takes its cue from the ministry of Jesus. Their ministry is actually a continuation of the earthly ministry of Jesus (9.35-11.1; 28.18-20). Moreover, as we noted above, the structure of the Gospel emphasizes the life and ministry of the earthly Jesus; all that came before is preparation, and all that follows is based upon that life and ministry.

NOTES

Notes to Chapter 1

1. For a brief survey of the history of investigation into Matthew's literary structure through 1974, see Kingsbury (1975: 1-39). A more extensive examination follows, in Chapter 2.

2. See Schlatter (1959); Lagrange (1948: xxv, xxx); Albright and Mann (1971: lxii-lxiii).

3. 7.28; 11.1; 13.53; 19.1; 26.1.

4. McKee (1949); Kümmel (1975: 105-106); Kingsbury (1975: 1-39); Lohmeyer (1967: 9-12); Schenk (1983: 71).

5. A helpful discussion regarding the relationship between literary criticism and redaction criticism can be found in Keegan (1985).

6. Gros Louis (1982: 17-18); Kessler (1982: 1-19); Perrin (1976: 122); Robbins (1984: 19-52); Dewey (1980).

7. For my understanding of many of the compositional relationships that follow I am especially indebted to Traina (1952: 50-59); Kuist (1939, and 1947: 80-87, 159-81).

8. Freedman (1971: 123); Muilenburg (1969: 16); Abrams (1981: 111); Culpepper (1983: 73, 87, 97, 128); Dewey (1980: 32); Gros Louis (1982: 23); N. Frye (1957: 77).

9. 1.6; 11.23; 14.2, 9, 13; 15.20; 16.4, 5, 8; 17.4, 6, 14; 18.2, 4, 7, 28; 19.1, 8, 9, 10, 23, 31, 39, 40, 48, 49, 51; 23.4; 24.30, 32.

10. 1.7, 8, 15, 19, 32, 34; 2.25; 3.11, 28, 32, 33; 4.39, 41, 44; 5.31, 32, 33, 34, 36, 37, 39; 7.7; 8.13, 14, 17, 18; 12.17; 15.26; 18.37; 19.35; 21.24.

11. Gros Louis (1982: 18); Auerbach (1957: 23); Abrams (1981: 10).

12. Repeated contrast between the covenant faithfulness of God and the unfaithfulness of Israel in 2.1-3.7, 9, 12, 15; 4.1, 15; 6.1, 6-10, 28-32; 8.22-34; 9.1-57; 10.6, 10-16; 13.1; 17.1-21.25. Repeated contrast between the God of Israel and the gods of the surrounding nations in 1.1-2, 6, 11-23; 3.6-12, 15; 4.1-3; 5.1-5, 31; 6.1, 7-10, 25-32; 8.22-34; 9.56-57; 10.7, 11-16; 13.1-24; 16.23-31; 18.7-31; 19.10-15. Repeated contrast between Israel and her neighbors in 1.1-2.5; 3.1-30; 4.2-5.31; 6.1-21; 10.6-12.6; 13.1-31; 18.7-31; 19.10-15.

13. Peter's description (1.12-5.11; 9.32-12.24) has striking similarities to that of Paul (9.1-31; 13.2-28.31). We recognize that this reconstruction is debatable, as are other examples included here. The purpose is not to argue for a particular interpretation of the texts, but to illustrate the nature of these compositional relationships. The latter is achievable so long as these relationships within the texts are at least conceivable.

14. 1.3, 5, 17; 3.7-13; 4.10, 14, 23; 11.12, 15, 20, 23; 14.2; 20.2; 21.3, 8.

15. E.g. 2.2-4; 3.1-14; 6.12-13; 8.24-26; 9.4-9; 11.1-12, 28-39; 13.33-34; 16.15-20; 20.42; 21.20-22.50.

16. For a discussion of the use of climax by literary critics, see Muilenburg (1969: 10-11); Abrams (1981: 10); Chronis (1982).

17. Achtemeier (1975: 88); Chronis (1982); Kingsbury (1983: 47-155).

18. Muilenburg (1969: 13); Abrams (1981: 139); Culpepper (1983: 89).

19. Taylor (1952: 152); Kingsbury (1983: 69); Achtemeier (1975: 49-50).

20. Culpepper (1983: 89); Dewey (1980: 32); R. Fowler (1981: 170); Genette (1980: 75-76); Petersen (1978: 55-80).

21. Perrin (1976: 122); Bright (1975: 241); Bruce (1954: 39); Culpepper (1983: 89). This use of 'summarization' involves the relationship between the content of these passages and the surrounding literary material, not the question of frequency or duration as such, as is found in discussions of summary in narrative time. Cf. Culpepper (1983: 71); Genette (1980: 95-98); Lanser (1981: 201); Chatman (1978: 224-25).

22. Soulen (1981: 94); Dewey (1980: 31); Muilenburg (1969: 9-10); Fenton (1959: 175-76); Lohr (1961).

23. Argument in 1.1-14; 2.5-3.6; 5.1-10; 7.1-10.18; exhortation in 2.1-14; 3.7-14; 5.11-6.20; 10.19-13.17.

24. Dewey (1980: 34); Achtemeier (1975: 23-26, 32-33); R. Fowler (1981: 165).

Notes to Chapter 2

1. Those who mark the break at 4.12 include E. Anderson (1909: xxi); Box (1922: 8); Burton (1898: 97-101); Conzelmann and Lindemann (1975: 251); Durand (1948: 1); Farmer (1982: 138-40); Harrison (1964: 159); Hunter (1972: 57); Kerr (1892: 25); Klostermann (1971: Contents page); Lagrange (1948: xxvi-xxix); Meinertz (1950: 167-68); Michaelis (1961: 25-26: 1948: I, vii-viii); Moffatt (1918: 244-45); Plummer (1909: lxiii); Schmid (1956: 23-30); Senior (1977: 15-16); B. Weiss (1888: II, 277); Wikenhauser (1958: 174); Zahn (1909: II, 541).

Those who mark the break at 4.17 include Battenhouse (1937: 93); McNeile (1938: xii); Jülicher (1894: 186); Robinson (1928: xix); Schweizer (1975: 5).

Those who mark the break at 5.1 include Davidson (1894: I, 345); Roux (1956).

2. Those who mark the break at 19.1 include E. Anderson (1909: 21); Battenhouse (1937: 93); Box (1922: 8); Burton (1898: 97-101); Davidson (1894:I: 345); Durand (1948); Farmer (1982: 138-40); Harrison (1964: 160); Hunter (1972: 57); Jülicher (1894: 186); Kerr (1892: 24); Lagrange (1948:

xxiii); McNeile (1938: xii); Meinertz (1950: 167-68); Plummer (1909: xviii); Wikenhauser (1958: 175).

Those who mark the break at 16.13 include Klostermann (1971: contents page).

Those who mark the break at 16.21 include Senior (1977: 15-16).

Those who mark the break at 17.1 include Robinson (1928: ix-xx).

3. Conzelmann and Lindemann (1975: 251); Michaelis (1961: 25-26); Schmid (1956).

4. Lagrange (1948: vi-xix, xxxiii-cxlviii); Zahn (1909: 506-30); Schlatter (1948); Kingsbury (1977: 1-3).

5. Plummer presents his outline of Matthew in the same fashion (1909: xviii). See also B. Weiss (1888: II, 263-82); McNeile (1938: xii).

6. Burton (1898: 93); Conzelmann and Lindemann (1975: 251); Farmer (1982: 139).

7. Allen and Grensted (1929: 33); Box (1922: 7); Burton (1898: 96); Davidson (1894: 366); Harrison (1964: 161-62); Hunter (1972: 56); Kerr (1892: 23); McNeile (1938: xvi-xvii); Meinertz, (1950: 168-69); Moffatt (1918: 250-51); Plummer (1909: xxv-xxxi); Robinson (1928: xi-xii); Senior (1977: 16); B. Weiss (1888: II, 282-84); Wikenhauser (1958: 186).

8. Allen and Grensted (1929: 33); Harrison (1964: 161-62); McNeile (1938: xvi-xvii); Meinertz (1950: 168-69).

9. Box (1922: 7); Conzelmann and Lindemann (1975: 251). Conzelmann and Lindemann (1975: 251-52), Hunter (1972: 56), and Wikenhauser (1958: 189) also discuss Jesus in terms of 'Teacher', or 'new Moses', yet these designations are connected to other observations on Matthew and not to their discussions on Matthean structure.

10. E.g. Box (1922: 6-7); Burton (1898: 97); Meinertz (1950: 168-69); Plummer (1909: xxv-xxi).

11. Petersen (1978: 24-32). It is probable, as we shall see below, that geography in Matthew does have some theological import, but to make this the ultimate basis for structuring Matthew's Gospel requires more thorough examination and more persuasive arguments than have been forthcoming. Cf. Conzelmann and Lindemann (1975: 251); Farmer (1982: 159).

12. Bacon (1912); Bacon (1918: 56-66); Bacon (1928: 203-31).

13. ἀνομία: 7.13-23; 13.41; 24.10-12. See Bacon (1928: 204, 223).

14. Bacon (1912: 153), 'Doctrine as well as history is subordinate to the one great aim of teaching men "to observe all things whatsoever Jesus commanded"'. Cf. Ingelaere (1979).

15. Alington (1946: 294); Argyle (1963: 2); Barr (1976: 351); Bauman (1961: 112); Beare (1981: 200); Benoit (1953: 7); Crapps, *et al.* (1969: 475); Enslin (1931); Enslin (1938: 391); Farrer (1954: 180); Franzmann (1961: 174); Fuller (1971: 115); F. Green (1936: 5); Gutbrod (1973: 17); Guthrie (1970: 30); Heard (1950: 66); Henshaw (1952: 124); Hunkin (1950: 73); Kee (1971: 610); Kee, *et al.* (1965: 276); Keegan (1982); Kilpatrick (1946: 75);

Levesque (1916: 387); Lohse (1972: 140); McKenzie (1968: 62); Marxsen (1968: 8-9); Milligan (1913: 147-48); Minear (1982: 12); Neill (1976: 94); Perrin and Duling (1982: 268); Radermakers (1972: II, 20); Rattey (1935: 65); Ridderbos (1958: 15); Riddle and Hutson (1946: 161); Rife (1975: 78); Selby (1971: 112); Waetjen (1976: 31).

16. Alington (1946: 306); Bauman (1961: 111); Bornkamm (1973: 60); Case (1909: 394, 399); Cox (1952: 20); Craig (1939: 43); Crapps, *et al.* (1969: 474); Enslin (1938: 389); Farrer (1954: 177-97); Fuller (1971: 115); Fuller and Perkins (1982: 33-34); F. Green (1936: 10-12); Gromacki (1974: 72); Gundry (1981: 83); Harvey (1977: 57); Heard (1950: 65-66); Henshaw (1952: 121); Hunkin (1950: 73); Hunter (1972: 56); Jones (1965: 19); Kee (1971: 609); Kee, *et al.* (1965: 285); Keegan (1982: 426); Kilpatrick (1946); Lohse (1972: 139); Loisy (1950: 111); McKenzie (1968: 62); Marxsen (1968: 8-10); Milligan (1913: 147); Minear (1982: 12); Neill (1976: 94); Perrin and Duling (1982: 274); Price (1961: 191-94); Radermakers (1972: II, 15-16); Rattey (1935: 65-66); Riddle and Hutson (1946: 161); Rolland (1972: 155, 164), Schelkle (1966: 55); Selby (1971: 110); Spivey and Smith (1982: 98, 130); Stendahl (1968: 20-29). Three exceptions are the avowedly literary critical studies by Barr (1976: 340); Waetjen (1976: 15-45); Combrink (1982: 1-20).

17. Alington (1946: 292); Barr (1976: 357); Bauman (1961: 111-12); Bornkamm (1973: 61); Case (1909: 391); Cox (1952: 22); Crapps, *et al.* (1969: 474, 478); Franzmann (1961: 174); Fuller (1971: 117); Fuller and Perkins (1982: 83); F. Green (1936: 2-3); Guthrie (1970: 23-24); Harvey (1977: 59); Henshaw (1952: 125); Hunter (1972: 58); Kee (1971: 609); Lohse (1972: 142); McKenzie (1968: 64); Perrin and Duling (1982: 270-71); Price (1961: 204); Riddle and Hutson (1946: 164-65); Selby (1971: 120); Spivey and Smith (1982: 98, 130-31); Tenney (1961: 151-52).

18. E.g. Enslin (1938: 389-90); Franzmann (1961: 171); F. Green (1936: 6); Gundry (1981: 84-85); Guthrie (1970: 31-32); Hunter (1972) 57-58; McKenzie (1968: 62); Rattey (1935: 67).

19. Argyle (1963: 3); Franzmann (1961: 180); Guthrie (1970: 25); Hunter (1972: 58); Rattey (1935: 65); Riddle and Hutson (1946: 162); Selby (1971: 112).

20. Those who see ch. 23 as the sixth discourse include Case (1909: 391); Heard (1950: 66); Ridderbos (1958: 78); Schelkle (1966: 55).

Those who identify seven discourses include Gromacki (1974: 71); G. Green (1968: 57-59).

21. E.g. Bauman (1961: 113-14); Franzmann (1961: 177); Gundry (1981: 88); Guthrie (1970: 50); Selby (1971: 149).

22. Graig (1939: 41-42); Gutbrod (1973: 20); Hunter (1972: 59); Kee (1971: 610); Levesque (1916: 398); Loisy (1950: 26-28); McKenzie (1968: 66); Meier (1980: xii); Neill (1976: 97-103); Price (1961: 196); Radermakers (1972: II, 21-22); Rolland (1972: 156-57); Tenney (1961: 141-43).

23. Alington (1946: 294); Argyle (1963: 1); Benoit (1953: 8); Cox (1952:

22); Crapps, *et al.* (1969: 475); Franzmann (1961: 174); F. Green (1936: 5); Guthrie (1970: 30); Hunter (1972: 57); Jones (1965: 20-21); Kee (1971: 610); Meier (1980: xii); Milligan (1913: 147-48); Minear (1982: 12-16); Spivey and Smith (1982: 99); Waetjen (1976: 33-34).

24. Gutbrod (1973: 16); Loisy (1950: 111); Radermakers (1972: II, 19-22); Rolland (1972: 156-57); Selby (1971: 148-49).

25. Hill (1972: 144-48); Price (1961: 194-96); and especially Barr (1976).

26. See also Bauman (1961: 111); Crapps, *et al.* (1969: 477); Heard (1950: 66); Kee, *et al.* (1965: 275).

27. Enslin (1938: 389); Fuller (1971: 117); Gundry (1981: 84); Henshaw (1952: 122-24); Hunter (1972: 58); Lohse (1972: 141); Loisy (1950: 113); McKenzie (1968: 62).

28. Farrer (1954: 179); Barr (1976: 351); Kümmel (1973: 106); Davies (1967: 214); Davies (1966: 25); Ogawa (1979: 17); Kingsbury (1975: 4).

29. Argyle (1963: 2); Enslin (1938: 399); Gundry (1981: 85).

30. As when Fuller and Perkins (1983: 83) speak of the passion as the climax to the Gospel, while at the same time declaring that ch. 23 is a denunciation of false teachers that characteristically comes at the *end* of a document.

31. Davies (1966: 92-93); Kingsbury (1975: 5); Barth (1963: 157-59); Barr (1976: 351); Kümmel (1973: 106).

32. Gutbrod (1973: 16); Loisy (1950: 111); Radermakers (1972: II, 12-22); Rolland (1972: 156-57); Selby (1971: 148-49); Farrer (1954: 180).

33. E.g. Bacon (1930: 81); Benoit (1953: 8); Cox (1952: 22).

34. Franzmann (1961: 175); Minear (1982: 17); Spivey and Smith (1982: 129); McKenzie (1968: 66).

35. Others who see the turning point of the chiasm at 13.35-36 are Fenton (1959: 175-79); Gaechter (1966: 70-80; 1963: 17); Lohr (1961).

36. E.g. Rolland (1972). Rolland identifies the turning point of Matthew at 4.17. For a survey of various chiastic approaches to Matthew, see Di Marco (1976).

37. Kingsbury (1975: 1-39). Others who have adopted this outline are Clogg (1940); Dillersberger (1953: I, 1-171); Dods (n.d.); Krentz (1964: 409-14); Kümmel (1973: 105-106); White (1905); Palmer (1947); McKee (1949); Farrar (1897); Rau (1976); Stonehouse (1944); Strong (1914); Lohmeyer (1956); Sabourin (1978); cf. Hill (1979).

38. In his investigation of the unity of 1.1-4.16, Kingsbury largely follows the study of Edgar Krentz. See n. 37.

39. For additional objections to Kingsbury's structure, see Hill (1984) and Kingsbury's response (1985). Other topical outlines have been put forward which do little more than catologue the basic contents of the Gospel and which make virtually no attempt to relate the parts to one another. These include Carr (1878); Efird (1980); Harless (1844); Ramaroson (1974); Schniewind (1954); Léon-Dufour (1965: 168-73); Smith (1933); Albright and Mann (1971: lxii-lxiii).

40. An exception is Filson (1960: 20-23). Filson is convinced that no topical outline can do justice to the structure of Matthew. But he identifies the central theme around which Matthew writes his Gospel not as salvation history, but as Matthew's didactic purpose. This didactic purpose is widely conceived, for Matthew is a book written for Christian teachers who will use it both within the church (catechesis, paraenesis) and for missionary work.

41. It is interesting to note that Kingsbury maintains the divisions of Krentz, but uses different nomenclature to designate the central thought in 4.17-16.20 and 16.21-28.20.

42. Kingsbury (1966: 504-506), see especially the consistent way in which the disciples (and those who approach Jesus in faith) address him by the confessional title, 'Lord' (e.g. 15.25; 16.22; 17.4; 18.21), and the references to the disciples and those of faith 'worshipping' Jesus (e.g. 2.11; 14.33; cf. 28.17).

43. See Deut. 1.1; 4.44; 28.69; 33.1, 24; 32.44-45.

44. Frankemölle (1974: 7-80). In this connection Frankemölle points to the inclusio between chs. 1-2 and chs. 26-28. He notes especially the recurrence of μεθ᾿ ἡμῶν (ὑμῶν) at 1.23; 28.20 (pp. 321-25).

45. In other works Meier adopts the five-fold alternating pattern; cf. Meier (1980: xi-xii; 1979).

46. A few scholars have attempted to merge two or more of these structural approaches, all with limited success. See Barker, *et al.* (1969); Barnett (1946); Goodspeed (1937); Ingelaere (1979); Via (1980). Others divide the Gospel solely on the basis of Matthew's redactional activity, especially his decision to follow essentially the order of Mark from 13.52 on. See Gundry (1982); von Soden (1907: 181-83); Rigaux (1968: 33-34); Combrink (1983). Childs (1985: 63-64) argues, without adequate support, that it is inappropriate to identify a comprehensive structure in Matthew's Gospel; it is not at all clear how a lack of scholarly consensus regarding Matthew's structure necessarily leads to the conclusion that the Gospel lacks any sort of comprehensive structure whatsoever, nor is it clear why Childs declares that the investigation into Matthew's structure 'reflects a modern mentality and attitude to literature which were not shared to the same extent in the ancient world', while at the same time he finds discrete structural divisions in equally ancient documents, e.g. Mark (1985: 86) and John (1985: 122-23, 136-42).

Notes to Chapter 3

1. Obviously these acts of mission are not entirely identical. E.g. part of Jesus' mission involves 'giving his life as a ransom for many' (20.28) and thus 'saving his people from their sins' (1.21).

2. 4.23; 5.1, 19; 7.29; 9.35; 11.1; 13.54; 21.23; 22.16; 28.19.

3. Of disciples at 10.1; 17.14-20; of Jesus at 8.16; 9.32-34; 12.22-29; 15.21-28; 17.14-20.

4. Bornkamm, *et al.*, pp. 249-72; Gerhardsson (1979: 76); Schlatter (1948: 301).

5. Of Jesus at 4.23; 9.35; of the disciples at 24.14; 26.13; cf. 11.1.

6. For the use of the passive of divine circumlocution, see Zerwick (1963: par. 236); Blass and Debrunner (1961: par. 130[1], 313, 342[1]).

7. Of Jesus at 10.40; 15.24; 21.37; of the disciples at 10.2, 5, 16; 23.34, 37.

8. Of Jesus at 10.40; 18.5; of the disciples at 10.14, 40-41.

9. Of the disciples at 10.11-15; of Jesus at 12.15; 14.13; 15.21; 16.4; 10.17; and the motif of Jesus turning away from Israel, for instance, 17.17; 21.43; 23.37-39.

10. Bornkamm, *et al.* (1963: 275). Cf. 19.28 with 3.7-12; 7.21-23; 25.31-46, etc.

11. 10.17; cf. 10.19, 21; 24.9-10.

12. 10.4; 17.22; 20.18-29; 26.2, 15-16, 21, 23-25, 45-46, 48; 27.2-4, 26.

13. The Greek term ἡγεμών is used in both cases. See 27.2, 11, 14-15, 21, 27; 28.14.

14. 5.11; 10.18, 22, 39; 16.25.

15. Quell, *TDNT*, I, 21-35; Moffatt (1929). See 5.43-48, which climaxes 5.17-48; also 7.12; 22.36-40.

16. For the structure of Matthew's ethics, see Trilling (1968: 165-224); Strecker (1971: 130-47); Barth (1963: 58-164).

17. Throughout 1.1-4.16 Jesus is pictured as the one who brings Israel's history to fulfillment (e.g. 1.1-17; 2.16). Cf. Kingsbury (1975).

18. Also Bornkamm, *et al.* (1963: 255, 258); also, in 12.12 Jesus interprets his own actions by declaring that they are in accord with the law of God.

19. E.g. 18.1-4, 10-20; 24.45; 25.14-36.

20. 9.13, 27, 36; 14.14; 15.22, 25, 32; 17.15; 20.30-34. See Bornkamm (1963: 58-164).

21. The Lord's Prayer actually contains what the disciples are to say (6.9-13).

22. E.g. 11.25-28; 13.11, 16.17, 51; 16.13-17; 17.17.

Notes to Chapter 4

1. These other contrasts involve acceptance of Jesus' point of view (following him) or the acceptance of the point of view of his opponents. Many of these elements are important in Matthew's presentation and will be dealt with below in several places.

2. 1.1, 6, 17, 20.

3. 1.16, 18, 20, 21-23; 2.5; 3.17; 4.3, 6.
4. 1.1-17, 21-23; 2.15, 23.
5. 15.7; 22.18; 23.13-15, 23, 25, 27, 29.
6. Beare (1981: 530); Fenton (1963: 435); Gundry (1982: 562). See 4.24-25; 7.28; 8.1; 9.8, 33.34, 36; 12.15; 13.2; 14.13, 34-36; 21.1-17, 46; 26.4-5; 27.20.
7. Cf. 12.7; 21.35-39; 22.6; 23.29-36; chs. 26-27.
8. Cf. 9.34; 11.18-19; 12.24; 26.60-61, 64-65; 28.13.
9. πειράζω. See 16.1; 19.3; 22.18, 35.
10. εἰ υἱὸς εἶ τοῦ θεοῦ. See 27.40; cf. 4.3, 6; also 27.43.
11. 4.23-25; 7.28-29; 9.7-8, 33, 35-38; 21.1-16.
12. Jesus' opposition is not limited to the Jews. Jesus declares that he will be killed by Gentiles (20.19), and this in fact occurred (ch. 27). Matthew tells us that Pilate 'delivered him to to crucified' (παραδίδωμι) (27.26).
13. 5.17-18; 7.12, 29a; 12.2; 22.40.

Notes to Chapter 5

1. Lohmeyer (1956: 4); Brown (1977: 58-59); McNeile (1938: 1); Filson (1960: 52); Schrenk, *TDNT* (I, 682-84); Johnson (1969: 146); Gundry (1982: 13)
2. Gen. 5.1; 10.1; 11.10, 27; Ruth 4.18-19.
3. Kingsbury (1975: 10); Stendahl (1983: 60); Klostermann (1971: 1); Schlatter (1948: 1); Plummer (1909: 1).
4. Klostermann (1971: 1); Gaechter (1963: 34-35); Grundmann (1981: 61); Robinson (1928: 2); Davies (1966: 67-70); Frankemölle (1974: 364); Beare (1981: 65).
5. 1.25; 2.5-6, 15, 17-18, 23; 4.14-16; cf. 1.1-17.
6. E.g. Bonnard (1963: 16); Brown (1977: 67); Beare (1981: 65); Fenton (1963: 39); Gaechter (1963: 34-35); Gundry (1982: 13); Lagrange (1948: 13); Grundmann (1981: 62).
7. Plummer (1909: 3); Brown (1977: 74); Lohmeyer (1956: 5); see Johnson (1969: 154-55).
8. Fenton (1963: 37); Gundry (1982: 13); Malina (1970-71: 100).
9. 1.22-23; 2.5-6, 15, 17-18, 23.
10. Dreams are understood by Matthew to contain divine revelations (cf. 1.20; 2.12-13, 19, 22; 27.19).
11. Robertson (1934: 567, 582, 636) properly makes the distinction between ὑπό as expressing mediate agency and διά as expressing immediate agency. See also Moulton, *et al.* (1976: I, 106).
12. See 2.8, 11, 13, 20-21.
13. Most of those who follow Bacon's division of the Gospel discern a major break at 3.1. See above, pp. 27ff.

14. Krentz (1964: 412); Lohmeyer (1956: 33-34); Bonnard (1963: 31).
15. See Chapter 2, n. 1.
16. Bonnard (1963: 48); Schlatter (1948: 115-16); Allen (1912: 35); Grundmann (1981: 397); Trilling (1981: I, 55-56).
17. Gundry (1982: 61); Fenton (1963: 66-67); Beare (1981: 356).
18. 12.9-13, 15, 22; 14.14, 34-36.
19. We recognize that the proclamation of Jesus to Israel is the necessary, but not the sole and sufficient, cause of the responses. Jesus indicates that the reason for the rejection is found also in their stubbornness and in the will of God (11.16-27), while the acceptance of the disciples has to do with the revelation from the Father (13.10-12, 16-17; 16.16-20).
20. We agree neither with those who view the sermon on the mount as an example of Jesus' preaching (e.g. McNeile [1938: 46]) nor with those who see preaching in Jesus' comments in chs. 8-9 (e.g. Burger [1973: 282-83]). Matthew clearly and explicitly presents the sermon on the mount as Jesus' teaching (5.1-2; 7.24-28), and although it is assumed, there is no proclamation here that the kingdom of heaven is at hand, which is the substance of preaching (3.2; 4.17; 10.7). Moreover, Burger's contention that Jesus' words in chs. 8-9 expand the 'preaching' of 4.23 and 9.35 comes as a result of his redactional comparison of this material with Mark. It is unclear how an original reader of Matthew, not focusing on Matthew's redaction of Mark and Q, could have recognized these comments as preaching.
21. 4.25; 5.1; 7.28; 8.1, 10; 9.7, 32.
22. ἐν τῷ λαῷ. This phrase refers here to the people of Israel. See Schlatter (1948: 123); McNeile (1938: 47). The reference to Galilee, pointing back to 4.15-16 where Galilee is asociated with Gentiles, and the reference in 4.24-25 to people coming to Jesus from all around—including Gentile lands—could cause the reader to conclude that Jesus' ministry was directed to Gentiles. Matthew therefore carefully indicates that the ministry of Jesus was directed to Jews.
23. 4.18, 23; ch. 8; cf. 4.15-16.
24. 4.17, 23; 5.3, 10, 20; 6.10; 7.21; 8.12; 9.35.
25. Cf. 8.16, 28, 34; 9.32-34. See Gerhardsson (1979: 31).
26. τὰς πόλεις καὶ τὰς κώμας; 10.5, 11, 14-15, 23.
27. Trilling (1981: I, 200); Beare (1981: 256); Robinson (1928: 120).
28. 14.13-23; 15.10-20, 32-39; 16.5-20.
29. 3.4; cf. 2 Kgs 1.8; also Mt. 11.14; 17.11-13.
30. 2.17; 4.14-16; 11.13; 12.17; 13.17. See Kingsbury (1984).
31. The majority of commentators recognize the development at 16.21 vis-à-vis the preceding material. See Fenton (1963: 271); McNeile (1938: 244); Gaechter (1963: 541); Lohmeyer (1956: 264); Grundmann (1981: 397).
32. We agree with Dillersberger (1953: 21-22) when he maintains that the crucial geographical turning point in Matthew comes not at 19.1, when Jesus actually leaves Galilee and enters Judea, but at 16.21, where the journey

begins. Mt. 16.21 is the first reference to Jerusalem as the place of the passion.

33. Allen (1912: 217); Schlatter (1948: 597); Bonnard (1963: 296).

34. 1.1, 6, 20, 25.

35. For a detailed examination of the meaning of this phrase, see Catchpole (1971: 212-26).

36. 27.11, 29, 37, 42.

37. 16.21; 17.12, 23; 20.19; 21.37; 26.2, 28.

38. We note here the use of the passive voice and the reference to the veil being torn from top to bottom. See Schweizer (1975: 516); Gundry (1982: 575); Dahl (1983: 51); Hill (1972: 355); Lohmeyer (1956: 395-96).

39. A number of German commentators see the significance of δείκνυμι here as containing the element of apocalyptic divine revelation, noting the use of the term in Rev. 1.1 (Lohmeyer [1956: 264]; Grundmann [1981: 397]; Schweizer 1975: 345]). This view ignores the use of the term in the New Testament as a whole and fails to recognize its function in the book of Revelation. Its use there is in accord with its general use in the New Testament; the term is used not because the revelation is apocalyptic or hitherto hidden, but precisely because it comes to John through visions. The mere fact that the word appears in the Apocalypse of John does not make it apocalyptic everywhere it occurs in the New Testament.

40. 17.10; 18.33; 23.23, 25.

41. Mt. 4.10 reads: ὕπαγε Σατανᾶ. The difference between the two phrases—the addition of ὀπίσω μου in 16.23—points back to the journey image; Peter is not to stand in Jesus' way on the road to suffering.

42. 17.14-21; 19.1-30; 21.23-27; 22.15-22, 34-40; 24.45-25.30.

Notes to Chapter 6

1. Those who argue that all worship and all doubt include Grundmann (1981: 576); I.P. Ellis (1967-68: 574-77); Bonnard (1963: 418). Those who argue that only some of the eleven doubt include Malina (1970-71: 98); Blass-Debrunner (1961: par. 250).

2. Kingsbury (1974: 573-84); Hubbard (1974: 73); McNeile (1938: 435); cf. Malina (1970: 90-91).

3. For surveys of the history of interpretation, see Hubbard (1974: 3-17), and especially Friedrich (1983).

4. 1 Tim. 3.16; Heb. 1.5-14; Phil. 2.9-11.

5. See Vögtle (1964); Hubbard (1974: 83-84); Trilling (1968: 26-28); Plummer (1909: 429).

6. Cf. Gen. 15.1-6; 17.15-27; 26.63; 28.11-12; 35.9-15.

7. We are indebted in large part to Friedrich (1983: 161-62) for this critique of Hubbard.

8. Kümmel (1973: 108); Kingsbury (1977: 30-57); Childs (1985: 64-69).

9. Other themes in the Gospel of Matthew which come to expression in 28.16-20 include the tension between faith and doubt/understanding and incomprehension (cf. e.g. 14.22-23), the mission of the disciples (see above), and the commands of Jesus to his disciples (cf. e.g. chs. 5-7; ch. 18).

10. 3.11; 11.3; 21.9. In 23.39 this title is used explicitly in connection with the coming of Jesus in eschatological judgment as Son of man.

11. The verb ποιμαίνω is used at 2.6 and the noun ποιμήν at 26.31. Furthermore, there are references to the people who are without a shepherd at 9.36 and to the people as 'lost sheep' at 10.6 and 15.24. See Jeremias, *TDNT*, II, 489.

12. 1.1, 16-18; 2.4; 11.2; 16.16, 20; 22.42; 23.10; 26.63, 68; 27.17, 22.

13. See 2.2; 21.5; 25.34, 40; 27.11, 29, 37, 42; also 1.6.

14. 1.1; 9.27; 12.23; 15.22; 20.30-31; 21.9, 15. See Strecker (1971); Burger (1970: 72-90); Gibbs (1963-64: 446-62).

15. See 7.22; 8.2, 6, 8, 21, 25; 9.28; 10.24-25; 12.8; 13.27; 14.28, 30; 15.22, 25, 27; 16.22; 17.4, 15; 18.21; 20.33; 21.3, 9; 22.43-45; 24.42; 25.11.

16. 3.17; 14.33; 16.16; 17.5; 27.54; 28.12; also 2.15; 11.25-30; 16.27; 21.37; Kingsbury (1975: 48-83); Gerhardsson (1979: 88-91).

17. 8.20; 9.6; 10.23; 11.19; 12.8, 32, 40; 13.37, 41; 16.13, 27, 28; 17.9, 12, 22; 18.11; 19.28; 20.18, 28; 24.27, 30, 37, 39, 44; 25.31; 26.2, 24, 45, 64. Cf. Tödt (1965: 78-80).

18. 8.19; 9.11; 12.38; 17.24; 19.16; 22.16, 24, 36; 26.18, 25, 49; also 10.24-25.

19. Of course, one must not overlook the possibility that on occasion this term was meant to be understood facetiously or hypocritically; cf. 22.16-18. This hierarchy and categorization of the various titles is based on the discussion in Kingsbury (1975: 40-127). For another view, see Meier (1979).

20. 1.23; 2.6, 15, 18, 23; 4.15-16; 8.17; 12.18-21; 13.35; 12.5; 27.9-10.

21. We agree with Bornkamm (1964: 190) when he argues that the λαός of 1.21 refers not to the Jewish people *per se*, but to the community of those who were to believe in Jesus. Bornkamm points to the reference to 'my church' in 16.18 and to the transfer of the kingdom from the Jews to 'a nation that bears its fruit' (21.43). See also Frankemölle (1974: 16-17). We add that, on literary-critical grounds, prophecies from angels in Matthew are always reliable and find fulfillment. Since the Gospel teaches that the Jews as a whole have rejected Jesus and now suffer the consequent loss of the kingdom, this verse must point to the authority of Jesus to deliver his church from sin. This observation clarifies the notion of the authority of Jesus in relation to the church, a notion that is central in 28.16-20.

We recognize that the conception by the Holy Spirit is bound up with the divine Sonship of Jesus, as are many other elements in 1.1-4.16. In fact, almost every expression of the authority of Jesus is related to one christological category or another. For the sake of clarity and analysis, we have chosen to deal above with the titles of majesty themselves and to discuss at this point other, though related, descriptions of the authority of Jesus.

22. 1.20, 24; 2.12, 13-15, 19-23.
23. 8.2; 9.18; 14.33; 15.25; 18.26; 20.20; 28.9, 17.
24. See Michaelis (*TDNT, VI*, 163); Arndt-Gingrich (1957:665). Matthew, in other places, mentions two further indicators of the authority of Jesus in connection with persons who approach Jesus. First, the notion of 'bending the knee, kneeling' (γονυπετέω) is used once alone (27.29) and once in connection with the expression 'to approach' (προσέρχομαι, 17.14). According to Schlier (*TDNT*, I, 738), there is no distinction between bending the knee and full prostration. This genuflection reinforces the recognition of majesty; it expresses supplication and worship.

Second, Matthew sometimes employs προσέρχομαι ('to come to, to approach') in order to describe persons who come into the presence of Jesus (e.g. 8.19; 9.18). In the LXX this term has cultic overtones, and in Josephus it is often used of persons who approach a king. See Arndt and Gingrich (1957: 270); Kingsbury (1981: 76); Bornkamm, *et al.* (1963: 226); Schneider, (*TDNT*, II, 683).

25. προσφέρω. E.g., Lev. 1.2, 5; 2.8; Ezek. 44.15.
26. δῶρον. 2.11; 5.23-24; 8.4; 15.5; 23.18-19.
27. See also 7.21-22; 10.32-33; 13.41; 16.27.
28. 5.21-48; 9.13; 12.7: 22.15-22. One notes the recurring contrast, 'But I say unto you', vv. 21, 27, 31, 33, 38, 43.
29. This indicates that Jesus shares God's psychological point of view. See Uspensky (1973: 81-100).
30. 8.3, 13, 32; 9.7, 22, 25; 15.28; 17.18.
31. 8.3, 8, 13, 15, 26, 32; 9.6, 18, 20-21, 25, 29; 14.35.
32. Jones (1964: 141); McNeile (1938: 162); Johannes Weiss (1906: I, 299-300); Norden (1913: 277-308); Hill (1972: 206); Gundry (1982: 216); Fenton (1963: 187); Allen (1912: 123); Jeremias (1967: 49); Tasker (1961: 120).
33. Gaechter (1963: 379-80); Schlatter (1948: 384-85); Kingsbury (1975: 65); over against Kilpatrick (1946: 91); Tasker (1961: 120); Klostermann (1971: 108); Jeremias (1967: 49). Jeremias is correct when he observes that 'deliver' (παραδίδωμι) is often used technically for the transmission of doctrine. Yet such usage can be discerned with certainty only in those passages where it is expressly indicated, since this term is frequently used for giving over or handing over in general, with no indication of the transmission of tradition or knowledge. Moreover, 'all' (πάντα) stands here in an absolute position; the passage carries a formal resemblance to 28.18; and Matthew has a penchant for verbal anticipation (cf. e.g. 14.33 to 16.16). Finally, the putative connection of πάντα with (ταῦτα) 'these things' (v. 25), which in turn refers back to the underlying meaning of Jesus' mighty works (vv. 20-24),

provides πάντα with a very weak meaning: God has delivered to Jesus the significance of his work.

34. E.g. cf. 26.20-25 with 26.47-50; 26.30-35 with 26.56, 69-75.

35. Thus, the first and last reference to the opposition to Jesus leading to his death concern the charge of blasphemy.

36. 5.47; 6.7, 32; 18.17; 20.19, 25.

37. In the parable itself, Jesus emphasizes that the field belongs to the householder, i.e. to God (vv. 24, 27).

38. 1.16, 21, 23; 2.15; 3.17.

39. E.g. Hubbard (1974: 97); Grundmann (1981: 420); Kingsbury (1975: 71).

Notes to Chapter 7

1. Others besides Streeter who have recognized the transitional nature of the formula include Bultmann (1958: 334); Kingsbury (1975: 6); Barr (1976: 352).

2. E.g. 9.15-17; 11.4-30; 12.25-37, 39-45; 15.10-20; 16.24-28; 20.1-16; 21.28-22.14; 23.

3. E.g. Kümmel (1973: 106-107); Streeter (1925: 262); Davies (1966: 14-17).

4. Luz (1983: 98-128); Perrin and Duling (1982: 276); Harvey (1977: 56-57); Marxsen (1968: 146-53).

BIBLIOGRAPHY

Abrams, M.H. *A Glossary of Literary Terms.* 4th edn. New York: Holt, Rhinehart & Winston, 1981.

Achtemeier, P.J. *Mark.* Proclamation Commentaries. Philadelphia: Fortress, 1975.

Albright, W.F., and Mann, C.S. *Matthew: Introduction Translation, and Notes.* AB 26. Garden City: Doubleday, 1971.

Alington, C.A. *The New Testament: A Reader's Guide.* London: G. Bell, 1946.

Allen, W.C. *A Critical and Exegetical Commentary on the Gospel according to Matthew.* ICC. 3rd edn. Edinburgh: T. & T. Clark, 1912.

—and Grensted, L.W. *Introduction to the Books of the New Testament.* 3rd edn. Edinburgh: T. & T. Clark, 1929.

Alter, R. *The Art of Biblical Narrative.* New York: Basic Books, 1981.

Anderson, B. 'The New Frontier of Rhetorical Criticism: A Tribute to James Muilenburg'. In *Rhetorical Criticism: Essays in Honor of James Muilenburg,* pp. ix-xviii. Ed. Jared J. Jackson and Martin Kessler. Pittsburgh: Pickwick, 1974.

Anderson, E.E. *The Gospel according to St. Matthew: With Introduction and Notes.* Edinburgh: T. & T. Clark, 1909.

Argyle, A.W. *The Gospel according to Matthew.* Cambridge Bible Commentary. Cambridge: Cambridge University Press, 1963.

Arndt, W.F., and Gingrich, F.W. *A Greek-English Lexicon of the New Testament and other Early Christian Literature:* Chicago: University of Chicago, 1957.

Auerbach, Eric. *Mimesis: The Representations of Reality in Western Literature.* Trans. William Trask. Garden City: Doubleday, 1957.

Bacon, B.W. 'The "Five Books" of Matthew Against the Jews'. *Expositor* 15 (1918): 56-66.

—'Jesus and the Law: A Study of the First "Book" of Matthew (Mt. 3-7)'. *JBL* 47 (1928): 203-31.

—*The Making of the New Testament.* New York: Henry Holt, 1912.

—*Studies in Matthew.* New York: Henry Holt 1930.

Barker, G.W.; Lane, W.L.; and Michaels, J.R. *The New Testament Speaks.* New York: Harper & Row, 1969.

Barnett, A.E. *The New Testament: Its Making and Meaning.* New York: Abingdon-Cokesbury, 1946.

Barr, D.L. 'The Drama of Matthew's Gospel: A Reconsideration of its Structure and Purpose'. *TD* 24 (1976): 349-59.

Battenhouse, H.M. *New Testament History and Literature.* New York: Thomas Nelson, 1937.

Bauman, E.W. *An Introduction to the New Testament.* Philadelphia: Westminster, 1961.

Beardslee, W.A. *Literary Criticism of the New Testament.* Guides to Biblical Scholarship. Philadelphia: Fortress, 1970.

Beare, F.W. *The Gospel according to Matthew: Translation, Introduction and Commentary.* San Francisco: Harper & Row, 1981.

Benoit, P. *L'évangile selon Saint Matthieu,* La Sainte Bible, vol. 1. 2nd edn. Paris: Cerf, 1953.

Blair, E.P. *Jesus in the Gospel of Matthew.* New York: Abingdon, 1960.

Blass, F., and Debrunner, A. *A Greek Grammar of the New Testament and other Early Christian Literature*. Trans. and ed. Robert W. Funk. Chicago: University of Chicago, 1961.

Bonnard, P. *L'évangile selon Saint Matthieu*, Commentaire du Nouveau Testament, vol. 1. Neuchâtel: Delachaux et Niestle, 1963.

Booth, W. 'Distance and Point-of-View: An Essay in Classification'. *Essays in Criticism* 11 (1961): 60-79.

—*The Rhetoric of Fiction*. Chicago: University of Chicago, 1961.

Bornkamm, G., 'Der Auferstandene und der Irdische. Mt. 28, 16-20'. In *Zeit und Geschichte: Dankesgabe an Rudolf Bultmann zum 80. Geburtstag*, pp. 171-91. Ed. Erich Dinkler. Tübingen: J.C.B. Mohr, 1964.

—*The New Testament: A Guide to its Writings*. Trans. R.H. Fuller and I. Fuller. Philadelphia: Fortress, 1973.

Bornkamm, G.; Barth, F.; and Held, H.J. *Tradition and Interpretation in Matthew*. Trans. Percy Scott. New Testament Library. Philadelphia: Westminster, 1963.

Box, G.H. *St. Matthew: Introduction, Revised Version with Notes, Index, and Maps*. New Century Bible. New York: Henry Frowde, 1922.

Bright, J. *The Authority of the Old Testament*. Grand Rapids: Baker, 1975.

Brooks, O. 'Matthew xxviii.16-20 and the Design of the First Gospel'. *JSNT* 10 (1981): 2-18.

Brown, R.E. *The Birth of the Messiah: A Commentary on the Infancy Narratives in Matthew and Luke*. Garden City: Doubleday, 1977.

Bruce, F.F. *The Book of Acts*. NICNT Grand Rapids: Eerdmans, 1954.

Bultmann, R. *Die Geschichte der synoptischen Tradition*. FRLANT 29. 4th edn. Göttingen: Vandenhoeck & Ruprecht, 1958.

Burger, C. 'Jesu Taten nach Matthäus 8 und 9'. *ZThK* 70 (1973): 272-87.

—*Jesus als Davidssohn: Eine traditionsgeschichtliche Untersuchung*. Göttingen: Vandenhoeck & Ruprecht, 1970.

Burton, E.D. 'The Purpose and Plan of the Gospel of Matthew'. *BW* 11 (1898): 37-44, 91-101.

Carr, A. *The Gospel according to St. Matthew: With Maps and Introduction*. Cambridge Bible for Schools. Cambridge: Cambridge University Press, 1878.

Case, S.J. The Origin and Purpose of the Gospel of Matthew'. *BW* 34 (1909): 391-403.

Catchpole, D.R. 'The Answer of Jesus to Caiaphas'. *NTS* 17 (1971): 212-26.

Chatman, S. *Story and Discourse: Narrative Structure in Fiction and Film*. Ithaca: Cornell University, 1978.

Childs, B. *The New Testament as Canon: An Introduction*. Philadelphia: Fortress, 1985.

Chronis, H.L. 'The Torn Veil: Cultus and Christology in Mark 15.37-39'. *JBL* 101 (1982): 97-114.

Clogg, F.B. *An Introduction to the New Testament*. 2nd edn. London: University of London, 1940.

Combrink, H.J.B. 'The Structure of the Gospel of Matthew as Narrative'. *Tyndale Bulletin* 34 (1983): 61-90.

Conzelmann, H. *Die Mitte der Zeit—Studien zur Theologie des Lukas*. BHTL, 17. Tübingen: J.C.B. Mohr, 1954.

—and Lindemann, A. *Arbeitsbuch zum Neuen Testament*. Tübingen: J.C.B. Mohr, 1975.

Cope, O.L. *Matthew: a Scribe Trained for the Kingdom of Heaven*. CBQMS, 5. Washington, D.C.: Catholic Biblical Association, 1976.

Cox, G.E.P. *The Gospel of St. Matthew*. Torch Bible Commentaries. London: SCM, 1952.

Craig, C.T. *The Study of the New Testament*. New York: Abingdon-Cokesbury, 1939.

Crapps, R.W.; McKnight, E.V.; and Smith, D.A. *Introduction to the New Testament*. New York: Ronald Press, 1969.

Culpepper, R.A. *Anatomy of the Fourth Gospel: A Study in Literary Design*. Foundations & Facets: New Testament. Philadelphia: Fortress, 1983.

Dahl, N.A. 'The Passion Narrative in Matthew'. In *The Interpretation of Matthew*, pp. 42-55. Ed. Graham Stanton. Issues in Religion and Theology, 3. Philadelphia: Fortress, 1983.

Dahood, M. *Psalms*. AB, 3 vols. Garden City: Doubleday. 1966.

Dalman, G. *The Words of Jesus: Considered in Light of Post-Biblical Jewish Writings and the Aramaic Language*. Trans. D.M. Kay. Edinburgh: T. & T. Clark, 1909.

Davidson, S. *An Introduction to the Study of the New Testament: Critical, Exegetical, and Theological*. 3rd edn. 2 vols. London: Kegan Paul, Trench, Trübner, 1894.

Davies, W.D. *Invitation to the New Testament: A Guide to its Main Witnesses*. London: Darton, Longman & Todd, 1967.

—*The Setting of the Sermon on the Mount*. Cambridge: Cambridge University Press, 1966.

Delling, G. 'ἄρχω'. In *Theological Dictionary of the New Testament* 10 vols. I: 478-89. Trans. G. Bromiley. Ed. G. Kittel. Grand Rapids: Eerdmand, 1971.

Dewey, J. *Markan Public Debate*. SBLDS, no. 48. Chico: Scholars, 1980.

'Point of View and the Disciples in Mark'. In *Society of Biblical Literature, 1982 Seminar Papers*, pp. 97-106. Ed. K.H. Richards. Chico: Scholars, 1982.

Dibelius, M. *Die Formgeschichte des Evangeliums*. 3rd edn. Tübingen: J.C.B. Mohr, 1959.

Dillersberger, J. *Matthäus: Das Evangelium des heiligen Matthäus in theologischer und heilsgeschichtler Schau*. I: *Sein Kommen in Vielfalt (die Vorgeschichte)*. Salzburg: Otto Müller, 1953.

Di Marco, A. 'Der Chiasmus in der Bibel, 3. Teil'. *LB* 39 (1976): 37-58.

Dods, M. *An Introduction to the New Testament*. Theological Educator. London: Hodder & Stoughton, n.d.

Dupont, J. 'L'évangile de saint Matthieu: quelques clés de lecture'. *CL* 57 (1975): 3-40.

Durand, A. *Evangile selon Saint Matthieu: Traduction et Commentaire*. Verbum Salutis: Commentaire de Nouveau Testament, 1. Paris: Beauchnesne, 1948.

Easton, B.S. *The Gospel Before the Gospels*. New York: Scribner's 1928.

Efird, J.M. *The New Testament Writings: History, Literature and Interpretation*. Atlanta: John Knox, 1980.

Egan, K. 'What is a Plot?' *New Literary History* 9 (1978): 455-73.

Ellis, I.P. 'But Some Doubted'. *NTS* 14 (1968): 574-80.

Ellis, P.F. *Matthew: His Mind and His Message*. Collegeville: Liturgical, 1974.

Enslin, M.S. '"The Five Books of Matthew": Bacon on the Gospel of Matthew'. *HTR* 24 (1931): 67-97.

—*The Literature of the Christian Movement: Part III of Christian Beginnings*. New York: Harper & Brothers, 1938.

Farmer, W.R. *Jesus and the Gospel: Tradition, Scripture, and Canon*. Philadelphia: Fortress, 1982.

—'A "Skeleton in the Closet" of Gospel Research'. *BR* 6 (1961): 18-42.

—*The Synoptic Problem: A Critical Analysis*. New York: Macmillan, 1964.

Farrar, F.W. *The Messages of the Books: Being Discourses and Notes on the Books of the New Testament*. New York: E.P. Dutton, 1897.

Farrer, A. *St. Matthew and St. Mark*. London: Dacre, 1954.

Fenton J.C. 'Inclusio and Chiasmus in Matthew'. In *Studia Evangelica [I]: Papers Presented to the International Congress on 'The Four Gospels in 1957'*, pp. 174-79. Kurt Aland, *et al*. TU, 73. Berlin: Akademie, 1959.

—*Saint Matthew*. Westminster Pelican Commentaries. Philadelphia: Westminster, 1963.

Filson, F.V. *The Gospel according to St. Matthew*. Black's New Testament Commentaries. London: A. & C. Black, 1960.

—*Opening the New Testament*. Philadelphia: Westminster, 1952.

Foerster, W. 'εξουσία'. In *Theological Dictionary of the New Testament*, 10 vols. II: 562-74. Trans. G. Bromiley. Ed. G. Kittel. Grand Rapids: Eerdmans, 1971.

Fowler, A. 'The Selection of Literary Constructs'. *New Literary History* 7 (1975): 39-55.

Fowler, R.M. *Loaves and Fishes*. SBLDS 54. Chico: Scholars, 1981.

Frankemölle H. *Jahwebund und Kirche Christi: Studien zur Form- und Traditionsgeschichte des 'Evangeliums' nach Matthäus*. Neutestamentliche Abhandlungen, 10. Münster: Aschendorff, 1974.

Franzmann, M.H. *The Word of the Lord Grows: A First Historical Introduction to the New Testament*. St. Louis: Concordia, 1961.

Freedman, W. 'The Literary Motif: A Definition and Evaluation'. *Novel* 4 (1971): 123-31.

Frei, H.W. *The Eclipse of Biblical Narrative*. New Haven: Yale University, 1974.

Friedrich, G. 'Die formale Struktur von Mt. 28.18-20'. *ZThK* 80 (1983): 137-83.

Frye, N. *Anatomy of Criticism: Four Essays*. Princeton: Princeton University, 1957.

Frye, R.M. 'A Literary Perspective for the Criticism of the Gospels'. In *Jesus and Man's Hope*, II: 193-221. Edited by Donald G. Miller and Dikran Y. Hadidian. 2 vols. Pittsburgh: Pittsburgh Theological Seminary, 1971.

Fuller, R.H. *A Critical Introduction to the New Testament*. London: Duckworth, 1971.

Fuller, R.H., and Perkins, P. *Who Is This Christ?: Gospel Christology and Contemporary Faith*. Philadelphia: Fortress, 1983.

Gaechter, P. *Die literarische Kunst im Matthäus-Evangelium*. Stuttgarter Bibelstudien, 7. Stuttgart: Katholisches Bibelwerk, 1966.

—*Das Matthäus Evangelium: Ein Kommentar*. Innsbruck: Tyrolia, 1963.

Genette, G. 'Boundaries of Narrative'. *New Literary History* 8 (1976): 1-13.

—*Narrative Discourse: An Essay in Method*. Trans. Jane E. Lewin. Ithaca: Cornell University, 1980.

Gerhardsson, B. *The Mighty Acts of Jesus according to Matthew*. Trans. Robert Dewsnap. Scripta Minora, 5. Lund: GWK Gleerup, 1979.

Gibbs, J.M. 'Purpose and Pattern in Matthew's Use of the Title "Son of David"'. *NTS* 10 (1963-64): 446-62.

Goodspeed, E.J. *An Introduction to the New Testament*. Chicago: University of Chicago, 1937.

Grant, F.C. *Form Criticism: A New Method of New Testament Research*. Chicago: Willett, Clark, 1934.

Green, F.W. *The Gospel according to St. Matthew: In the Revised Version with Introduction and Commentary*. The Clarendon Bible. Oxford: Clarendon, 1936.

Green, H.B. 'The Structure of St. Matthew's Gospel'. In *Studia Evangelica IV: Papers Presented to the Third International Congress on New Testament Studies. Part I: The New Testament Scriptures*, pp. 47-59. Ed. Frank L. Cross. TU, 102. Berlin: Akademie, 1968.

Greeven, H. 'προσκυνέω'. In *Theological Dictionary of the New Testament*. 10 vols. II: 758-66. Trans. G. Bromiley. Ed. G. Kittel. Grand Rapids: Eerdmans, 1971.

Gromacki, R.G. *New Testament Survey*. Grand Rapids: Baker, 1974.

Gros Louis, K.R.R. and Ackerman, J.S., ed. *Literary Interpretations of Biblical Narratives*, vol. II. Nashville: Abingdon, 1982.

Grundmann, W. *Das Evangelium nach Matthäus*. Theologischer Handkommentar zum Neuen Testament, 1. 5th edn. Berlin: Evangelische Verlagsanstalt, 1981.

—'δεῖ'. In *Theological Dictionary of the New Testament*. 10 vols. II: 22-25. Trans. G. Bromiley. Ed. G. Kittel. Grand Rapids: Eerdmans, 1971.

—'σύν-μετά'. In *Theological Dictionary of the New Testament*. 10 vols. VII: 766-97. Trans. G. Bromiley. Ed. G. Friedrich. Grand Rapids: Eerdmans, 1971.

Gundry, R.H. *Matthew: A Commentary on His Literary and Theological Art*. Grand Rapids: Eerdmans, 1982.

—*A Survey of the New Testament*. Grand Rapids: Zondervan, 1981.

Gutbrod, K. *Kurze Biblekunde des Neuen Testaments*. Stuttgart: Calwer, 1973.

Guthrie, D. *New Testament Introduction*. 3rd edn. Downer's Grove: Inter-Varsity Press, 1970.

Harless, C.A. 'The Structure of the Gospel according to Matthew'. Trans. H.B. Smith. *BS* 1 (1844): 86-97.

Harrison, E.F. *Introduction to the New Testament*. Grand Rapids: Eerdmans, 1964.

Harvey, A.E. *Something Overheard: An Invitation to the New Testament*. Atlanta: John Knox, 1977.

Heard, R. *An Introduction to the New Testament*. London: A. & C. Black, 1950.

Henshaw, T. *New Testament Literature: In the Light of Modern Scholarship*. London: Allen & Unwin, 1952.

Hermerén, G. 'Intention and Interpretation in Literary Criticism'. *New Literary History* 7 (1975): 57-82.

Hernadi, P. 'Literary Theory: A Compass for Critics'. *Critical Inquiry* 3 (1976): 369-86.

Hill, D. *The Gospel of Matthew*. New Century Bible Commentary. Grand Rapids: Eerdmans, 1972.

—'Some Recent Trends in Matthean Studies'. *Irish Biblical Studies* 1 (1979): 139-49.

—'The Figure of Jesus in Matthew's Gospel: A Response to Professor Kingsbury's Literary-Critical Probe'. *JSNT* 21 (1984): 37-52.

Hubbard, B.J. *The Matthean Redaction of a Primitive Apostolic Commissioning: An Exegesis of Matthew 28.16-20*. SBLDS, 19. Missoula: Scholars, 1974.

Hummel, R. *Die Auseinandersetzung zwischen Kirche und Judentum im Matthäusevangelium*. Beiträge zur Evangelischen Theologie, 33. München: Kaiser, 1963.

Hunkin, J.W. *The New Testament: A Conspectus*. The Calet Library of Modern Christian Thought and Teaching. London: Duckworth, 1950.

—'"Pleonastic *archomai*" in the New Testament'. *JTS* 25 (1924): 391-95.

Hunter, A.M. *Introducing the New Testament*. 3rd edn. Philadelphia: Westminster, 1972.

Ingelaere, J.C. 'Structure de Matthieu et histoire du Salut'. *Foi et Vie* 78 (1979): 10-33.

Iser, W. *The Act of Reading: A Theory of Aesthetic Response*. Baltimore: Johns
     Hopkins University, 1978.
—*The Implied Reader: Patterns of Communication in Prose Fiction from Bunyan to
     Beckett*. Baltimore: Johns Hopkins University, 1974.
Jeremias, J. 'ποιμή'. In *Theological Dictionary of the New Testament*. 10 vols. VI: 485-
     502. Trans. G. Bromiley. Ed. G. Kittel. Grand Rapids: Eerdmans, 1971.
—*Jesus' Promise to the Nations*. Trans. S.H. Hooke. Studies in Biblical Theology, 24.
     Naperville: Allenson, 1958.
—*The Prayers of Jesus*. Trans. J. Bowden, C. Burchard, and J. Reumann. Philadelphia:
     Fortress, 1967.
—*Rediscovering the Parables*. Trans. S.H. Hooke and F. Clarke. New York: Scribner's,
     1966.
Johnson, M.D. *The Purpose of Biblical Genealogies, With Special Reference to the
     Genealogies of Jesus*. SNTSMS, 8. Cambridge: Cambridge University Press,
     1969.
Jones, A. *The Gospel according to St. Matthew: A Text and Commentary for Students*.
     New York: Sheed & Ward, 1964.
Jülicher, A. *Einleitung in das Neue Testament*. Freiburg: Akademische Verlagsbuch-
     handlung von J.C.B. Mohr, 1894.
Kee, H.C.; Young, F.W.; and Froelich, K. *Understanding the New Testament*. 2nd edn.
     Englewood Cliffs: Prentice-Hall, 1965.
Keegan, T.J. *Interpreting the Bible: A Popular Introduction to Biblical Hermeneutics*.
     New York: Paulist, 1985
—'Introductory Formulae for Matthean Discourses'. *CBQ* 44 (1982): 415-30.
Kelber, W. 'Redaction Criticism: On the Nature and Exposition of the Gospels'. *PRS*
     6 (1979): 4-16.
Kermode, F. *The Genesis of Secrecy: On the Interpretation of Narrative*. Cambridge,
     Mass.: Harvard University, 1979.
Kerr, J.H. *An Introduction to the Study of the Books of the New Testament*. 2nd edn.
     New York: Revell, 1892.
Kessler, M. 'A Methodological Setting for Rhetorical Criticism'. In *Art and Meaning:
     Rhetoric in Biblical Literature*, pp. 1-19. Ed. D.J.A. Clines, D.M. Gunn, and A.J.
     Hauser. JSOTS, 19. Sheffield: JSOT, 1982.
Kilpatrick, G.D. *The Origins of the Gospel of St. Matthew*. Oxford: Clarendon,
     1946.
Kingsbury, J.D. *The Christology of Mark's Gospel*. Philadelphia: Fortress, 1983.
—'The Composition and Christology of Matt. 28.16-20'. *JBL* 93 (1974): 573-84.
—'The Figure of Jesus in Matthew's Story: A Rejoinder to David Hill'. *JSNT* 25
     (1985): 61-81.
—'The Figure of Jesus in Matthew's Story: A Literary-Critical Probe'. *JSNT* 21
     (1984): 3-36.
—'The Gospel of Mark in Recent Research'. *RSR* 5 (1979): 101-106.
—*Jesus Christ in Matthew, Mark, and Luke*. Proclamation Commentaries. Phila-
     delphia: Fortress, 1981.
—'The "Jesus of History" and the "Christ of Faith", in Relation to Matthew's View of
     Time—Reaction to a New Approach'. *CTM* 37 (1966): 502-508.
—*Matthew*. Proclamation Commentaries. Philadelphia: Fortress, 1977.
—*Matthew: Structure, Christology, Kingdom*. Philadelphia: Fortress, 1975.
—*The Parables of Jesus in Matthew 13: A Study in Redaction-Criticism*. St. Louis:
     Clayton, 1969.

Klostermann, E. *Das Matthäus-Evangelium*. Handbuch zum Neuen Testament, 4. 4th edn. Tübingen: J.C.B. Mohr, 1971.

Krentz, E. 'The Extent of Matthew's Prologue: Toward the Structure of the First Gospel'. *JBL* 83 (1964): 409-15.

Kümmel, W.G. *Introduction to the New Testament*. Trans. H.C. Kee. Nashville: Abingdon, 1973.

—*The New Testament: The History of the Investigation of its Problems*. Trans. S.M. Gilmour and H.C. Kee. Nashville: Abingdon, 1972.

Kuist, H.T. *How to Enjoy the Bible*. Richmond: John Knox, 1939.

—*These Words Upon Thy Heart: Scripture and the Christian Response*. Richmond: John Knox, 1947.

Lagrange, Marie-Joseph. *Évangile selon Saint Matthieu*. 7th edn. Paris: J. Gabalda, 1948.

Lanser, S.S. *The Narrative Act: Point of View in Prose Fiction*. Princeton: Princeton University, 1981.

Léon-Dufour, X. 'The Synoptic Gospels'. In *Introduction to the New Testament*, pp. 140-321. Ed. A. Robert and A. Feuillet. Trans. P.W. Skeban, *et al*. New York: Desclée, 1965.

Levesque, E. 'Quelques procédés littéraires de Saint Matthieu'. *RB* 25 (1916): 387-405.

Lohmeyer, E. *Das Evangelium des Matthäus*. Ed. W. Schmauch. Kritisch-exegetischer Kommentar über das Neue Testament. 4th edn. Göttingen: Vandenhoeck & Ruprecht, 1956.

Lohr, C.H. 'Oral Techniques in the Gospel of Matthew'. *CBQ* 23 (1961): 403-35.

Lohse, E. *The Formation of the New Testament*. Trans. M. Eugene Boring. Nashville: Abingdon, 1972.

Loisy, A. *The Origins of the New Testament*. Trans. L.P. Jacks. London: Allen & Unwin, 1950.

Lotman, J.M. 'Point of View in a Text'. *New Literary History* 6 (1975): 339-52.

Lund, N.W. *Chiasmus in the New Testament: A Study in Formgeschichte*. Chapel Hill: University of North Carolina, 1942.

—'The Influence of Chiasmus Upon the Structure of the Gospel according to Matthew'. *ATR* 13 (1931): 405-33.

Luz, U. 'The Disciples in the Gospel according to Matthew'. Trans. R. Morgan. In *The Interpretation of Matthew*, pp. 98-128. Ed. G. Stanton. Issues in Religion and Theology, 3. Philadelphia: Fortress, 1983.

McKee, D.G. 'Studia Biblica VI. The Gospel according to Matthew'. *Int* 3 (1949): 194-205.

McKenzie, J.L. 'The Gospel according to Matthew'. In *The Jerome Bible Commentary*, pp. 62-114. Ed. R.E. Brown, J.A. Fitzmyer, and R.E. Murphy. Englewood Cliffs: Prentice-Hall, 1968.

McKnight, E.V. *What is Form Criticism?* Guides to Biblical Scholarship. Philadelphia: Fortress, 1969.

McNeile, A.H. *The Gospel according to Matthew: The Greek Text with Introduction, Notes, and Indices*. London: Macmillan, 1938.

Malina, B.J. 'The Literary Structure and Form of Matt. xxviii. 16-20'. *NTS* 17 (1970): 87-103.

Marxsen, W. *Introduction to the New Testament: An Approach to its Problems*. Trans. G. Buswell. Philadelphia: Fortress, 1968.

Meier, J.P. *Matthew*. New Testament Message, 3. Wilmington: Michael Glazier, 1980.

—'Salvation History in Matthew: In Search of a Starting Point'. *CBQ* 37 (1975): 203-13.
—*The Vision of Matthew: Christ, Church, and Morality in the First Gospel.* New York: Paulist, 1979.
Meinertz, M. *Einleitung in das Neue Testament.* 5th edn. Paderborn: Ferdinand Schöning, 1950.
Michaelis, Wilhelm. *Einleitung in das Neue Testament: Die Entstehung, Sammlung und Überlieferung der Schriften des Neuen Testaments.* 3rd edn. Berlin: Berchtold Haller, 1961.
—*Das Evangelium nach Matthäus.* Prophezei: Schweizerisches Bibelwerk für Gemeinde. Zürich: Zwingli, 1948.
—'πίπτω'. In *Theological Dictionary of the New Testament*, 10 vols. VI: 161-73. Trans. G. Bromiley. Ed. G. Friedrich. Grand Rapids: Eerdmans, 1971.
Michel, O. 'The Conclusion of Matthew's Gospel: A Contribution to the History of the Easter Message'. Trans. Robert Morgan. In *The Interpretation of Matthew*, pp. 30-41. Ed. G. Stanton. Issues in Religion and Theology, 3. Philadelphia: Fortress, 1983.
Milligan, G. *The New Testament Documents: Their Origin and Early History.* London: Macmillan, 1913.
Minear, P.S. *Matthew: The Teacher's Gospel.* New York: Pilgrim, 1982.
Moffatt, J. *Introduction to the Literature of the New Testament.* International Theological Library. 3rd edn. Edinburgh: T. & T. Clark, 1918.
—*Love in the New Testament.* London: Hodder & Stoughton, 1929.
Morgan, G.C. *The Analyzed Bible.* Westwood: Revell, 1964.
Moule, C.F.D. *An Idiom-Book of New Testament Greek.* 2nd edn. Cambridge: Cambridge University Press, 1959.
Moulton, J.H.; Howard, W.F.; and Turner, N. *A Grammar of New Testament Greek.* 4 vols. Edinburgh: T. & T. Clark, 1976. Vol. I: *Prolegomena*, by J.H. Moulton. Vol. IV: *Style*, by N. Turner.
Mowinckel, S. *The Psalms in Israel's Worship.* Trans. D.R. Ap-Thomas. 2 vols. Oxford: Blackwell, 1962.
Muilenburg, J. 'Form Criticism and Beyond'. *JBL* 88 (1969): 1-18.
—'A Study of Hebrew Rhetoric: Repetition and Style'. *Vetus Testamentum Supplement* 1 (1953): 97-111.
Neill, S. *Jesus Through Many Eyes: Introduction to the Theology of the New Testament.* Philadelphia: Fortress, 1976.
Norden, E. *Agnostos Theos: Untersuchungen zur Formgeschichte religiöser Rede.* Leipzig: Teubner, 1913.
Ogawa, A. *L'histoire de Jesus chez Matthieu: La signification de l'histoire pour la théologie matthéenne.* Publications Universitaires Européennes, Europäische Hochschulschriften, 23/16. Frankfurt: Peter Lang, 1979.
Palmer, C.L. *Emmanuel: Studies in the Gospel by Matthew.* Atlanta: Committee on Women's Work, Presbyterian Church in the United States, 1947.
Perrin, N. 'The Evangelist as Author: Reflections on Method in the Study and Interpretation of the Synoptic Gospels and Acts'. *BR* 17 (1972): 5-18.
—'The Interpretation of the Gospel of Mark'. *Int* 30 (1976): 115-24.
—*What is Redaction Criticism?* Guides to Biblical Scholarship. Philadelphia: Fortress, 1969.
—and Duling, D.C. *The New Testament, An Introduction: Proclamation and Parenesis, Myth and History.* 3rd edn. New York: Harcourt Brace Jovanovich, 1982.

Pesch, R. 'Der Gottessohn im matthäischen Evangelienprolog: Beobachtungen zu den Zitationsformeln der Reflexionszitate'. *Biblica* 48 (1967): 395-420.

Petersen, N.R. *Literary Criticism for New Testament Critics*. Guides to Biblical Scholarship. Philadelphia: Fortress, 1978.

—'Literary Criticism in Biblical Studies'. In *Orientation by Disorientation: Studies in Literary Criticism and Biblical Literary Criticism, Presented in Honor of William A. Beardslee*, pp. 25-50. Ed. Richard A. Spencer. Pittsburgh Theological Monograph Series, 35. Pittsburgh: Pickwick, 1980.

—'Point of View in Mark's Narrative'. *Semeia* 12 (1978): 97-121.

Plummer, A. *An Exegetical Commentary on the Gospel according to Matthew*. London: Robert Scott, 1909.

Price, J.L. *Interpreting the New Testament*. New York: Rinehart & Winston, 1961.

Quell, G. 'ἀγαπάω'. In *Theological Dictionary of the New Testament*, 10 vols. I: 21-35. Trans. G. Bromiley. Ed. G. Kittel. Grand Rapids: Eerdmans, 1971.

Radermakers, J. *Au fil de l'évangile selon saint Matthieu*. 2 vols. Louvain: Heverlee, 1972.

Ramaroson, L. 'La structure du premier Évangile'. *Science et Esprit* 26 (1974): 69-112.

Rattey, B.K. *The Growth and Structure of the Gospels*. Oxford: Oxford University Press, 1935.

Rau, C. *Das Matthäus-Evangelium: Entstehung, Gestalt, Essenischer Einfluss*. Stuttgart: Urachhaus, 1976.

Rhoads, D. 'Narrative Criticism and the Gospel of Mark'. *JAAR* 50 (1982): 411-34.

— and Michie, D. *Mark as Story: An Introduction to the Narrative of a Gospel*. Philadelphia: Fortress, 1982.

Ridderbos, H. *Matthew's Witness to Jesus Christ: The King and the Kingdom*. New York: Association, 1958.

Riddle, D.W., and Hutson, H.H. *New Testament Life and Literature*. Chicago: University of Chicago, 1946.

Rife, J.M. *The Nature and Origin of the New Testament*. New York: Philosophical Library, 1975.

Rigaux, B. *The Testimony of St. Matthew*. Trans. P.J. Oliguy. Chicago: Franciscan Herald, 1968.

Robbins, V. *Jesus the Teacher: A Socio-Rhetorical Interpretation of Mark*. Philadelphia: Fortress, 1984.

—and Patton, J.H. 'Rhetoric and Biblical Criticism'. *Quarterly Journal of Speech* 66 (1980): 327-50.

Robertson, A.T. *A Grammar of the Greek New Testament in the Light of Historical Research*. Nashville: Broadman, 1934.

Robinson, T.H. *The Gospel of Matthew*. Moffatt New Testament Commentary. London: Hodder & Stoughton, 1928.

Rohde, J. *Rediscovering the Teaching of the Evangelists*. Trans. D.M. Barton. New Testament Library. London: SCM, 1968.

Rolland, P. 'From the Genesis to the End of the World: The Plan of Matthew's Gospel'. *BTB* 2 (1972): 155-76.

Rothfuchs, W. *Die Erfüllungszitate des Matthäusevangeliums: Eine biblisch-theologische Untersuchung*. Stuttgart: Kohlhammer, 1969.

Roux, H. *L'Évangile du Royaume*. 2nd edn. Geneva: Labor et Fides, 1956.

Sabourin, L. *L'Évangile selon Saint Matthieu et ses principaux parallèles*. Rome: Pontificii Instituti Biblici, 1978.

Schelkle, K.H. *Das Neue Testament: Seine literarische und theologische Geschichte.* 3rd edn. Kevelaer, Rhineland: Butzon & Bercker, 1966.

Schenk, W. 'Das "Matthäusevangelium" als "Petrusevangelium"'. *BZ* 27 (1983): 58-80.

Schlatter, A. *Der Evangelist Matthäus, seine Sprache, sein Ziel, seine Selbständigkeit: Ein Kommentar zum ersten Evangelium.* Stuttgart: Calwer, 1948.

Schlier, H. 'ἀρνέομαι'. In *Theological Dictionary of the New Testamenet* 10 vols. I: 469-71. Trans. G. Bromiley. Ed. G. Kittel. Grand Rapids: Eerdmans. 1971.

—'γονυπετέω'. In *Theological Dictionary of the New Testament.* 10 vols. I: 738-40. Trans. G. Bromiley. Ed. G. Kittel. Grand Rapids: Eerdmans, 1971.

Schmid, J. *Das Evangelium nach Matthäus.* Regensburger Neues Testament, 1. 3rd edn. Regensburg: Pustet, 1956.

Schmidt, K.L. *Der Rahmen der Geschichte Jesu: literarische Untersuchungen zur ältesten Jesusüberlieferung.* Berlin: Trowitzsch, 1919.

Schneider, J. 'προσέρχομαι'. In *Theological Dictionary of the New Testament*, 10 vols. II: 683-84. Trans. G. Bromiley. Ed. G. Kittel. Grand Rapids: Eerdmans, 1971.

Schniewind, J. *Das Evangelium nach Matthäus.* Das Neue Testament Deutsch. Neues Göttinger Bibelwerk, 2. 7th edn. Göttingen: Vandenhoeck & Ruprecht, 1954.

Schrenk, G. 'γένεσις'. In *Theological Dictionary of the New Testament.* 10 vols. I: 682-83. Trans. G. Bromiley. Ed. G. Kittel. Grand Rapids: Eerdmans, 1971.

Schweitzer, A. *The Quest of the Historical Jesus: A Critical Study of its Progress from Reimarus to Wrede.* Trans. W. Montgomery. 8th edn. London: A. & C. Black, 1945.

Schweizer, E. *The Good News according to Matthew.* Trans. D.E. Green. Atlanta: John Knox, 1975.

Selby, D.S. *Introduction to the New Testament.* New York: Macmillan, 1971.

Senior, D. *Invitation to Matthew: A Commentary on the Gospel of Matthew with Complete Text from the Jerusalem Bible.* Garden City: Doubleday, 1977.

—*What Are They Saying About Matthew?* New York: Paulist, 1983.

Sider, J.W. 'Rediscovering the Parables: The Logic of the Jeremias Tradition'. *JBL* 102 (1983): 61-83.

Silberman, L.H. 'Listening to the Text'. *JBL* 102 (1983): 3-26.

Smith, B.T.D. *The Gospel according to St. Matthew: With Introduction and Notes.* Cambridge Bible for Schools and Colleges. Cambridge: Cambridge University Press, 1933.

Soden, H. von *Book of the New Testament: Contributions to Early Christian Literature.* New York: Williams & Norgate, 1907.

Soulen, R.N. *Handbook of Biblical Criticism.* 2nd edn. Atlanta: John Knox, 1981.

Spivey, R.A., and Smith, D.M., Jr. *Anatomy of the New Testament: A Guide to its Structure and Meaning.* 3rd edn. New York: Macmillan, 1982.

Stendahl, K. 'Quis et Unde? An Analysis of Mt 1-2'. In *The Interpretation of Matthew*, pp. 56-66. Ed. G. Stanton. Issues in Religion and Theology, 3. Philadelphia: Fortress, 1983.

—*The School of St. Matthew: And its Use of the Old Testament.* Philadelphia: Fortress, 1968.

Stonehouse, N.B. *The Witness of Matthew and Mark to Christ.* Philadelphia: Presbyterian Guardian, 1944.

Strecker, G. 'The Concept of History in Matthew'. *JAAR* 35 (1967): 219-30.

—*Der Weg der Gerechtigkeit: Untersuchung zur Theologie des Matthäus.* FRLANT, 82. 3rd edn. Göttingen: Vandenhoeck & Ruprecht, 1971.

Streeter, B.H. *The Four Gospels: A Study of Origins.* New York: Macmillan, 1925.

Strong, A.H. *Popular Lectures on the Books of the New Testament*. Philadelphia: Griffith & Rowland, 1914.

Talbert, C.H. *Literary Patterns, Theological Themes, and the Genre of Luke-Acts*. SBLMS, 20. Missoula: Scholars, 1974.

—*Reading Luke: A Literary and Theological Commentary on the Third Gospel*. New York: Crossroad, 1982.

Tannehill, R.C. 'The Disciples in Mark: The Function of a Narrative Role'. *JR* 57 (1977): 386-405.

—'The Gospel of Mark as Narrative Christology'. *Semeia* 16 (1979): 57-92.

Tasker, R.V.G. *The Gospel according to St. Matthew: An Introduction and Commentary*. Tyndale New Testament Commentaries. Grand Rapids: Eerdmans, 1961.

Taylor, V. *The Gospel according to Mark*. London: Macmillan, 1952.

Tenney, M.C. *New Testament Survey*. Grand Rapids: Eerdmans, 1961.

Thompson, W.G. 'An Historical Perspective in the Gospel of Matthew'. *JBL* 93 (1974): 243-62.

—*Matthew's Advice to a Divided Community: Mt. 17.22-18.35*. Analecta Biblica: Investigationes Scientificae in Res Biblicas, 44. Rome: Biblical Institute Press, 1970.

Tödt, H.E. *The Son of Man in the Synoptic Tradition*. Trans. D.M. Barton. New Testament Library. Philadelphia: Westminster, 1965.

Traina, R.A. *Methodical Bible Study: A New Approach to Hermeneutics*. New York: Ganis & Harris, 1952.

Trilling, W. *The Gospel according to Matthew*. Trans. Kevin Smyth. New Testament for Spiritual Reading, 2. 2 vols. London: Burns & Oates, 1981.

—*Das Wahre Israel: Studien zur Theologie des Matthäus-Evangeliums*. Studien zum Alten und Neuen Testament, 10. München: Kösel, 1968.

Uspensky, B. *A Poetics of Composition: The Structure of the Artistic Text and Typology of a Compositional Form*. Trans. V. Zavarin and S. Wittig. Berkeley: University of California, 1973.

Via, D.O. 'Structure, Christology, and Ethics in Matthew'. In *Orientation by Disorientation: Studies in Literary Criticism and Biblical Literary Criticism, Presented in Honor of William A. Beardslee*, pp. 199-215. Ed. R.A. Spencer. Pittsburgh Theological Monograph Series, 35. Pittsburgh: Pickwick, 1980.

Vögtle, A. 'Das christologische und ecclesiologische Anliegen von Mt. 22.18-20'. In *Studia Evangelica II: Papers Presented to the Second International Congress on New Testament Studies*, pp. 266-94. Ed. Frank L. Cross. TU, 87. Berlin: Akademie, 1964.

Waetjen, H.C. *The Origin and Destiny of Humanness: An Interpretation of the Gospel according to Matthew*. San Rafael: Crystal, 1976.

Walker, R. *Die Heilsgeschichte im ersten Evangelium*. FRLANT, 91. Göttingen: Vandenhoeck & Ruprecht, 1967.

Weiss, B. *A Manual of Introduction to the New Testament*. Trans. A.J.K. Davidson. Foreign Biblical Library. 2 vols. London: Hodder & Stoughton, 1888.

Weiss, J. 'Das Matthäus Evangelium'. In *Die drei älteren Evangelien*, pp. 222-392. Die Schriften des Neuen Testament, 1. 4th edn. Ed. O. Baumgarten, *et al*. Göttingen: Vandenhoeck & Ruprecht, 1929.

Westcott, B.F. *The Gospel according to St. John: The Authorized Version with Introduction and Notes*: London: James Clarke, 1958.

White, W.W. *Thirty Studies in the Gospel by Matthew*. N.p.: S.M. Henderson, 1905.

Wikenhauser, A. *New Testament Introduction*. Trans. Joseph Cunningham. New York: Herder & Herder, 1958.

Wrede, W. *Das Messiasgeheimnis in den Evangelien*. 3rd edn. Göttingen: Vandenhoeck & Ruprecht, 1963.

Zahn, T. *Introduction to the New Testament*. Trans. J.M. Trout, *et al*. 3 vols. Edinburgh: T. & T. Clark.

Zerwick, M. *Biblical Greek*. Trans. J. Smith. Scripta Pontificii Instituti Biblica, 114. 4th edn. Rome: Pontifical Biblical Institute, 1963.

INDEXES

(References to the Notes section are not included in the Indexes.)

INDEX OF BIBLICAL REFERENCES

INDEX OF AUTHORS

Strecker, G. 12, 45-48, 51
Streeter, B.H. 33, 129

Talbert, C.H. 16
Thompson, W.G. 12, 52
Traina, R.A. 8
Trilling, W. 12, 48, 49, 112, 126

Turner, N. 86

Vögtle, A. 111, 113

Walker, R. 12, 49-51, 69
Wikenhauser, A. 22, 24

JOURNAL FOR THE STUDY OF THE NEW TESTAMENT
SUPPLEMENT SERIES